Dear Future Exam Success Story

First of all, **THANK YOU** for purchasing Mometrix study materials!

Second, congratulations! You are one of the few determined test-takers who are committed to doing whatever it takes to excel on your exam. **You have come to the right place.** We developed these study materials with one goal in mind: to deliver you the information you need in a format that's concise and easy to use.

In addition to optimizing your guide for the content of the test, we've outlined our recommended steps for breaking down the preparation process into small, attainable goals so you can make sure you stay on track.

We've also analyzed the entire test-taking process, identifying the most common pitfalls and showing how you can overcome them and be ready for any curveball the test throws you.

Standardized testing is one of the biggest obstacles on your road to success, which only increases the importance of doing well in the high-pressure, high-stakes environment of test day. Your results on this test could have a significant impact on your future, and this guide provides the information and practical advice to help you achieve your full potential on test day.

Your success is our success

We would love to hear from you! If you would like to share the story of your exam success or if you have any questions or comments in regard to our products, please contact us at **800-673-8175** or **support@mometrix.com**.

Thanks again for your business and we wish you continued success!

Sincerely,
The Mometrix Test Preparation Team

Written and edited by the Mometrix Exam Secrets Test Prep Team
Printed in the United States of America

Mometrix
TEST PREPARATION

STAAR

Test Prep Guide Grade 8 Reading Language Arts

TABLE OF CONTENTS

Introduction

Thank you for purchasing this resource! You have made the choice to prepare yourself for a test that could have a huge impact on your future, and this guide is designed to help you be fully ready for test day. Obviously, it's important to have a solid understanding of the test material, but you also need to be prepared for the unique environment and stressors of the test, so that you can perform to the best of your abilities.

For this purpose, the first section that appears in this guide is the **Success Strategies**. We've devoted countless hours to meticulously researching what works and what doesn't, and we've boiled down our findings to the four most impactful steps you can take to improve your performance on the test. We start at the beginning with study planning and move through the preparation process, all the way to the testing strategies that will help you get the most out of what you know when you're finally sitting in front of the test.

We recommend that you start preparing for your test as far in advance as possible. However, if you've bought this guide as a last-minute study resource and only have a few days before your test, we recommend that you skip over the first two Success Strategies since they address a long-term study plan.

If you struggle with **test anxiety**, we strongly encourage you to check out our recommendations for how you can overcome it. Test anxiety is a formidable foe, but it can be beaten, and we want to make sure you have the tools you need to defeat it.

Strategy #1 – Plan Big, Study Small

There's a lot riding on your performance. If you want to ace this test, you're going to need to keep your skills sharp and the material fresh in your mind. You need a plan that lets you review everything you need to know while still fitting in your schedule. We'll break this strategy down into three categories.

Information Organization

Start with the information you already have: the official test outline. From this, you can make a complete list of all the concepts you need to cover before the test. Organize these concepts into groups that can be studied together, and create a list of any related vocabulary you need to learn so you can brush up on any difficult terms. You'll want to keep this vocabulary list handy once you actually start studying since you may need to add to it along the way.

Time Management

Once you have your set of study concepts, decide how to spread them out over the time you have left before the test. Break your study plan into small, clear goals so you have a manageable task for each day and know exactly what you're doing. Then just focus on one small step at a time. When you manage your time this way, you don't need to spend hours at a time studying. Studying a small block of content for a short period each day helps you retain information better and avoid stressing over how much you have left to do. You can relax knowing that you have a plan to cover everything in time. In order for this strategy to be effective though, you have to start studying early and stick to your schedule. Avoid the exhaustion and futility that comes from last-minute cramming!

Study Environment

The environment you study in has a big impact on your learning. Studying in a coffee shop, while probably more enjoyable, is not likely to be as fruitful as studying in a quiet room. It's important to keep distractions to a minimum. You're only planning to study for a short block of time, so make the most of it. Don't pause to check your phone or get up to find a snack. It's also important to **avoid multitasking**. Research has consistently shown that multitasking will make your studying dramatically less effective. Your study area should also be comfortable and well-lit so you don't have the distraction of straining your eyes or sitting on an uncomfortable chair.

The time of day you study is also important. You want to be rested and alert. Don't wait until just before bedtime. Study when you'll be most likely to comprehend and remember. Even better, if you know what time of day your test will be, set that time aside for study. That way your brain will be used to working on that subject at that specific time and you'll have a better chance of recalling information.

Finally, it can be helpful to team up with others who are studying for the same test. Your actual studying should be done in as isolated an environment as possible, but the work of organizing the information and setting up the study plan can be divided up. In between study sessions, you can discuss with your teammates the concepts that you're all studying and quiz each other on the details. Just be sure that your teammates are as serious about the test as you are. If you find that your study time is being replaced with social time, you might need to find a new team.

Strategy #2 – Make Your Studying Count

You're devoting a lot of time and effort to preparing for this test, so you want to be absolutely certain it will pay off. This means doing more than just reading the content and hoping you can remember it on test day. It's important to make every minute of study count. There are two main areas you can focus on to make your studying count.

Retention

It doesn't matter how much time you study if you can't remember the material. You need to make sure you are retaining the concepts. To check your retention of the information you're learning, try recalling it at later times with minimal prompting. Try carrying around flashcards and glance at one or two from time to time or ask a friend who's also studying for the test to quiz you.

To enhance your retention, look for ways to put the information into practice so that you can apply it rather than simply recalling it. If you're using the information in practical ways, it will be much easier to remember. Similarly, it helps to solidify a concept in your mind if you're not only reading it to yourself but also explaining it to someone else. Ask a friend to let you teach them about a concept you're a little shaky on (or speak aloud to an imaginary audience if necessary). As you try to summarize, define, give examples, and answer your friend's questions, you'll understand the concepts better and they will stay with you longer. Finally, step back for a big picture view and ask yourself how each piece of information fits with the whole subject. When you link the different concepts together and see them working together as a whole, it's easier to remember the individual components.

Finally, practice showing your work on any multi-step problems, even if you're just studying. Writing out each step you take to solve a problem will help solidify the process in your mind, and you'll be more likely to remember it during the test.

Modality

Modality simply refers to the means or method by which you study. Choosing a study modality that fits your own individual learning style is crucial. No two people learn best in exactly the same way, so it's important to know your strengths and use them to your advantage.

For example, if you learn best by visualization, focus on visualizing a concept in your mind and draw an image or a diagram. Try color-coding your notes, illustrating them, or creating symbols that will trigger your mind to recall a learned concept. If you learn best by hearing or discussing information, find a study partner who learns the same way or read aloud to yourself. Think about how to put the information in your own words. Imagine that you are giving a lecture on the topic and record yourself so you can listen to it later.

For any learning style, flashcards can be helpful. Organize the information so you can take advantage of spare moments to review. Underline key words or phrases. Use different colors for different categories. Mnemonic devices (such as creating a short list in which every item starts with the same letter) can also help with retention. Find what works best for you and use it to store the information in your mind most effectively and easily.

Strategy #3 – Practice the Right Way

Your success on test day depends not only on how many hours you put into preparing, but also on whether you prepared the right way. It's good to check along the way to see if your studying is paying off. One of the most effective ways to do this is by taking practice tests to evaluate your progress. Practice tests are useful because they show exactly where you need to improve. Every time you take a practice test, pay special attention to these three groups of questions:

- The questions you got wrong
- The questions you had to guess on, even if you guessed right
- The questions you found difficult or slow to work through

This will show you exactly what your weak areas are, and where you need to devote more study time. Ask yourself why each of these questions gave you trouble. Was it because you didn't understand the material? Was it because you didn't remember the vocabulary? Do you need more repetitions on this type of question to build speed and confidence? Dig into those questions and figure out how you can strengthen your weak areas as you go back to review the material.

Additionally, many practice tests have a section explaining the answer choices. It can be tempting to read the explanation and think that you now have a good understanding of the concept. However, an explanation likely only covers part of the question's broader context. Even if the explanation makes perfect sense, **go back and investigate** every concept related to the question until you're positive you have a thorough understanding.

As you go along, keep in mind that the practice test is just that: practice. Memorizing these questions and answers will not be very helpful on the actual test because it is unlikely to have any of the same exact questions. If you only know the right answers to the sample questions, you won't be prepared for the real thing. **Study the concepts** until you understand them fully, and then you'll be able to answer any question that shows up on the test.

It's important to wait on the practice tests until you're ready. If you take a test on your first day of study, you may be overwhelmed by the amount of material covered and how much you need to learn. Work up to it gradually.

On test day, you'll need to be prepared for answering questions, managing your time, and using the test-taking strategies you've learned. It's a lot to balance, like a mental marathon that will have a big impact on your future. Like training for a marathon, you'll need to start slowly and work your way up. When test day arrives, you'll be ready.

Start with the strategies you've read in the first two Success Strategies—plan your course and study in the way that works best for you. If you have time, consider using multiple study resources to get different approaches to the same concepts. It can be helpful to see difficult concepts from more than one angle. Then find a good source for practice tests. Many times, the test website will suggest potential study resources or provide sample tests.

Test-Taking Strategies

This section contains a list of test-taking strategies that you may find helpful as you work through the test. By taking what you know and applying logical thought, you can maximize your chances of answering any question correctly!

It is very important to realize that every question is different and every person is different: no single strategy will work on every question, and no single strategy will work for every person. That's why we've included all of them here, so you can try them out and determine which ones work best for different types of questions and which ones work best for you.

Question Strategies

⊘ Read Carefully

Read the question and the answer choices carefully. Don't miss the question because you misread the terms. You have plenty of time to read each question thoroughly and make sure you understand what is being asked. Yet a happy medium must be attained, so don't waste too much time. You must read carefully and efficiently.

⊘ Contextual Clues

Look for contextual clues. If the question includes a word you are not familiar with, look at the immediate context for some indication of what the word might mean. Contextual clues can often give you all the information you need to decipher the meaning of an unfamiliar word. Even if you can't determine the meaning, you may be able to narrow down the possibilities enough to make a solid guess at the answer to the question.

⊘ Prefixes

If you're having trouble with a word in the question or answer choices, try dissecting it. Take advantage of every clue that the word might include. Prefixes can be a huge help. Usually, they allow you to determine a basic meaning. *Pre-* means before, *post-* means after, *pro-* is positive, *de-* is negative. From prefixes, you can get an idea of the general meaning of the word and try to put it into context.

⊘ Hedge Words

Watch out for critical hedge words, such as *likely, may, can, often, almost, mostly, usually, generally, rarely,* and *sometimes.* Question writers insert these hedge phrases to cover every possibility. Often an answer choice will be wrong simply because it leaves no room for exception. Be on guard for answer choices that have definitive words such as *exactly* and *always.*

⊘ Switchback Words

Stay alert for *switchbacks.* These are the words and phrases frequently used to alert you to shifts in thought. The most common switchback words are *but, although,* and *however.* Others include *nevertheless, on the other hand, even though, while, in spite of, despite,* and *regardless of.* Switchback words are important to catch because they can change the direction of the question or an answer choice.

✓ Face Value

When in doubt, use common sense. Accept the situation in the problem at face value. Don't read too much into it. These problems will not require you to make wild assumptions. If you have to go beyond creativity and warp time or space in order to have an answer choice fit the question, then you should move on and consider the other answer choices. These are normal problems rooted in reality. The applicable relationship or explanation may not be readily apparent, but it is there for you to figure out. Use your common sense to interpret anything that isn't clear.

Answer Choice Strategies

✓ Answer Selection

The most thorough way to pick an answer choice is to identify and eliminate wrong answers until only one is left, then confirm it is the correct answer. Sometimes an answer choice may immediately seem right, but be careful. The test writers will usually put more than one reasonable answer choice on each question, so take a second to read all of them and make sure that the other choices are not equally obvious. As long as you have time left, it is better to read every answer choice than to pick the first one that looks right without checking the others.

✓ Answer Choice Families

An answer choice family consists of two (in rare cases, three) answer choices that are very similar in construction and cannot all be true at the same time. If you see two answer choices that are direct opposites or parallels, one of them is usually the correct answer. For instance, if one answer choice says that quantity *x* increases and another either says that quantity *x* decreases (opposite) or says that quantity *y* increases (parallel), then those answer choices would fall into the same family. An answer choice that doesn't match the construction of the answer choice family is more likely to be incorrect. Most questions will not have answer choice families, but when they do appear, you should be prepared to recognize them.

✓ Eliminate Answers

Eliminate answer choices as soon as you realize they are wrong, but make sure you consider all possibilities. If you are eliminating answer choices and realize that the last one you are left with is also wrong, don't panic. Start over and consider each choice again. There may be something you missed the first time that you will realize on the second pass.

✓ Avoid Fact Traps

Don't be distracted by an answer choice that is factually true but doesn't answer the question. You are looking for the choice that answers the question. Stay focused on what the question is asking for so you don't accidentally pick an answer that is true but incorrect. Always go back to the question and make sure the answer choice you've selected actually answers the question and is not merely a true statement.

✓ Extreme Statements

In general, you should avoid answers that put forth extreme actions as standard practice or proclaim controversial ideas as established fact. An answer choice that states the "process should be used in certain situations, if…" is much more likely to be correct than one that states the "process should be discontinued completely." The first is a calm rational statement and doesn't even make a definitive, uncompromising stance, using a hedge word *if* to provide wiggle room, whereas the second choice is far more extreme.

⊘ BENCHMARK

As you read through the answer choices and you come across one that seems to answer the question well, mentally select that answer choice. This is not your final answer, but it's the one that will help you evaluate the other answer choices. The one that you selected is your benchmark or standard for judging each of the other answer choices. Every other answer choice must be compared to your benchmark. That choice is correct until proven otherwise by another answer choice beating it. If you find a better answer, then that one becomes your new benchmark. Once you've decided that no other choice answers the question as well as your benchmark, you have your final answer.

⊘ PREDICT THE ANSWER

Before you even start looking at the answer choices, it is often best to try to predict the answer. When you come up with the answer on your own, it is easier to avoid distractions and traps because you will know exactly what to look for. The right answer choice is unlikely to be word-for-word what you came up with, but it should be a close match. Even if you are confident that you have the right answer, you should still take the time to read each option before moving on.

General Strategies

⊘ TOUGH QUESTIONS

If you are stumped on a problem or it appears too hard or too difficult, don't waste time. Move on! Remember though, if you can quickly check for obviously incorrect answer choices, your chances of guessing correctly are greatly improved. Before you completely give up, at least try to knock out a couple of possible answers. Eliminate what you can and then guess at the remaining answer choices before moving on.

⊘ CHECK YOUR WORK

Since you will probably not know every term listed and the answer to every question, it is important that you get credit for the ones that you do know. Don't miss any questions through careless mistakes. If at all possible, try to take a second to look back over your answer selection and make sure you've selected the correct answer choice and haven't made a costly careless mistake (such as marking an answer choice that you didn't mean to mark). This quick double check should more than pay for itself in caught mistakes for the time it costs.

⊘ DON'T RUSH

It is very easy to make errors when you are in a hurry. Maintaining a fast pace in answering questions is pointless if it makes you miss questions that you would have gotten right otherwise. Test writers like to include distracting information and wrong answers that seem right. Taking a little extra time to avoid careless mistakes can make all the difference in your test score. Find a pace that allows you to be confident in the answers that you select.

⊘ KEEP MOVING

Panicking will not help you pass the test, so do your best to stay calm and keep moving. Taking deep breaths and going through the answer elimination steps you practiced can help to break through a stress barrier and keep your pace.

Final Notes

The combination of a solid foundation of content knowledge and the confidence that comes from practicing your plan for applying that knowledge is the key to maximizing your performance on test day. As your foundation of content knowledge is built up and strengthened, you'll find that the strategies included in this chapter become more and more effective in helping you quickly sift through the distractions and traps of the test to isolate the correct answer.

Now that you're preparing to move forward into the test content chapters of this book, be sure to keep your goal in mind. As you read, think about how you will be able to apply this information on the test. If you've already seen sample questions for the test and you have an idea of the question format and style, try to come up with questions of your own that you can answer based on what you're reading. This will give you valuable practice applying your knowledge in the same ways you can expect to on test day.

Good luck and good studying!

Reading

Vocabulary

Dictionary

A print or digital dictionary can be used to find out many things about a word. A dictionary will show the correct pronunciation of a word, provide its meaning, and identify what part of speech the word is. It will also tell how the word was derived—that is, what words it came from originally. A dictionary will have a **pronunciation guide** for each word that shows how to sound it out and where its syllables start and end. It will use symbols to indicate sounds, and will also use sample sounds (the "a" in "bad," for instance). A dictionary lists all of the meanings of a word and the parts of speech the word can be used as.

Example

Philippe used his dictionary to check the various meanings of the word *eliminate*. He found this entry:

> eliminate \ i-ˈli-mə-ˌnāt \ verb
> 1. to put an end to or get rid of
> 2. to expel from the living body
> 3. to cause to disappear by combining two or more equations

Identify which definition of *eliminate* is used in the following sentence:

> Harold couldn't wait to *eliminate* the other team from the playoffs by winning the first two games.

The correct answer is meaning 1: "to put an end to or get rid of." If you substitute that definition for the word, the sentence makes sense. Meanings 2 and 3 do not fit with the context of the sentence. When considering which meaning is being used, always check for context clues in the sentence or in the sentences before or after the sentence in which the word is used. Dictionaries also tell you how to pronounce words and often the derivation of the word, although that is not given here.

Thesaurus

A thesaurus is a reference book that gives **synonyms** of words. It is different from a dictionary because a thesaurus does not give definitions. A thesaurus can be helpful in finding the meaning of an unfamiliar word when reading. If the meaning of a synonym is known, then the meaning of the unfamiliar word will be known. Another time in which a thesaurus can be helpful is when writing. Using a thesaurus helps authors to vary their word choice.

Glossary

A glossary is a **list of terms and their definitions** that can be found **at the back** of certain types of books, such as textbooks or reference books. A glossary does not have the definitions of all words, like a dictionary, but instead gives the definitions of the important terms within that particular book which are either uncommon or newly introduced. One may use a glossary when reading a book about economics or a chapter in a science textbook, for example, to define some of the technical terms within the text.

Denotative and Connotative Meanings

The **denotative meaning** of a word is the exact dictionary definition of the word. The **connotative meaning** of a word is the emotion conveyed by the use of the word in context. The word may have associated meaning in addition to its dictionary definition. A good way to remember the difference between denotative and connotative is to think "direct" or "dictionary" in relation to denotative.

An example of a denotative meaning for the adjective *ablaze* would be "burning", as in the logs burning in a fireplace. A connotative meaning for the adjective *ablaze*, based on the context of the word, may indicate a level of comfort while sitting in front of a fireplace. For instance, in the context: "A logs were *ablaze* in the fireplace, radiating heat out into the corners of the snow-enclosed room", the word *ablaze* implies comfort and coziness within the space described. The connotative meaning of a word can often have an emotional association for the reader.

Example

Define the denotative and connotative meaning of the word *palace* in the following sentence:

> The golden *palace* gates opened slowly to reveal an expansive garden that was well-tended by precise gardeners all wearing the king's insignia.

In the example, the denotative meaning of the word is that a *palace* is literally a place where royalty lives. A *palace* implies, or connotes, a place of riches and is usually associated with wealth. The words "golden", "expansive garden", and "king's insignia" all give clues that the *palace* can be viewed as a place of importance, one that is well taken care of.

When looking for the denotative meaning of a word, remember to think "direct", or the literal meaning of the word. The connotative meaning of the word is implied and not directly stated; the connotative meaning is often associated with emotion and feeling about the typical context of the word.

Using Context to Determine the Meanings of Words

Readers of all levels will encounter words that they have either never seen or that they have seen before but still don't know what it means. The best way to define a word in **context** is to look for nearby words that can assist in learning the meaning of the word.

Context Clues

Context clues are hints about the meaning of a word. They are the words or phrases in the sentence or sentences before and after a new or unfamiliar word. Context clues give the reader an idea about what a word means. A context clue may also contain words that help define the new word or an example of what the new word means. A context clue in the form of an example may contain the words including 'such as', a dash, or a colon before stated information.

Using context clues to figure out meaning can be helpful when learning a new set of vocabulary words or reading a difficult text. The dictionary definition of a word can always be looked up to double-check intended meaning.

Review Video: Reading Comprehension: Using Context Clues
Visit mometrix.com/academy and enter code: 613660

EXAMPLE

Determine the meaning of *cordial* in the following excerpt.

> The salesperson smiled when the couple came into the store. She told them to take their time in choosing a ring. She chatted with them about their future plans. She was the most *cordial* salesperson they had ever met.

The excerpt states that the salesperson smiled. It says that she told them to take their time and that she chatted with them. Obviously, the word *cordial* has a positive meaning based on these context clues. They seem to like the salesperson. She seems very pleasant. If you put the word "pleasant" in place of *cordial*, the sentences make sense. Through this process it is possible to use context clues to help the reader understand the meaning of an unknown word. The same process can be used to decipher the meanings of unknown expressions or sayings.

EXAMPLE

Read the sentence and explain the meaning of *sense of foreboding:*

> All day long Ron kept thinking about Sue. For some unknown reason he was worried about her. He had a strong *sense of foreboding* that something was about to go wrong in Sue's city. Then he heard about the earthquake there. Luckily Sue was not injured.

To figure out the meaning of the phrase *sense of foreboding*, the reader needs to look for context clues in just the same way the reader would do to figure out the meaning of a single word. The excerpt says that Ron was "worried" about Sue for "some unknown reason." It also says that he felt that "something was going to go wrong in Sue's city." Ron also heard about an earthquake taking place in Sue's city. A "sense of foreboding" must mean that Ron had an idea that something bad was going to happen. The context clues help the reader figure out the meaning of the phrase.

SUBSTITUTION TO FIND MEANING

One way to find out if you have figured out the correct meaning of a new word is to **substitute** the meaning for the word. Using the example for *basin*, if the reader substituted in "depression in the earth," the sentence would read

> The "depression in the earth" had filled with water over the summer months, so that the rocky bottom was no longer visible to the casual hiker.

This is a way for the reader to confirm that they have used the context clues in the sentence correctly.

SYNONYMS AND ANTONYMS

When you understand how words relate to each other, you will discover more in a passage. This is explained by understanding **synonyms**, which are words that mean the same thing, and **antonyms**, which are words that mean the opposite of one another. As an example, *dry* and *arid* are synonyms, and *dry* and *wet* are antonyms.

> **Review Video: What are Synonyms and Antonyms?**
> Visit mometrix.com/academy and enter code: 105612

Definition Within a Text

An author may **define** a word in the text. For example, an author may write, "The company did not have sufficient capital, that is, available money, to continue operating." The author defined "capital" as "available money." Authors will use words and phrases, such as "that is," "or," "meaning," and "which is," to let the reader know that they are defining the word.

Analogy

Analogies are used to **compare relationships**. For example, the analogy "restaurant is to eating as store is to shopping." A restaurant is a place where you eat, and a store is a place where you shop. The analogy compares locations and the things people do at those locations. **Analogies** can also be used to show the meaning of unfamiliar words. For example, consider the analogy "author is to writing as artisan is to crafting." *Artisan* may be an unfamiliar word to some. However, this analogy begins with "author is to writing." An author writes to create books, articles, and poems. The first part of the analogy pairs a person's job title with the action that their job requires. Based on this, a reader can conclude that an artisan is someone who crafts things.

Examples That Clarify Meaning

An author may use a word and then give examples that reveal its meaning. Consider this text: "Those who do not know sign language can communicate with people who are deaf or hard of hearing by using gestures. These may include pointing their fingers to indicate which direction to look or go or holding up a hand to indicate stopping." The author of this text has used the word *gestures* and then followed it with examples. This shows a reader who is unfamiliar with the word that gestures are hand motions. Readers can find examples by looking for signal words like "for example," "for instance," "like," and "such as."

Contrast

Readers can use these **contrasting** words and **opposites** as context clues to help them understand unfamiliar words. For example, an author may write, "Our conversation was not cheery. We sat and talked very solemnly about the events." Because the author says the conversation was "not cheery," a reader who is not familiar with the word "solemnly" can see that "solemn" means the opposite of cheery. This shows that *solemn* must mean serious or sad.

Cause and Effect

A text that discusses a **cause and effect** can also show the meaning of an unfamiliar word. Consider the following sentence: "The student was mortified after she learned that she accidentally sang the wrong song at the talent show." *Mortified* may be an unfamiliar word. However, this sentence shows that the student became mortified as a result of her mistake. The reader can understand that making a mistake in front of many people is the cause. Usually, this would have the effect of making someone very embarrassed. *Mortified* means "extremely embarrassed," which is supported by the event in the sentence.

Multiple-Meaning Words

Some words are spelled exactly the same but have different meanings in different contexts. One needs to use the context of the situation to determine the correct meaning of the word in each case. Often, these words can be used as either a noun or a verb and their grammatical usage determines the meaning.

A **homonym** is defined as a word that has more than one meaning, but is spelled and pronounced the same in all contexts. For example, the word *degree* has at least three different meanings, depending on the situation in which the word is used: (a) a *degree* is the incremental measurement of temperature; (b) a *degree* is a title awarded upon graduation from college; and (c) *degree* can mean the extent or amount of something. Here are three different sentences, each using one of these meanings of the word *degree*:

1. You probably don't notice a difference when the temperature rises one *degree*.
2. The employer is only willing to hire someone with a *degree* in mathematics.
3. It was hard to tell the *degree* to which he really cared about the outcome.

Similar Words

Homophones are words that are pronounced the same, but may be spelled differently. An example of two homophones would be *heir* (someone due to inherit an estate) and *air* (the invisible substance people breathe).

Homographs are words that are spelled the same, but may be pronounced differently. An example of a homograph is the word *row*, which is pronounced one way when used to mean a horizontal grouping and is pronounced another way when used to mean an argument.

Root Words and Affixes

A **root word** is a word that can be added onto. An **affix** is a prefix or suffix that is added onto a root word. Often, the affixes in the English language come from Latin or Greek origins. A **prefix** is added to the beginning of a root word and a **suffix** is added to the end of a root word.

For example, the word "inscription" is made up of three sections. The root *script* means "write" or "writing." There are two affixes in the word. The prefix *in-* can mean various things such as "not," but also "on." In this case it means "on." The suffix *-tion* means "action" or "process." So, put together, the word "inscription" means "the act of writing on." Studying roots and affixes is important because it allows you to decode words you might not otherwise understand with relative ease.

Common Greek and Latin Root Words

Root	Meaning	Example
ast	related to stars	astronaut (someone who travels through outer space)
duc	to lead	conductor (someone who leads a musical group, such as an orchestra)
gen	born	genealogy (the study of ancestry)
log/logue	spoken	monologue (a speech performed by one person)
mand/mend	to instruct	command (to give someone stern instructions to do something)
mis/mit	to send	transmit (to send something to another place)
omni	all	omniscient (all knowing)
path	related to sickness or feelings	pathology (the study of diseases)
phil	loving	philanthropist (someone that acts for the good of others)
photo	light	photon (a small particle of light)

Root	Meaning	Example
qui	to rest	quiet (to make less noise)
scrib/script	to write	transcript (a written copy of spoken words)
vac	empty, void	vacant (the state of being empty)
vid/vis	related to sight	video (a recording that is viewed, or watched)

COMMON PREFIXES

Prefix	Meaning	Example
dis-	not	disagree (not agree)
im-	not	impossible (not possible)
in-	in, into, not	injustice (an action that is not just)
mis-	wrongly	misspell (to spell wrongly)
non-	not	nonpaid (not paid)
pre-	before	preview (to view before)
sub-	under	submerge (to sink below the surface)
super-	over or greater than	superhuman (greater than a regular human)
trans-	across, through, or change	translate (to write or say in a different language)

COMMON SUFFIXES

Suffix	Meaning	Example
-able	can be done	likeable (can be liked)
-er	a person connected with	teacher (a person connected with teaching)
-ful	full of	wonderful (full of wonder)
-it/ity	state of	activity (state of being active)
-ive	cause to, tend to, or doing	creative (a person who tends to make new things or think of new ideas)
-logy	study of	biology (study of life)
-ment	the result	payment (the result of being paid)
-ness	state of being	darkness (being dark)

Suffix	Meaning	Example
-y	characterized by	cloudy (characterized by clouds)

EXAMPLE

Use knowledge of affixes to figure out the meaning of the word *mournful* in the following sentence:

> "Well, it being away in the night and stormy, and all so mysterious-like, I felt just the way any other boy would a felt when I see that wreck laying there so *mournful* and lonesome in the middle of the river." (From *The Adventures of Huckleberry Finn* by Mark Twain).

Mourn means to grieve for something, while *-ful* refers to being "full of". Putting the two components together, *mournful* means "full of grief or sadness". This definition makes sense in the context of the sentence. The "wreck" in the sentence is sad looking because it is in the river by itself.

When trying to determine the meaning of a word, always look for a root word and any prefixes or suffixes that have been added on to the root word. If a component of a word is not familiar, decipher what is clear about the word, then look at the word as used in context.

CHAPTER QUIZ

1. A thesaurus can do all of the following, EXCEPT:

a. Give synonyms of words
b. Give word definitions
c. Help find the meaning of an unfamiliar word
d. Help authors vary their word choice when writing

2. Which of the following are words that sound alike, but are spelled differently and have different meanings?

a. Synonyms
b. Antonyms
c. Homophones
d. Homographs

3. What common suffix indicates state of being?

a. -ness
b. -y
c. -ful
d. -er

CHAPTER QUIZ ANSWER KEY

1. B: See section **Thesaurus**

2. C: See section **Similar Words**

3. A: See section **Common Suffixes**

Comprehension Skills

Making Predictions

When you read a story, you should look for clues to make a prediction about what will happen. At the end of the story, you may even think about what will happen next to the main character, and use the clues in the story to make a prediction. You can also use personal experience to help make a prediction.

Suppose there is a story about a boy going swimming, and he swims too far out. Suppose the story says the boy can't get back to shore and starts to yell. Suppose the lifeguard comes and helps him. Suppose the story stops after the boy goes back in the water again. The reader might make the prediction that the boy won't swim as far out this time. This may not be true, but it is the most likely thing to happen.

Example

Describe what prediction can be made based on the following sentences:

> When Glen is sick, his mother keeps him home from school. He stays in bed all day and takes medicine. Glen woke up this morning with a sore throat. His head was hot, and he felt achy.

The story says that Glen's mother keeps him home when he is sick and that Glen spends the day in bed when he is sick. The story says that Glen woke up this morning with a sore throat. His head was hot, and he felt achy. The reader can figure out that Glen was sick. Because Glen's mother always keeps him home when he is sick, the reader can predict that Glen will be staying home from school and spending the day in bed.

You can also use text features find information to make predictions and verify conclusions determined about different texts. Using key words as clues, looking for bold print words, looking for sentences that include captions, and words that are written in italics are a few features that can be used to help understand and make predictions about a text.

Using Structure and Genre to Make Predictions

The structure and genre of a story can also help readers make predictions. Most stories follow the same structure. They have an exposition, rising action, a climax, falling action, and a resolution. Because most stories follow this structure, readers can predict that each of these parts will occur in the story. For example, rising action usually begins after the conflict of the story is introduced. This means that if characters have not faced any conflict, the reader can predict that something will go wrong for the characters. Likewise, stories in the same genre may contain similar events. For example, in a mystery, the characters work to solve a crime or explain a strange event. So, when reading a mystery, the reader can predict that the conflict will be a crime or event that the characters must learn more about.

Making Connections to Enhance Comprehension

Reading involves thinking. For good comprehension, readers make text-to-self, text-to-text, and text-to-world connections. Making connections helps readers understand text better and predict what might occur next based on what they already know, such as how characters in the story feel or what happened in another text. Readers can make connections before, during, and after reading. Venn diagrams and other graphic organizers can help readers visualize connections.

Text-to-Self

Reading while looking for connections with the reader's life and experiences makes literature more personally relevant and meaningful to readers. Sentences showing text-to-self connections may begin with these examples

- This is similar to a time when...
- I empathize with this character because...
- The setting makes me think of...
- I experienced this same thing when...

Text-to-Text

Reading while looking for connections to other texts helps the reader learn to identify the way authors use genre, setting, characters, plot elements, literary structure and devices, and themes to create meaning. Authors can also **allude** to other works by quoting or referencing events from a well-known source. Sentences showing text-to-text connections may begin with these examples

- The character shares the same flaw as the character in...
- This is an allusion to the events in...
- The conflict in this story is similar to the conflict in...
- The relationship between the protagonist and antagonist is different than the one in...

Text-to-World

Reading while looking for connections to the world helps the reader begin to see literature as a reflection of real life and notice patterns in history and current events. Sentences showing text-to-world connections may begin with these examples

- The event in this story sounds like the event in history when...
- The actions of this character sound like the historical tale of...
- This is like what happened in real life when...
- I heard about this on the news when...

Making Inferences

An **inference** is a **conclusion** or generalization that the reader makes based on the information provided within a text. Certain facts are included to help a reader come to a specific conclusion. It is what the story may hint about, and what a reader can conclude as a result of what the author says in the passage. It is also the best guess that a reader can make based on what happened or was said or in a story. A good inference is based on or supported by details in the passage.

Readers may come to their own conclusion about a topic, or the author may state a conclusion at the end of a story. When readers are in the middle of a story, they can predict what will happen at the end of it based on the events that have occurred so far and the typical characteristics that have been presented by the author up to that point. A reader needs to consider all of the information that an author has presented, including the main point and supporting points, to make logical conclusions and inferences about the story.

For instance, if a passage says that Joan is holding her mouth and moaning, you might conclude, or **infer,** that she has a sore mouth or a toothache. You cannot be sure of this, but it is the best conclusion that you can reach using the information at hand. Inferences are considered **implicit**

information. They are not found directly in a passage, but they can be supported by explicit information from the passage.

Review Video: Inference
Visit mometrix.com/academy and enter code: 379203

Finding Explicit Information

Explicit information is the term for information that is **directly stated** in a story or passage. It is what **the author tells you**. It is not information that is hinted at or that you have to make a conclusion about. Explicit information can be facts or details about an event, something or someone. There is usually a lot of explicit information in a story and this information is often used to make an inference or draw a conclusion. to answer questions that ask about explicit information, simply reread the story until you find the answer. in fiction, details about characters, events, and setting are often explicit.

Example

Read the following excerpt and identify which information is explicit.

> In ancient times the value of an ox was the basis for the monetary systems of the Greeks, Assyrians, Mesopotamians, and the Egyptians. Each of these territories had their own currency. For instance, Egypt traded in gold and Greece in silver or copper.

All of the information in the excerpt is explicit. Nothing is hinted at. It says that the value of an ox was the basis for the monetary system for ancient Greeks, Assyrians, Mesopotamians, and the Egyptians. It adds that each of these territories had their own currency. It further informs that Egypt traded in gold and Greece in silver or copper. All of this information is factual. There are no opinions in the excerpt. There is nothing with which to make an inference

Implicit Information

Implicit information is information that is **not directly stated** in a text, but can be inferred from something that the author explicitly states. For instance, the author may say "Seth buys a new TV, laptop, and home theater system every year." from this the reader could infer several things. For instance, Seth probably likes electronics and has a lot of spending money.

Example

Draw a conclusion based on the implicit information in the following sentence from the *Adventures of Tom Sawyer* by Mark Twain:

> He had discovered a great law of human action, without knowing it—namely, that in order to make a man or a boy covet a thing, it is only necessary to make the thing difficult to attain.

The reader can clearly see from the sentence that the character did not set out to learn something, but through an action, the character learned that people will want what is hard to attain. Although it's not explicitly stated, the reader can draw the conclusion that the character gained the experience of coveting (or desiring) something that was hard to get.

EXAMPLE

An inference can be made about the character of the narrator based on the following excerpt from David Copperfield by Charles Dickens:

> My father's eyes had closed upon the light of this world six months, when mine opened on it. There is something strange to me...in the shadowy remembrance that I have of my first childish associations with his white grave-stone in the churchyard, and of the indefinable compassion I used to feel for it lying out alone there in the dark night, when our little parlour was warm and bright with fire and candle, and the doors of our house were - almost cruelly, it seemed to me sometimes - bolted and locked against it.

In order to make an inference, the reader must use clues from the passage to come to a conclusion. It is explicitly stated in the passage that David's father died before he was born. Based on the excerpt, the reader can infer that David Copperfield feels sadness over the loss of his father, even though he never knew him. This inference about David's character can be made using context clues from the passage: David feels "indefinable compassion" for his father's gravestone. The phrase "almost cruelly" indicates that David feels that his family is perhaps too harsh in their treatment of his father. He feels a connection to his father's gravestone and feels bad that the stone is left out in the cold when his house is warm.

EXAMPLE

An inference can be made about the character Pip based on the following excerpt from Great Expectations by Charles Dickens:

> I never had one hour's happiness in her society, and yet my mind all round the four-and-twenty hours was harping on the happiness of having her with me unto death.

In order to make an inference, the reader must use clues from the passage to come to a conclusion. This excerpt shows the reader Pip, who is thinking about a romantic relationship with a woman. The words "yet my mind all round the four and twenty hours" and "harping" lead the reader to infer that he has a crush on this woman and cannot get her out of his thoughts. Pip has never enjoyed her company, yet he dreams of their happiness together. From this, the reader can infer that Pip is unrealistic about romantic relationships.

EXAMPLE

Draw a conclusion based on the following sentence.

> New Orleans then was a mere huddle of buildings around Jackson Square; but with the purchase of the Louisiana territory from France, and the great influx of American enterprise that characterized the first quarter of the last century, development was working like yeast...

The reader needs to use prior experience and background information to draw an accurate conclusion about the sentence. The sentence describes how New Orleans grew after the "purchase of the Louisiana territory" and how "development was working like yeast". Yeast multiplies rapidly, so the reader can conclude that New Orleans was growing rapidly.

KEY IDEAS AND SUPPORTING DETAILS

Identifying **key ideas** helps the reader see what a text or story is mostly about. They are the **most important ideas** in a text, and everything else in the text builds around and supports them. Every piece of writing has key ideas. The **supporting details** in a story, such as the characters, events, and settings, will work together to reveal the key ideas. The details are not key ideas, themselves. They make the key ideas clear and show the reader the author's purpose for writing the text.

SYNTHESIZING A TEXT WITH EXISTING KNOWLEDGE

Synthesizing is similar to summarizing but it takes it one step further. Synthesizing involves taking the main points of a text and comparing it with existing knowledge to create a new idea, perspective, or way of thinking.

Another term for knowledge that you already have is **schema**. The plural form of this word is **schemata**. Schemata contain all the ideas you have about something. Synthesizing is all about how schemata change over time with the introduction of new information.

EXAMPLE

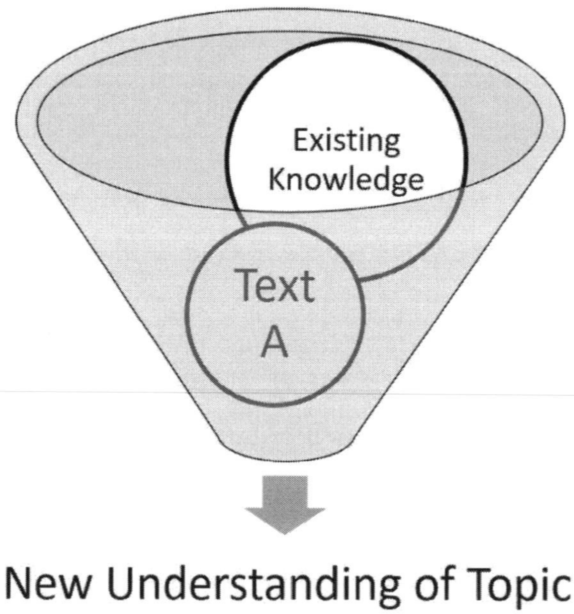

Using self-questioning strategies can help readers synthesize texts with their schemata to increase or change their understanding of topics. These questions include

- What do I already know about this topic?
- Is any of this new information?
- Has my perspective changed now that I've read this?
- What do I understand now that I didn't before?
- What are the main ideas of this text?
- How do the parts of the text fit together to create meaning?
- Are there any text-to-text, text-to-self, or text-to-world connections here?

SYNTHESIZING TEXTS WITHOUT EXISTING KNOWLEDGE

If the reader is completely unfamiliar with the topic, they will have no background knowledge. In this case, instead of using existing knowledge, synthesizing may instead be done by combining the ideas provided in two or three different texts. The reader must make connections between the texts, determine how the ideas fit together, and gather evidence to support the new perspective.

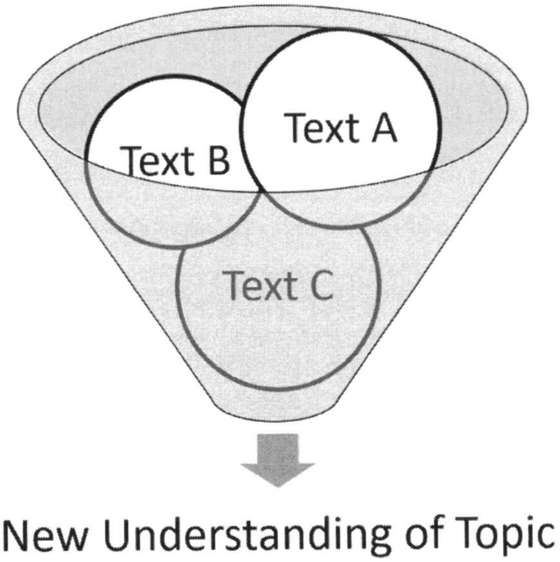

Using self-questioning strategies can help readers synthesize texts to increase their understanding of topics. In this case, readers are creating new schemata as they read. These questions include

- What do these texts have in common?
- What is different between these texts?
- What new information have I learned?
- What do I understand now that I didn't before?
- How do these texts relate to one another?
- If I think of these texts as parts of one whole, what meaning do they create together?
- What predictions can I make about this topic?

Chapter Quiz

1. Which of the following helps the reader learn to identify ways authors use genre, setting, characters, plot elements, literary structure and devices, and themes to create meaning?

a. Reading while looking for connections to the reader's life
b. Reading while looking for connections to other texts
c. Reading while looking for connections to the world
d. Reading while looking for connections to history

2. Which of the following is a conclusion that the reader makes using clues in the text?

a. Thesis
b. Prediction
c. Inference
d. Guess

3. What term refers to knowledge that you already have?

a. Cognition
b. Glossary
c. Schema
d. Explicit information

Chapter Quiz Answer Key

1. B: See section **Making Connections to Enhance Comprehension**

2. C: See section **Making Inferences**

3. C: See section **Synthesizing a Text with Existing Knowledge**

Response Skills

Text Evidence

The term **text evidence** refers to information found in a text that supports a reader's claim about the text. A reader can draw conclusions or inferences based upon information found in a text. Often, the author will deliberately include information that supports the main point of the text to help the reader make conclusions and inferences that align with the author's purpose for writing the text.

Drawing Conclusions Based on Text Evidence

Readers often need to use prior experience and background information to draw an accurate conclusion about the passage they are reading. Sometimes interpreting the information in a sentence can be difficult, especially if the reader is unfamiliar with some of the words used in a sentence. Looking at the words that the reader does understand in the sentence can help. By taking a pen or pencil and underlining important information in a sentence, the reader can better understand what the author is trying to say and draw a clearer conclusion from that.

Example

Draw a conclusion based on the following sentence.

> New Orleans then was a mere huddle of buildings around Jackson Square; but with the purchase of the Louisiana territory from France, and the great influx of American enterprise that characterized the first quarter of the last century, development was working like yeast...

The sentence describes how New Orleans grew after the "purchase of the Louisiana territory" and how "development was working like yeast". Yeast multiplies rapidly, so the reader can conclude that New Orleans was growing rapidly.

Example

Read the following sentence. Draw a conclusion based upon the information presented.

> "A rosy-faced servant-maid opened the door, and smiled as she took the letter which he silently offered."

The reader can conclude, based on the sentence, that the servant-maid is friendly. The words "rosy-faced" and "smiled" lead the reader to this conclusion. People who are friendly are often described as having rosy complexions and smiling as a common sign of pleasantness. The reader can also assume, from the sentence, that the letter does not present any threat or unpleasantness to the servant-maid. The person presenting the letter does not have anything to say upon offering it, so perhaps he is waiting to see how the servant-maid will react.

When interpreting a sentence, always look for key words that describe a character. The author carefully crafts a description of each character, to form a picture in the reader's mind about what the character is like.

Paraphrasing and Summarizing

Paraphrasing and summarizing are two ways readers can work to understand what they read. Both involve reading a text and recalling the main points in an accurate way, but they differ in several ways.

How to Paraphrase	How to Summarize
State the message in the text in the reader's own words, while keeping the original meaning of the text Take all of the original ideas and word them in a way that the reader can better understand Put what the reader has read into their own words, rephrasing what the author has written	State main points of the text clearly and to-the-point. Take information and state it simply, in a much shorter form. Put information in a short form that keeps the main points of the whole text. Do not include many details, just the main idea of the text

Paraphrasing is often done for individual ideas, while summarizing is done for an entire block of text or ideas. Often times, a summary can be done in just one sentence, boiling down the author's words into just main idea.

Review Video: Summarizing Text
Visit mometrix.com/academy and enter code: 172903

Example

Read the following paragraph and then give a one sentence summary statement:

> When choosing a pet, people need to think about what type of home they can offer the animal. For example, a small apartment might not be a good fit for a large dog, but could be a comfortable home for a kitten. A house that has a big yard would be great for a puppy, but a rabbit does not need a large yard.

In order to summarize, one has to identify the main idea and any supporting ideas in the author's work. The summary is an overview of the author's paragraph and will tell what it is about without getting into any of the details. The summary needs to be broad enough to cover all of the information in the author's paragraph. Here is a possible summary statement for the above paragraph:

> People need to consider a number of factors, particularly the available space they have, when choosing a pet.

EXAMPLE

Read the following sentences and then paraphrase the material:

> The government is debating a new health care system for our country. The Senate and the House of Representatives have both passed bills; now they need to resolve these two bills into one bill that a majority can agree on.

When paraphrasing information, one needs to read carefully and pay attention to details, then put the material away and write or tell it in their own words. One does not want to look at the material while paraphrasing to avoid plagiarizing by accident. Here is one example of a way to paraphrase the sentences:

> Our government is trying to adopt a new health care system. The Senate has passed a bill and so has the House of Representatives. Their bills are different so now they have to compromise on one bill that can be passed.

EXAMPLE

Read the summary and explain how to improve it.

> Edgar Degas was a great artist who broke with tradition and became an Impressionist. His paintings and sculptures are included in the collections of major museums everywhere. In his forties, his vision became poor and he worked more on sculptures because he could feel them. He died in 1917 at the age of 83. His father was a banker.

This summary is quite good. It has a main idea and includes some of the important details. The main idea is that Degas was a great artist. Supporting details include that his paintings and sculpture are included in collections of major museums as well as the fact that he had poor vision and turned to sculpting because he could feel the sculptures. While the information about his death is not perhaps the most important, it is of interest that he lived to the age of 83. The one glaring error with the summary is that it mentions the fact that his father was a banker. This does not directly relate to the main idea. It is not a supporting detail and is unimportant to the central thesis of the passage. It should be deleted.

SUMMARIZING LITERATURE TO SUPPORT COMPREHENSION

When reading literature, especially demanding works, summarizing helps readers identify important information and organize it in their minds. They can also identify themes, problems, and solutions, and can sequence the story. Readers can summarize before, during, and after they read. They should use their own words, as they do when describing a personal event or giving directions. Previewing a text's organization before reading by examining the book cover, table of contents, and illustrations also aids summarizing. So does making notes of key words and ideas in a graphic organizer while reading. Graphic organizers are another useful method; readers skim the text to determine main ideas and then narrow the list with the aid of the organizer. Unimportant details should be omitted in summaries. Summaries can include description, problem-solution, comparison-contrast, sequence, main ideas, and cause-and-effect.

CHAPTER QUIZ

1. If a reader takes an author's original idea and then restates it, putting the idea into their own words, this is an example of:

a. Outlining text
b. Paraphrasing text
c. Summarizing text
d. Abstracting text

2. Which of the following is NOT true of summarizing?

a. A summary can be just one sentence that boils down the author's words into the main idea.
b. Summarizing helps readers work to understand what they have read.
c. A summary typically involves restating the main points of a text in a simpler, shorter fashion.
d. A summary should be subjective and include brief personal opinions on the subject.

CHAPTER QUIZ ANSWER KEY

1. B: See section **Paraphrasing and Summarizing**

2. D: See section **Paraphrasing and Summarizing**

Literary Elements

THEME

The **theme** of a story is a unifying idea that is used throughout the text; it can take the form of a common setting, idea, symbol, design, or recurring event. The theme of a story may vary according to place, time, and characters, but theme is often based on common human experience. A plot line is built around the theme of a story. Most themes are about life, society, or human nature. The theme is often why a passage is written. It helps give a passage unity. The theme is created through the development of the story. The events of a story help shape the kind of theme the passage. A theme is not usually stated explicitly. The reader **infers** the theme from the topic, information, or plot of a passage.

For example, a series of events in a story may be based upon people being willing to trust the actions of others. The story may be centered on why people need to trust others in order to carry out important actions. For example, a character may trust that a bus driver will stay on the road while the bus driver, in turn, trusts that the passengers stay in their seats so that they do not distract him.

The theme of a story is not the same as the topic of a story. The topic is what the story is about, but the theme is what a reader is meant to learn. When readers are discussing theme, they can determine both theme topics as well as theme statements.

Theme topics are broad ideas that apply to the text. Examples include:

- Love changes people
- Man versus man
- Man versus nature
- Man versus himself
- Fate versus free will
- Triumph over adversity

- Coming of age
- The importance of friendship
- Good vs. evil
- The circle of life

Themes may also be complete statements written in sentence form. Examples are:

- Acts of courage can bring positive changes to the world.
- True friendship can withstand the hardest challenges.
- What is on the inside is what makes a person beautiful.

> **Review Video: Themes in Literature**
> Visit mometrix.com/academy and enter code: 732074

Example

Tell why the theme of the following excerpt should be "Overconfidence can lead to a fall."

> Bella was happy. She auditioned for the starring role in the school play and she felt sure she'd got the part. Afterwards, she told her friends she would be starring in the play. But on Tuesday when the director said they had offered the part to Sara Goodwin, she started crying.

The excerpt tells the story of a girl who has an audition and thinks she got the starring role. She is so confident that she even tells her friends that she has the part. But then she learns that the role was offered to someone else and she starts to cry. She was overly confident about her success and was subsequently devastated when she learned of her failure, and that is the lesson of the story. If you are overly confident you may have a fall. That is the theme of the story. A theme is the lesson that a story teaches. This particular theme is found often in literature. A theme is not stated in a passage: the reader must deduce it from the plot of the story.

Example

Determine the theme of the following short paragraph:

> Matt had spent a lot of time preparing for his first babysitting experience. Matt stayed fully attentive to his young cousin, Toby, while he played outside. When his aunt returned, Matt was proud to report that all had gone well. He had acted in the adult role.

The short paragraph shown here is a coming of age story. This means that the protagonist goes through some kind of experience that changes him or her from a child into an adult. By preparing to care for his cousin Toby and keeping him safe while his aunt was away, Matt became more of an adult and less of a child. Taking care of someone else is an adult thing to do and Matt was successful. This was a defining moment in his life.

Universal Themes

Some themes are fairly common. These themes are called **universal themes** and they suggest things about life, society, and human nature. If a reader is trying to decide whether a theme is universal or not, they must consider whether the theme they have identified can be applied to other works as well. Some examples of universal theme topics are:

Good Versus Evil

- The universal theme of a small number of people invested in doing good works becoming a powerful force against those doing evil works can be seen in multiple texts, including the *Harry Potter* series by J.K. Rowling, *The Hunger Games* by Suzanne Collins, and *Cinder* by Marissa Meyer.

Change Versus Tradition

- *The Giver* by Lois Lowry, the *Divergent* series by Veronica Roth, and *Children of Eden* by Joey Graceffa all reveal the universal theme of the ongoing struggle for societies to welcome change rather than being stuck in tradition.

Man Versus Man

- Learning that people are capable of committing horrifying acts against other people is a universal theme evident in *The Boy in the Striped Pajamas* by John Boyne, *A Long Walk to Water* by Linda Sue Park, and *All the Light We Cannot See* by Anthony Doerr.

Characters and Theme

What a character says either to another character or about a situation may help the reader determine the theme of the text by revealing what a character is thinking or what he may do. Dialogue in the text can also help the reader determine the theme of the story by showing what the character intends to do in the future. For instance, as you read, ask yourself if a character is doing something wrong and, if so, ask yourself if the character is punished at the end of a story.

Characters

Character Trait

The traits of a character may include how they act and physical characteristics; a character trait is a behavior or physical characteristic that is unique to a specific character. For example, a character may be outgoing, which means he or she likes to talk a lot, or they may have bright red hair. These are both character traits.

An author uses character traits to describe a character in a story and help the reader to learn more about how the character acts and what they look like. By comparing the character traits in a story, the reader can see similarities and differences between characters. The author includes character traits to help the reader understand why a character may act a certain way in the story. For example, a character who is shy may not want to talk with a lot of people in a new classroom, but a character who is outgoing may want to talk with many people.

An author typically provides many details about a character so that the reader can learn more about the character's traits, motivations, relationships, and any conflicts they may have in the story. The traits of a character may include how they act and how they look. Characters are often motivated by things that have already happened in their life or how they feel about a topic. The author will often give the reader enough information about the character so that the reader can figure out why the character responds to a situation in a certain way. The author will also often give details about the relationships between characters and points they may conflict on. For example, a character may be good friends with another character; however, the two characters may disagree on where to play outside if one character likes being near the water and the other character does not.

Example

Read the following description of a character and decide, logically, whether the character is likely to go hiking outdoors:

> Jeremy lived in a high-rise in Chicago. He was studious, and not very athletic. Jeremy preferred to stay indoors and read a book, rather than enjoy outdoor weather.

Based on the description of the character's traits, preferences, and personality, he is not likely to go hiking outdoors. The description indicates that the character prefers reading, rather than enjoying outdoor weather. In addition, the character lives in a tall building in the middle of a large city, in order for him to enjoy the outdoors, he would have to travel away from where he lives. The character is not likely to change his preferences. A situation may lead the character to go hiking, but he is not likely to initiate the action on his own. A description of a character that is likely to go hiking outdoors may include a preference for outdoor activity and living near trails.

Character Changes and Responses

Characters can change in a multitude of ways throughout a story; however, there are main aspects of a character that change. A character's identifying **characteristics**, such as personality or behavior traits, may change as the result of a prominent event in the story, current **motivations**, and conflicts. As **conflicts** change or are resolved, a character may no longer be motivated by striving toward a goal that was previously important to them. Furthermore, a character's development may also lead them to make **different choices**, which can **impact the plot**. As the plot of a story moves along, characters can constantly change in relation to events that occur. Relationships between characters and the points of view of characters may change throughout a story as well.

Each story will have many different types of characters and each of these characters will have a different relationship with other characters. Stories usually have a protagonist, antagonist, and a variety of other characters including round, flat, and stock characters.

Protagonist

The main character in a drama, movie, novel, or other fictional text. The author portrays the protagonist in a way that the audience is most like to identify with themselves. The protagonist is generally undertaking some type of personal challenge throughout the story. The author writes the story so that the reader becomes aware of the protagonist's emotions and is generally able to empathize with the personal challenge.

Antagonist

The character that actively opposes the protagonist by trying to prevent them from succeeding. The antagonist is usually presented in such a way as to make the audience dislike them, and want them to fail at stopping the protagonist. The protagonist and antagonist oppose each other, so their relationship is almost always one of dislike.

Flat Character

Does not have any substantial changes throughout the story. They stay the same despite the conflict, and do not learn any lessons. They are usually minor characters that might interact with the main character in some way.

Round Character

Major characters in the story that will be more fully developed than other minor characters. They will usually encounter some type of conflict that they must overcome, and usually learn a lesson about life or themselves along the way.

Stock Characters

Often get their characteristics and mannerisms from stereotypes of people that are widely recognized. These types of characters are often repeated and well-known. Readers should be aware that stereotypes are rarely accurate in reality, and are generally intended to be humorous or dramatic. Some examples are evil stepmothers, unintelligent blondes, rude athletes, and loyal servants.

Characters' Influence on the Plot

There are many ways in which the action of a story may be driven. Dialogue is one of them. What a character says either to another character or about a situation may propel the action by revealing what a character is thinking or what he may do. Similarly, what a character says will tell the audience what he is like. His manner of speaking, what he says, and how he says it are all clues to his personality. Dialogue can also provoke a decision by showing what the character intends to do in the future. Incidents in a story also propel the action because the plot is made up of events that build on events. Incidents such as a confrontation could reveal aspects of a character or provoke a decision.

Example

Read the excerpt and tell how this incident propels the action of the story and provokes a decision.

> It was a perfect day it seemed, until Sam saw the thunderheads roll in. He knew that it would be dangerous to be in a rowboat in the middle of the lake during a thunder and lightning storm. Suddenly the sky became darker and he heard a clap of thunder.

This incident certainly propels the action of the story. It would appear that Sam is in a rowboat in the middle of the lake having a lovely time when he hears a clap of thunder. He realizes that a lake is a dangerous place to be so this event means that Sam must take action. What that action is would be of interest to the reader because it will help form the plot of the story. The incident also forces Sam to make a decision about what he should do. This will help the reader better understand Sam as a character.

Plot

The storyline of any text is also called a **plot**. The characters and events in the story determine what the plot will be. When events occur in a **linear** way, the story is generally told in chronological order and the order of events make sense. In texts with linear plots, readers may find a **plot line** useful as they try to put the events in the text in order and determine the relationships between events.

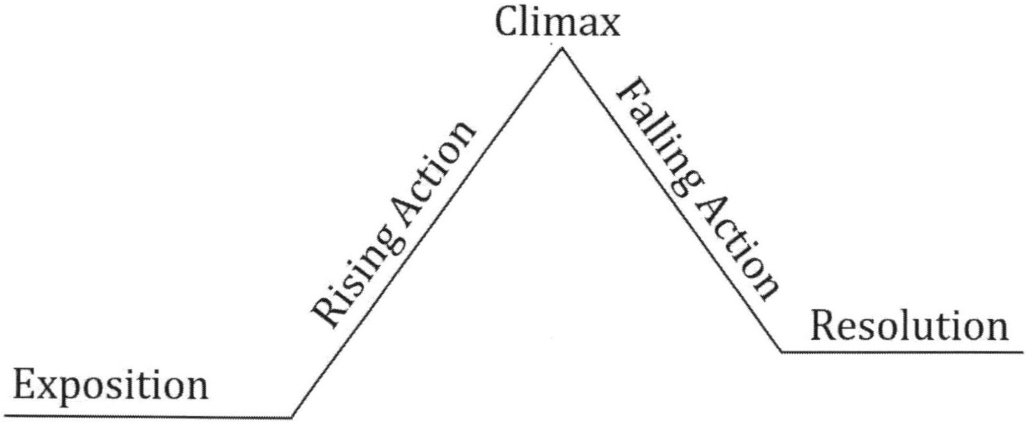

Review Video: Plot Line
Visit mometrix.com/academy and enter code: 944011

Linear plots will begin with **exposition**, which introduces the characters and the setting of the story. The plot will continue to develop as new ideas and events centered on the main conflict in the story are revealed, which is called the **rising action**. The action in the story will rise until a **climax** is reached within the conflict. The climax can also be referred to as the turning point in the story, since the climax is where each character makes an important decision. After the climax, the action starts to wind down during the **falling action**. At this point, the characters begin to follow the paths they chose in during climax. The events of the story reach **resolution** in some way by the end of the story. Some conflicts are left open-ended, so that the reader is left to decide what really happened at the end of the story. Keep in mind that not all resolutions are happy or peaceful.

Conflict

An important part of analyzing the plot of a passage is identifying the **main conflict**. There will likely be many smaller conflicts in the story, but there will be one main problem that influences the characters and events. To identify the main conflict, first look at who the main character is. Now ask yourself what they want. They may want to something to happen or not happen, another character to do or not do something, or to confront or avoid a problem, among other things. Once you know what they want, now ask yourself what is standing in the character's way. It may be a person, an event, or something less tangible like the passing of time. Combining what the main character wants and why they do not currently have leaves the reader with a summary of the main conflict.

Example

Read the following sentence from *The Call of the Wild* by Jack London and describe the main conflict in the sentence. Explain how the conflict may be resolved.

> The breaking down of discipline likewise affected the dogs in their relations with one another.

Based on the information in the sentence, an event has caused the dogs, the characters in the story, to not follow their regular routine. The sentence indicates that there has been a breaking down of discipline which is affecting how the dogs relate to each other. In order to solve this conflict, discipline needs to be restored. However, in order to return to previous relations between the dogs, any problems that are in the way of conflict resolution need to be taken care of. The word *likewise* means *also*, which tells the reader that other parts of the story are being affected besides the relations between the dogs.

RESOLUTION

The term **resolution** usually indicates the result of a conflict in a story. Conflict between characters, within a character, or against an external element is necessary in order to have a plot for a story. without conflict, no events would occur to form the story. A conflict will come to a climax, and then conclude in some way. The resolution of a problem may be open-ended, end tragically, or end in a way that is good for everyone involved. The problem resolution typically occurs near the end of a story, after the climax has happened. A problem may be resolved by the characters involved within the conflict or by an external event; an upcoming resolution may be foreshadowed in the text, or may be completely unexpected by the reader. If the resolution is completely unexpected, it is considered to be a **twist** in the story.

NON-LINEAR PLOT DEVELOPMENT

Some texts contain a **non-linear plot**, which means the plot is not told in chronological order, or is not told from "beginning to end" in one straight line. There are several devices that authors can use to make their plot non-linear, including:

- **Foreshadowing:** the author gives the reader hints early on in a work about something that will become clearer (or more important) later on.
- **Flashback:** the author shows the reader an event that happened in the past to explain something about the present.
- **Subplot:** a side story, usually about a supporting character, is told along with the main story. Sometimes subplots occur within flashbacks.
- **Parallel plot:** two stories are told alongside each other, often narrated by two different characters in alternating chapters. The events in the stories usually end up overlapping or coming together at some point, most often the climax of the text.

SETTING

The setting is where a story **takes place**. The setting of a story may stay the same for the entire story, or change as events in the story unfold. For example, an entire story may take place in one room or cross continents as the reader follows the characters along on a trail of events.

The setting of a story is described by the author in terms of what it looks like, how the character feels, and anything else that is happening at that location at the time. For example, a character may be caught on a doorstep on a cold, rainy day. The character may feel frustrated as they shiver in the doorway, waiting for the heavy rain to let up a bit.

SHAPING A CHARACTER WITH SETTING OR PLOT

The setting of a story shapes character because it helps to define the situation that a character finds herself in. A character is limited to the setting of a story. For example, if a story takes place in a cold environment filled with snow and ice, this is certain to impact what actions a character can and will take. Frequently, the setting changes the way characters behave based on time. For example, the character of a woman who is a single mother in 1920 would be seen and behave very differently than a single mother in 2020.

EXAMPLE

Read the excerpt and determine how the setting influences the character in this excerpt.

> She had swum too far out. The waves were higher than she thought. She was struggling hard to get to shore. She wondered if she would make it. She thought of her childhood. Had she been right to run away from home, she wondered? Just then, a lifeguard grabbed her and helped her to shore.

The setting of the ocean and the high waves creates a conflict in the character. She is worried. She thinks about her childhood and her parents. She doesn't know if she will make it to shore. This is how the setting affects the character in this excerpt. Without the high waves and the struggle, she would not become so worried and start to think about her past. She probably would not have questioned herself. This is an example of how a setting influences a character. If the waves had not been high, there probably would not have been a struggle or any self-searching of the swimmer's past.

HISTORICAL AND CULTURAL SETTING

Historical context influences literature in a number of ways. The style of the author's writing can be impacted by the historical period during which it was written (e.g., Dickens wrote at a time when authors were paid by the word; this is why his novels are so long). Obviously, the setting of the book includes its historical context. In addition, dialect may be a function of the historical period of the book. When a reader understands the historical context of a particular book, he or she can have a deeper understanding of the novel. Knowing about the time period during which the author wrote, as well as the time period discussed in the novel, helps the reader understand some of the author's choices, including character motivations.

EXAMPLE

Slavery used to be the norm in Southern states. One of the major ways in which the historical context of slavery impacted literature coming out of the South was the birth of the slave narrative. Slaves wanted to have their experiences documented. After the Civil War, former slaves wrote their stories. These slave narratives have given historians valuable firsthand accounts of life in the South. From a literary perspective, slave narratives are one of the most important genres of African-American writing. Slavery influenced literature by delving into themes of power, racial injustice, and equality. Literature from this time period can help the reader better understand the perspectives and experiences of the slaves themselves, as well as the slave holders.

PATTERNS RELATED TO SETTINGS

The setting of a story can allow the reader to draw on personal experience about where the story takes place. If a story takes place on a farm, the reader will likely picture a rural, peaceful setting, which may go along with (or be in contrast to) the actual plot of the story. For example, a reader would not expect a scary story to occur on a farm on a sunny day. Conversely, a reader may view a dark subway as a dangerous place, while the plot of a story set there may be based on a very calm series of events. When an author is crafting a story, they need to consider what the audience may already think about a particular setting in order to properly present the events of a story for greatest impact.

Chapter Quiz

1. What type of character often gets their characteristics and mannerisms from stereotypes of people that are widely recognized?

a. Minor characters
b. Stock characters
c. Flat characters
d. Round characters

2. Every plot will begin with ___________, which introduces the characters and the setting of the story.

a. Conflict
b. Rising action
c. Foreshadowing
d. Exposition

3. What plot device that authors can use to make their plot non-linear, is a side story told along with the main story?

a. Anecdote
b. Flashback
c. Subplot
d. Parallel plot

4. Which of the following would most likely convey a peaceful setting to the reader?

a. Sunny farm
b. Damp basement
c. Loud construction site
d. Dark subway

Chapter Quiz Answer Key

1. B: See section **Stock Characters**

2. D: See section **Plot**

3. C: See section **Non-Linear Plot Development**

4. A: See section **Patterns Related to Settings**

Literary Genres

Literary Genres

Literature contains many different **genres**, which are categories that texts can be divided into. Genres are used to group types of writing together for purposes of study, reading, or simple organization. Some common literary genres are

- **Realistic fiction** -A story that could actually happen and reflects life in a realistic way.
- **Adventure stories** -Short, mostly fictional stories that follow characters as they go on an adventure or quest.
- **Historical fiction** -Often strays from historical reality in order to tell a story and make a true historical event more interesting to the reader.
- **Mysteries** -Fiction stories about solving crimes or revealing secrets.

- **Humor** –Stories, mostly fictional, full of fun and excitement meant to entertain readers. Can be seen in stories from all genres.
- **Myth** -A legend or traditional narrative, often based on a historical event. The story reveals something about human behavior or the natural world, and often involves actions of gods.
- **Fantasy** -Fictional stories that contain unusual and other worldly settings and characters. The sense of "realness" in other stories is not present. The fantasy genre is known for including elements like magic and imaginary creatures like fairies, dragons, and elves.
- **Science fiction** -Fiction based on what could happen if actual, imagined, or possible scientific advances occurred. Usually set in the future, a modified past, or on other planets.
- **Short Story** -a fictional narrative that is shorter than a novel. However, there is not a definite page or word count that defines the short story category. Short stories tend to focus on one or few elements of a story in order to efficiently tell the story. Though they are often brief, short stories may still contain a moral or impact their readers.

POETRY

POET VERSUS SPEAKER

The author of a poem is called a **poet**. Many poems are written in first person, which means the **stanzas** (groups of lines) include words like "I" and "me." However, the poet is not always the **speaker** of the poem. In a novel, the author can create characters with different points of view. The characters can argue or have different roles to play in telling the story. Similarly, a poet may write a poem from a different point of view or even include more than one voice. The speaker is the voice of the poem, and is not always the same person as the poet him or herself. The reader or listener should know that the person telling the story is a character, and not always a real person.

For example, this excerpt from a poem by Dr. Seuss reads:

> When you think things are bad,
> when you feel sour and blue,
> when you start to get mad...
> you should do what I do!
> Just tell yourself, Duckie,
> you're really quite lucky!
> Some people are much more...
> oh, ever so much more...
> oh, muchly much-much more
> unlucky than you!

Even though one line has the word "I" in it, the poem is not from the perspective of Dr. Seuss. He is the author of the poem, but not the speaker. The person saying "I" is a character, just like in a story.

METER, RHYME, AND REPETITION IN POETRY

The **meter** of a poem refers to the number of syllables per line as well as the pattern of emphasis on those syllables. The use of meter gives a poem a rhythmic context and contributes to the poem's flow. Certain types of meter can also make a poem more appealing to the reader or represent natural speech rhythms.

Rhymes repeat the ending sound of words: "So very soon/We will fly to the moon." Here the "oo" sound is repeated in the words *soon* and *moon*. Rhymes are frequently used in poetry, mostly older forms of poetry rather than modern poems.

Another type of repetition is **alliteration**. Alliteration repeats beginning sounds, usually consonants: "Rah, rah, rah," the crowd cried, "rah, rah, rah." It is often used in poetry as well as in spoken forms of writing.

Rhyme Scheme

When determining what a poem's rhyme scheme is, readers should look at the last word of each line to see which words rhyme with each other. Words that rhyme are assigned a letter of the alphabet, beginning with "a." The next time words rhyme, if the rhyme is different than the last one, they assigned a new letter, going forward in order of the alphabet until the poem is over or there are no more rhymes. This sounds complicated, but it's easy with practice.

Let's take a look at an excerpt from Dylan Thomas' poem "Do not go gentle into that good night":

> Do not go gentle into that good night,
> Old age should burn and rave at close of day;
> Rage, rage against the dying of the light.
>
> Though wise men at their end know dark is right,
> Because their words had forked no lightning they
> Do not go gentle into that good night.

The words at the end of the lines are *night, day, light, right, they,* and *night.*

We know that the first rhyme is assigned the letter "a," and can clearly see that *night, light,* and *right* all rhyme, so we can mark the poem like this

> Do not go gentle into that good night, **a**
> Old age should burn and rave at close of day;
> Rage, rage against the dying of the light. **a**
>
> Though wise men at their end know dark is right, **a**
> Because their words had forked no lightning they
> Do not go gentle into that good night. **a**

Now, we'll look at the only other rhyme in the poem, which is made up of the words *day* and *they.* This rhyme does not rhyme with the first set of words, so it gets a new letter, "b."

> Do not go gentle into that good night, **a**
> Old age should burn and rave at close of day; **b**
> Rage, rage against the dying of the light. **a**
>
> Though wise men at their end know dark is right, **a**
> Because their words had forked no lightning they **b**
> Do not go gentle into that good night. **a**

After looking at all six lines and determining how they rhyme, we can confidently say that the rhyme scheme for this excerpt is a, b, a, a, b, a.

Rhymes are used at the discretion of the poet and are not always mandatory. Many modern poems—actually, most of them—use a blank verse, where there are no rhyme schemes. However, there are many formal poetic types, such as the sonnet, that have a specific rhyme scheme that poets must follow to achieve that kind of poetic form.

EXAMPLE

Explain the rhyme scheme of the following excerpt from a poem entitled "Alone" by Edgar Allan Poe.

> From childhood's hour I have not been
> As others were; I have not seen
> As others saw; I could not bring
> My passions from a common spring.
> From the same source I have not taken
> My sorrow; I could not awaken
> My heart to joy at the same tone;
> And all I loved, I loved alone.

The rhyme scheme that Edgar Allan Poe uses in this excerpt from his poem "Alone" is: a, a, b, b, c, c, d, d, e, e. Every two lines rhyme, but the rhyme is not repeated in the other lines. This is a rather unusual rhyme scheme; many others have lines that repeat the rhyme scheme, but not in a consecutive order, such as a, b, a, b or a, b, c a, b, c.

GRAPHICAL ELEMENTS IN POETRY

Graphic elements in a poem such as capitalization, line length, and word position can call special attention to words or phrases. **Capitalization** can signal the beginning of a sentence, or all caps may be used to provide emphasis. **Line length** can be used to help create a shape, like in concrete poems, or to create a bold statement, like a one-word line. A poet can create tension by using line length and punctuation independently of one another. **Word position** can be used to contribute to a feeling, or it can also be used to help create a shape, so poets are often careful where they end lines.

LINE BREAKS

Line breaks are used to end a line of poetry. Poets use **line breaks** to control the **length** of **each line**. The length of lines in a poem can impact the poem's meaning and the **speed** at which the poem is read. **Long** lines are usually read more **quickly**, while **short** lines cause the reader to briefly pause and look to the next line, so their reading is **slowed**. These effects often contribute to the reader's experience when reading the poem, so poets aim to make the effects match the tone of their message in the poem.

PUNCTUATION

The punctuation in each line of a poem causes the reader to **pause** after certain words. This lets the poet **emphasize** specific **ideas** or **images**. Similar to the effects of line length, punctuation at the end of a line can guide the **speed** at which the reader reads each line. Lines with a punctuation mark at the end cause readers to pause, while lines that do not end with a punctuation mark carry a sentence to the next line. This creates an effect that is like the effect of long lines.

CAPITALIZATION

Poets also use capitalization to **highlight** certain words in their poetry. Authors will often capitalize words that are not proper nouns so that the reader pays more attention to them. While this is not grammatically correct, it is used in poetry to create a certain effect and guide the reader as they read and form their understanding of the poem.

Epic Poetry and Lyric Poetry

An **epic poem** is a lengthy, narrative poem that usually tells a story about a serious or heroic deed. These types of poems are important within specific cultures or groups of people. In an epic, the hero tends to go on a journey or a quest. The hero meets many adversaries and enemies along the way. Through each encounter the hero may learn something new. When the hero returns home, he has changed significantly through his journey. Most often the hero's trials are related to morals that were important to the specific culture.

Lyric poetry is a type of poetry that expresses the author's personal feelings. This type of poetry is almost always emotional. They author will use sensory language to influence the audience's emotions. Originally, lyric poetry was written to be sung along with a lyre, a type of stringed instrument. It is a type of poetry that doesn't have to rhyme or even be set to music.

Drama

Dramas are texts that are written to be performed by people reading the lines or acting the stories out. They can also be presented as monologues (one character speaks), dialogues (two character speak to each other), or pantomimes (body movements are used instead of spoken words). Dramatic texts are called plays or **scripts**, and they are written differently than other texts.

Text Structure in Drama

Plays are divided into **acts** (large units) and **scenes** (small sections inside acts) instead of chapters. There are also **stage directions**, which are instructions from the playwright about where items go, where actors should move, and what the characters should be doing during the scene. Stage directions are usually in italics to set them apart from other parts of the play. When it is time for a character in a play to speak, there will be **character tag** on the left side of the page which shows the name of the character (all letters of the name are capitalized) followed by a colon.

Here is an example of how a page from a play might look:

Title of Play

Act Number

Scene Number

The setting of the scene is being described here. The reader is being introduced to the characters and the things happening around them. Characters will enter speak to one another during the scene.

CHARACTER 1:

I am speaking. These are words I say. *(stage directions)* I am still speaking.

CHARACTER 2 *enters and does something.*

CHARACTER 2:

Now I am speaking. This is my dialogue.

Dialogue and Stage Directions

Dialogue refers to what the characters say in a play when they are talking to each other, talking to themselves, or even talking to the audience. The type of speech, word choice, and accent a character uses is specific to the role he is playing. For example, a person cast to play a cowboy would have certain words in his vocabulary that a character from a big city in the North would not have.

A playwright also uses stage directions to make the play flow smoothly. Character interaction helps the viewer to understand the mood of the scene. If two characters are confrontational, the viewer is aware that there is some type of conflict occurring. Stage directions create order when all the characters are on stage together.

INFORMATIONAL TEXT

CONTROLLING IDEA

The controlling idea, also called the main idea or thesis, of a passage is usually located in the first paragraph or two of text. Having the controlling idea near the beginning of the passage allows the author to grab the reader's attention and let them know what the rest of the passage will discuss.

To find the controlling idea in a passage, there are questions the reader can ask while reading: What is this passage about? What does the author want the reader to know about the topic? The supporting details will provide evidence that the controlling idea is correct and are found in the body of a passage. The supporting details often provide examples of the controlling idea.

For example, a passage may contain the controlling idea: "Ellis Island was an entry-point to America for many immigrants during the Industrial Revolution." A supporting detail for the controlling idea may be "Immigrants were examined for contagious diseases at Ellis Island before being granted entry to America."

Review Video: Thesis Statements
Visit mometrix.com/academy and enter code: 691033

EXAMPLE

Determine the controlling idea the following sentence tells the reader and indicate what details support the controlling idea:

> Her breath billowed out in clouds of white and disappeared into the quiet air.

The controlling idea is what the author wants the reader to understand about the text. Details help to explain or support that controlling idea. A controlling idea usually states the point of an entire essay, article, or book, but can be simply stated in one sentence. The controlling idea in the sentence above is that a girl is outside in the cold. Details to support this statement include the word 'her,' showing that the character is a girl, and 'clouds of white,' which indicate that the air is cold. in order to conclude that the girl is out in the cold, the reader needs to understand that breath can be seen when the air is cold.

SUPPORTING DETAILS

Authors use supporting details to provide evidence and backing for the main point. All texts contain details, but they are only classified as supporting details when they serve to reinforce some larger point. Supporting details are most commonly found in informative and persuasive texts. in some cases, they will be clearly indicated with words like **for example** or **for instance**, or they will begin with words like **first**, **second**, and **last**. However, these special words are not a requirement. As a reader, it is important to consider whether the author's supporting details really back up his or her main point. Supporting details can be factual and correct but still not relevant to the author's point. Sometimes, supporting details can seem important but they might not support the controlling idea in the story well because they are based on opinion that cannot be proven.

Example

Decide whether the following sentence is the main point or a supporting point of a text, and state where the information would be placed in an outline:

> One type of horseback riding, bareback horseback riding, involves sitting on a moving horse without a saddle and grasping the horse's mane.

This sentence is a supporting point, with the main point of the entire text likely about horseback riding in general. As a supporting point, this sentence would go further down in an outline, next to any numeral after numeral I. This sentence can be followed by additional sub-points that further explain the concept of bareback horseback riding. When a supporting point is used to clarify a main point or topic, the supporting point helps to break the topic down into smaller pieces.

Structural Features of Informational Text

Texts which intend to inform the reader about a topic are often accompanied by visual aids or graphics. Some common examples are listed below.

- **Prefaces** are written to provide the reader with supporting information that was not included in the text. This information may help the reader better understand the text or may show the reader why the topic of the text is important or interesting to the author.
- **Introductions** usually appear as the first paragraph in a text. An introduction is used to catch the reader's attention and let the audience know what the text is about and how the topic will be covered by the text.
- **Insets and sidebars** show additional information related to the text in boxes or on the sides of the page. Insets can contain pictures or text, and sometimes have different colored backgrounds or font types to make them stand out from the text.
- **Visual aids** include features like diagrams, graphs, and charts. These can help the user think about information in a different way. They do this by visually presenting the relationship between the information in the text.
- **Citations** are used when an author includes information or ideas from other sources in his or her writing. A citation shows the reader which part of the text came from another source and which source it came from. Citations may come in different formats, and the format an author uses may depend on the subject and purpose of his or her work. Citations are usually linked to a bibliography or works cited page that gives more information about each source the author used.
- **Footnotes** are located at the bottom of a page. A footnote is referenced in the text by a superscript number, which is a small number that appears right above the end of a word. The footnote that has the same number is the one referenced by that part of the text. Footnotes may contain comments about the text or point the reader to a source that is relevant to the text.
- **Endnotes** are located after the conclusion of the text. These may be on the last page of the text or on a later page. Endnotes may give the reader more information about a text or direct the reader to an outside source that is relevant to the text.
- **References** are the sources of the information the author included in the text. In most works, the references will all be listed after the last page of the main text. These may be included on a page titled "Bibliography," "Works Cited," or, simply, "References." Reviewing the author's sources and reviewing their credibility can show the reader whether the work itself is credible, unbiased, and accurate.

Organizational Patterns

When writing there are a variety of ways that an author can choose to organize their text. It is important for them to choose the pattern that best presents their information, as not all patterns will work for every piece of writing. Some examples are

Advantage/Disadvantage

The author chooses a topic or concept and addresses both the advantages and disadvantages (or pros and cons) of the subject. In this type of text the author is not trying to persuade their audience to choose a side, but rather, to inform the reader of all the possible positive and negative effects.

Cause and Effect

The author will write about relationship between two events that occur, where the second event occurs as a result of the first.

For example, a text may discuss a school policy stating that when a student is late to school too many times, they receive a detention. Later in the text, we might see a student repeatedly arriving late to school, after which he is given a detention. In this example, the **cause** is the student being late to school, and the **effect** is the student receiving a detention.

Classification

The author chooses a topic and divides it into smaller parts or groups in order to discuss them individually. These types of texts address how parts work within a whole, or what characteristics can be used to classify a given subject or concept.

Chronological Order

The author organizes the progression of events based upon when they occurred and what was included in each step of the story. By organizing the text in this way the author presents all necessary information about the six questions readers can ask to help themselves understand the text: who, what, when, where, why, and how.

Compare and Contrast

The author will show similarities and differences between items or events.

For example, the author may write about cats and dogs. They might start by giving a brief description of the two. Then they will want to point out all of the similarities, such as; they both have tails, and both are kept as pets. Next, they will explain the differences, such as; dogs are canines, while cats are felines. They will try to provide as much detail as possible about both the similarities and the differences.

Definition

Authors introduce a concept or word and then explain or describe it. This type of text often included examples that will help the reader gain understanding of what is presumably a new concept for them.

Inductive / Deductive

Authors organize ideas from general to specific or specific to general. If ideas are organized **inductively**, they are arranged from specific facts to general conclusions. If ideas are organized from general conclusions to specific facts, they are organized **deductively**. A reader can make a logical assumption about a topic based on the facts that are presented in the text.

For example, in these two sentences the ideas are organized deductively, from general to specific.

> Many canoers use the lake in the summer. Jeff learned how to canoe last summer, and is on his way to the lake now.

The idea that "Many canoers use the lake in the summer" is a general idea. The facts that Jeff already knows how to canoe and is headed to the lake are specific to him as a character.

ORDER OF IMPORTANCE

The author puts the information in the text in order of what is most important. Order of importance can be either increasing or decreasing, depending on how the writer wants to structure the work.

PROPOSITION AND SUPPORT

The author states a proposition that they believe to be true, and then provides support for that proposition in the paper. The topics that use this type of structure are generally things that reader might feel uncertain about or might not already have an opinion about. The support that the author gives for the proposition should include facts, statistics, logic, and reasoning. The more hard evidence an author can give the reader, the better it will help convince them to see things from the author's point of view.

IDENTIFYING ORGANIZATIONAL STRATEGIES

EXAMPLE

Explain which organization pattern would be the best choice for this writer and why.

> Sara is writing a report on sea turtles. She has researched the various dangers that they face: their predators, the difficulties they encounter in their life cycle starting with their birth, their migration to the ocean, and the dangers that await them as they mature. She is unsure of how to organize her report.

A cause and effect order would seem to be the best idea for Sara because she would be able to identify the causes and effects of the dangers that sea turtles encounter. She could organize the report so that each paragraph deals with a different threat, using headings to identify what would be in each section. A chart would also be useful because it puts the same information in a clear format so that readers would be able to refer to it. She might also consider using a video showing baby turtles migrating towards the open sea, which would give her audience an even greater understanding of the turtles' plight.

EXAMPLE

Identify the text structure that is used in the following sentences:

> Madison and her brother Jake used to live on a wind-torn island in the Chesapeake Bay. Last year they moved to Baltimore, a city in Maryland. Next summer they plan to visit the island where they grew up.

Chronological order is used as a text structure in the example sentences, as they are organized according to the passage of time. Note that each sentence refers to a point in time. The first sentence refers to where the siblings lived in the past. The second sentence refers to the siblings' move to Baltimore last year. The final sentence refers to what the siblings plan to do in the future. By referring to a specific place in time, the reader can see what occurred in the story during that time period. An author will often use flashback to indicate what happened in the past, and foreshadowing to give the reader a glimpse of what may occur in the future.

Argumentative Texts

Identifying the Claim

In a persuasive or argumentative text, the author is writing in order to make and support a claim. A claim is similar to the key idea of an informational text. However, a claim can be argued, which means that some readers may not agree with it. The author of the text will need to use the body of the text to support the claim and show readers why they should agree with it. To identify the claim of a text, first identify the topic. Then, read the introduction text to see what the author writes about the topic.

The claim should be clearly stated in the introduction. However, if the claim is still not clear, read the body to see what kind of evidence the author uses to support the claim. The way that the author gives and applies evidence may also show what the claim of the text is.

Call to Action

Another strategy is to look for a call to action in the text. A call to action is a statement that instructs the reader to do something after reading the text. Often, the call to action will tell the reader to do something that shows that he or she agrees with the author's claim. For example, if an author's claim is that reading is better than watching a movie, the author may include a call to action that says "Turn off the TV and dig in to a new book today!" By including this statement, the author is telling the readers to show their agreement by choosing to read rather than watch a movie.

Identifying How the Author Supports a Claim

In a persuasive or argumentative text, the author must use information to support his or her claim. This information is called evidence. Below are common types of evidence an author may use to support a claim:

- **Facts:** Authors may use facts that show that their claim is true. For example, a claim that fish are better pets than dogs can be supported by the fact that fish cannot make a mess inside a house.
- **Personal Anecdotes:** A personal anecdote is a story from a person's own experience. Authors can use personal anecdotes to tell stories that show why their claim is true. For example, an author can support the claim that people should wear elbow pads when riding a bike can be supported by sharing a story about their experience of scraping their elbow after falling off of a bicycle.
- **Statistics:** Statistics are observations that are based on a collection of data. Statistics can show trends or preferences among members of a group. An author can use statistics to support a claim by sharing the statistic says is likely to happen or be true for many people.
- **Examples:** Authors may give examples of events or experiences that suggest that their claim is true. For example, an author may claim that people should exercise because it will make them healthier. The author could give an example of how exercise can improve a person's health in order to support this claim.
- **Quotes:** An author can support a claim by using quotes from other people or texts. If the person or text makes a statement that shows that the author's claim is true, the author can include that quote in his or her text. When authors include quotes in their work, they must always tell the reader where the quote came from.

The author must use enough evidence to support the claim. If the evidence does not fully support the claim in the text, then the author must continue working to find evidence for the claim. The evidence used to support a claim must also be believable and come from a reliable source.

Counterarguments

A counterargument is a claim that seeks to disprove another claim. Sometimes, an author of a persuasive or argumentative text will include a **counterargument** to their own claim in a text. Doing this allows the author to show why someone may disagree with his or her claim and then show why the counterargument is wrong. Authors include counterarguments in order to strengthen their own argument and show the reader why claims that oppose their own are incorrect.

Identifying the Intended Audience

Authors of persuasive and argumentative texts want to convince others to agree with a claim or take a certain action. Because of this, they will often write to a specific audience. Often, the target audience will include people who disagree with the author's claim. The author's desire is to give these people information that will lead them to change their minds or actions.

Strategies for Identifying the Intended Audience

One way to identify the intended audience of a persuasive or argumentative text is to first identify the author's claim. Then, consider who would disagree with the author's claim. This group of people is likely the group that the author wants to persuade.

Another way to identify the audience is to look for clues in the text. Sometimes, authors will clearly state which people are included in the intended audience. For example, imagine that an author includes the statement, "Teachers should reward their students every time they make a good grade on a test." This shows that the text is written to persuade teachers who do not already reward their students for good test grades. Similarly, a call to action may show who the target audience is by instructing the members of the audience to take a certain action.

Chapter Quiz

1. Literature in what genre is often based on historical events, reveals something about human behavior or the natural world, and often involves actions of gods?

a. Historical fiction
b. Myth
c. Fantasy
d. Adventure

2. In dramatic texts (plays or scripts), which of the following are usually in italics to set them apart from other parts of the play?

a. Dialogues
b. Acts and scenes
c. Stage directions
d. Character tags

3. In what organizational pattern does the author choose a topic and then divide it into smaller parts or groups in order to discuss them individually?

a. Deductive
b. Inductive
c. Classification
d. Definition

4. If an author writes about cats and dogs, showing their similarities and differences, this would be an example of what type of organizational pattern?

a. Cause and effect
b. Problem and solution
c. Proposition and support
d. Compare and contrast

5. In an informational text, when is the main idea of a passage often presented?

a. In the first sentence
b. In the first one to two paragraphs
c. In the middle
d. At the end/conclusion

Chapter Quiz Answer Key

1. B: See section **Literary Genres**

2. C: See section **Text Structure in Drama**

3. C: See section **Classification**

4. D: See section **Compare and Contrast**

5. B: See section **Controlling Idea**

Author's Purpose and Craft

Author's Purpose

The purpose of a text is the author's main reason for writing the text. As the reader reads a text, they should always try to figure out the author's purpose for writing as this will help them to better understand the message that the author is trying to convey.

Informational Texts

- Inform the reader on a topic that they previously knew nothing about, such as many non-fiction texts.
- The author will usually include sources of information for an informative piece.
- For example, an informative paper on early Native American Indian tribes would detail where Native American Indians lived, what types of foods they ate, how they bartered for goods, and other aspects of their culture.

Persuasive Texts

- Influence the reader to think a certain way about a topic, calling them to action or pointing them toward resources that would help them to learn more about the topic.
- A Proposition and Support paper would be an example of this, where an author gives their opinion and then tries to convince the reader to see something from their point of view.
- An author will often use positive expert testimonials when trying to persuade the reader to accept a given point-of-view.
- For example, an author may try to persuade the reader that technology is negatively affecting social interaction, and that limits should be set on how much people can use their technological devices.

Expressive Texts

- Express the author or speaker's opinion or emotions about a topic. Generally, expressive texts include descriptive words to clearly show the reader how the author or speaker feels.
- For example, the author may think that history is important for all people to study, and express the opinion that education without history class would be incomplete.

Entertaining Texts

- Entertain the reader, such as in most fictional texts.
- For example, Lois Lowry, the author of *The Giver,* entertains his readers with the story of a young boy named Jonas who is learning how to navigate his unexpected life assignment.
- Entertaining texts can be either fiction or non-fiction, but are usually stories such as a fairy tale or fictional piece of writing. Entertaining texts usually follow a chronological order.

Authors usually write to entertain, to inform, or to persuade their readers. The organization structure or pattern they use is related to what the author's purpose is. It is important to choose the pattern that best presents the information, as not all patterns will work for every piece of writing.

Review Video: Understanding the Author's Intent
Visit mometrix.com/academy and enter code: 511819

Determining the *Purpose of a Text*

While reading a text, you should always try to determine its purpose. To do so, ask yourself why the author wrote the text and what affect the writing has on you. Is the purpose to explain something or tell how to do something? Does the text try to persuade you of something? Perhaps the text is making an appeal to your emotions. The signs that a text is attempting to persuade you include an author offering an opinion and telling why she thinks that way. On the other hand, if a text is simply informative, it will have many facts that will give details about an event or person or a thing, but not try to persuade you of anything. Manuals that come with equipment are clearly not persuasive; they simply are instructive.

Example

Read the following sentence. State the author's point in writing the sentence, whether it is to inform, entertain, persuade, or state an opinion.

> Bristlecone pines are remarkable. They are the longest-lived form of plant life in the world. These trees can live as long as 5,000 years. Some bristlecone pines standing today in the western United States were seedlings when the Egyptian pyramids were being built. They were mature trees by the year 1 AD.

The purpose of the excerpt is to inform. The way in which a reader can tell this is that the text has concrete facts and details about the bristlecone pines. It does not have any opinions, other than the obvious one, that "bristlecone pines are remarkable." The author of the excerpt is not trying to persuade the reader of anything other than that. And the details that she includes make the pines very remarkable. The formal language is to the point and the information is interesting. The writer wants people to learn about the bristlecone pines; she is not selling them nor is she asking people to protect them.

EXAMPLE

Read the following sentence. State the author's point in writing the sentence, whether it is to inform, entertain, persuade, or state an opinion.

> Softsuds is the best shampoo on the market. It will leave your hair tangle-free and shiny. Try it out to see for yourself. Pick some up today!

The sentences shown here contains persuasive language about a certain brand of shampoo, which might be used in a commercial or other advertisement. The author is not trying to give factual information about the shampoo. He is not trying to describe the aroma or feeling of the shampoo's lather. The author is not telling a story about an experience using the shampoo either. Thus, from this deduction, one can determine that the author is writing with the purpose of influencing or persuading the reader to use the Softsuds brand of shampoo.

PRINT AND GRAPHIC FEATURES

An author may show information in a chart, a graph, in paragraph format, or as a list. Information may also be shown in a picture or a diagram. The way an author chooses to show information is often based on the purpose of the text and the audience that the text is meant to reach.

A reader may be asked to answer questions based on the graphic by itself, how the graphic relates to the text, or how the text would best be shown in a graphic form. Some common examples of graphics are cause and effect organizers, circle graphs, bar graphs, illustrations, and diagrams.

CAUSE AND EFFECT GRAPHIC ORGANIZERS

Cause-and-effect graphic organizers are often used to map the **elements of a story**. A reader might read a story about a string of events and then be asked to correctly fill in either the **cause** or **effect** of an event in the story.

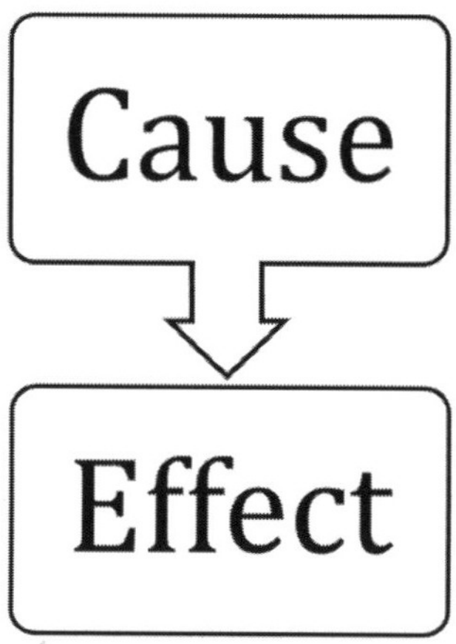

EXAMPLE

Read the following excerpt from *Ramona Quimby, Age 8* by Beverly Cleary and decide what the cause of the hectic morning at the Quimby house is.

> With all four members of the family leaving at different times in different directions, mornings were flurried in the Quimby household.

A **cause and effect** graphic organizer for this excerpt might look something like this:

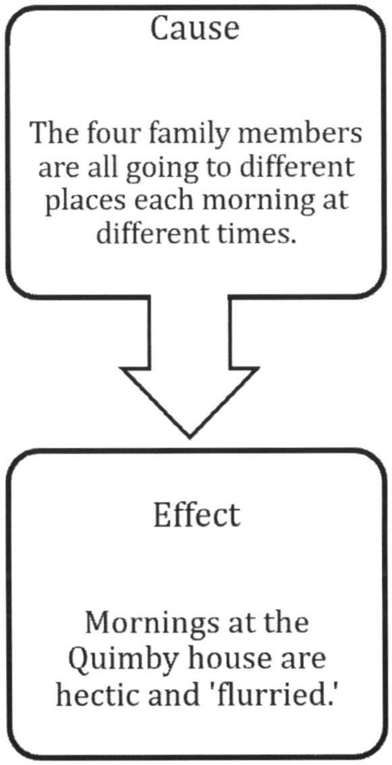

LINE GRAPHS

Line graphs are used for measuring general **trends over time**. For example, this line graph shows an overall upward trend in the amount of candy bars sold for four weeks.

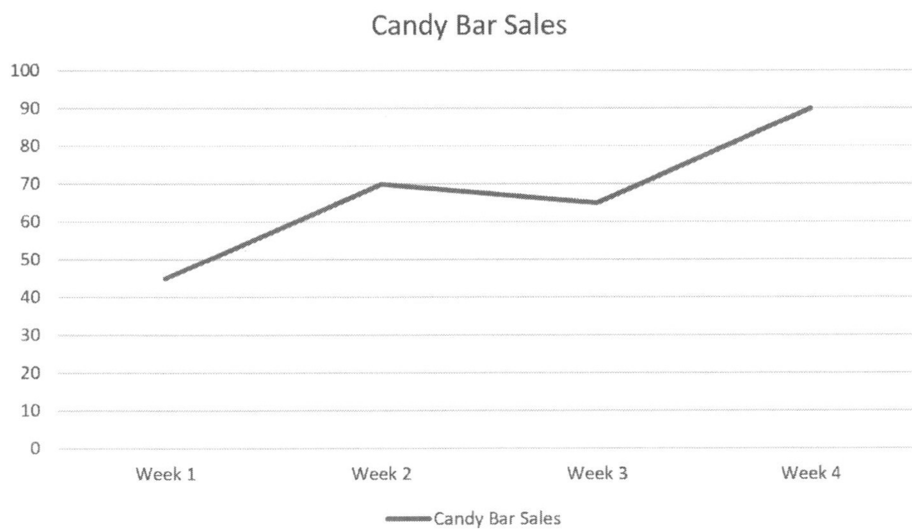

Circle Graphs

Circle graphs, also called pie charts, are often used to represent information that can be shown as **parts of a whole**. For example, this graph shows the results of people being asked about their favorite color:

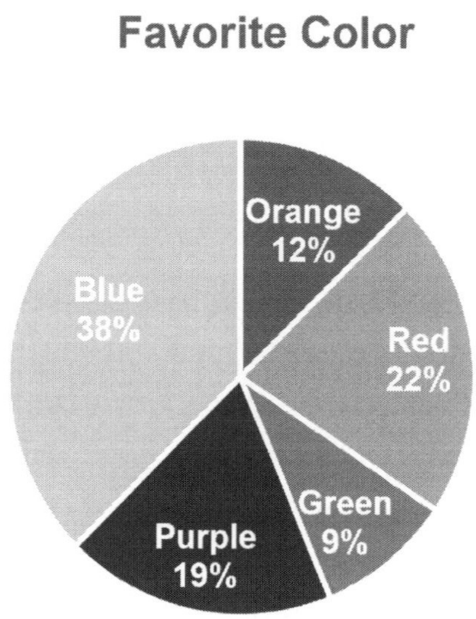

Bar Graphs

Bar graphs are used to show information about **numbers**. For example, this graph is a different way of representing the same results as those in the circle graph.

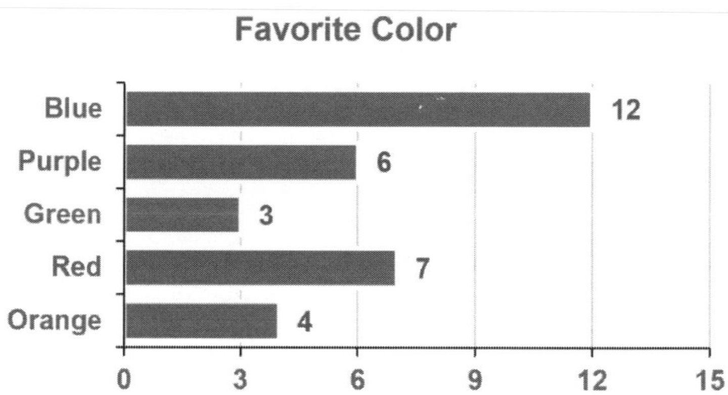

Illustrations and Photographs

Authors may choose to include **illustrations** or **photographs** (or both) with their texts. These two image types both show something from the text or give more information about the text.

Illustrations are drawings of an object. They may be based on reality, or they may represent an artist's abstract idea. For example, this is an illustration of a 1903 automobile:

Photographs are pictures of objects. They are generally extremely realistic, and most often show an object as it actually existed at that moment in time. For example, this is a photograph of a 1917 automobile:

Both illustrations and photographs give the reader another way to relate to and understand the text. The reader may be asked how the image relates to the text, what type of caption the image should be given, or why the author chose to include the image with the text.

Diagrams

Diagrams are used to show information in a visual way. There are many different types of diagrams, including:

Diagrams that show the parts of an object, how they work together, or how they should be put together. This is an example of a diagram which shows how gears turn together

Diagrams that show how information is related are called **Venn Diagrams**. These are ways to visually see the way in which two different ideas overlap. This is an example of a Venn Diagram comparing cats and dogs:

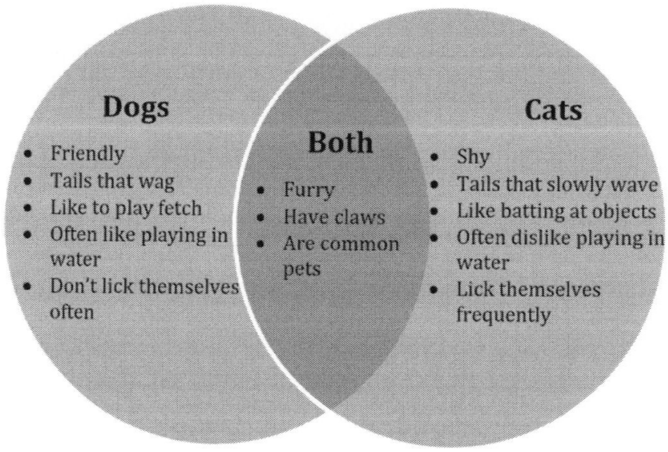

IMAGERY

Imagery is the use of **descriptive language** to add life or feeling to a work of literature. Many authors add literary and sound devices to create vivid pictures in the minds of their readers. Most of the time, imagery is thought to be one of the best ways to help readers fully understand and remember a work.

The most common forms of imagery are those that appeal to the sense of sight and sound. Imagery that appeals to the sense of sight, or **visual imagery**, helps the reader picture an event in their mind, usually by including specific details in the text that are not strictly necessary for the purpose of the story, but allow the reader to more easily "see" the scene. Some common forms of figurative language can help create visual imagery.

Review Video: Sensory Language
Visit mometrix.com/academy and enter code: 177314

LITERAL AND FIGURATIVE LANGUAGE

Many types of text use both **literal language**, which means just what it says, and **figurative language**, which allows the writer to expand the way in which he or she uses language. When an author uses figurative language, she connects things in an exaggerated and non-literal way in order to create a memorable image, which helps to describe a situation in a new way for the reader.

Review Video: Figurative Language
Visit mometrix.com/academy and enter code: 584902

SIMILE

- Shows similarity between two ideas or objects, using the words "**like**" or "**as**"
- For example, an author might write "The princess is as beautiful as a rose" to compare the appearance of a woman to a beautiful flower.

METAPHOR

- Puts one idea in place of another to draw a parallel between the two ideas.
- For example, an author might write "Her room was a pigsty," to compare a person's bedroom to a dirty spot where pigs sleep.
- Sometimes, an author will use multiple elements throughout the whole text, or a large part of the text, to build one metaphor. This is called an **extended metaphor**.

SYMBOLISM

- Using one object to stand for something else.
- For example, an author may include a flag flying high throughout a story to show pride in the characters' country and to represent the idea of patriotism.

HYPERBOLE

- An extreme exaggeration of an idea.
- For example, a character might say "I'm starving to death!" to show that they are really hungry. Most of the time a character who says this is not literally going to die from hunger, they are just ready for a snack.

PERSONIFICATION

- Gives life or human characteristics to an inanimate object
- For example, if an author writes "The trees whispered to each other across the wide blue sky," they are using personification to help the reader imagine the scene. Trees are not human beings, so they do not whisper, but the image created in the reader stands out more than a literal description would.

IRONY

- Uses sarcasm or humor (usually with an emphasis on the opposite) to show difference from literal meaning.
- For example, if a character says "Well today must be my lucky day!" after they left their homework on the kitchen table, they are being ironic. The irony used here helps show that it is definitely *not* the character's lucky day.

DRAMATIC IRONY

Dramatic irony refers to a situation when a character makes a remark about doing something that seems harmless in its context, but that the audience has more information about and realizes it could result in something unpleasant. This difference in knowledge can create suspense or humor depending on the circumstances. For instance, if a character says, "I will have a cup of tea now," and the audience knows that there is poison in the tea, it creates a situation that is suspenseful. That is an example of dramatic irony. The word "irony" comes from the Greek word for "dissembling" and it was used to describe what the Greeks thought was the gap between appearance and reality.

VERBAL IRONY AND PUNS

Verbal irony is a figure of speech which occurs when the intended meaning of a statement is different than, and usually the opposite of, what is said. It is often sarcastic in nature, as in the retort of the mother whose child is playing with her food and says, "Do I have to eat this food?" The mother simply says, "No, of course you don't have to eat it. Just eat it tomorrow when you are really hungry." The mother does not mean what she is actually saying, and is instead trying to make the point that if the child doesn't eat now, they will be extremely hungry later.

EXAMPLE

Discuss the kind of figurative language used by comedian Will Ferrell in this excerpt from his Harvard Commencement Address:

> I graduated from the University of Life, all right? I received a degree from the School of Hard Knocks. Our colors were black and blue, baby. I had office hours with the Dean of Bloody Noses, all right? I borrowed my class notes from Professor Knuckle Sandwich and his teaching assistant, Ms. Fat Lip Thanh Nguyen. That's the kind of school I went to for real, okay?

This excerpt is an example of an **extended metaphor**. While humorous in nature, Ferrell is comparing the idea of 'a formal education' to the idea of the 'real-world education' he received. These two ideas are unlike, and by placing them right next to one another for comparison, he highlights how different his experience was from the experiences of most of the graduates listening to him speak. This powerful metaphor serves his ultimate purpose of making sure the Harvard Class of 2003 recognized how lucky they were to be given so many educational opportunities.

EXAMPLE

Discuss the kind of figurative language used in the following poem by the Scottish poet Robert Burns.

> O my luve's like a red, red rose
> That's newly sprung in June;
> O my luve's like the melodie
> That's sweetly played in tune.

The poet uses **similes** to create an image in this poem. The two similes here occur when the speaker says that his love is "**like** a red, red rose" and that she is also "**like** the melodie." These are examples of similes because they use the comparing word 'like' to compare two things. They are not metaphors because metaphors do not use the comparing words 'like' or 'as.' The poem paints an image of the speaker's love by comparing her to a red rose that has newly sprung and a melody that is sweetly played.

EXAMPLE

Read the following excerpt from "The Raven" by Edgar Allan Poe, identify the metaphor, and discuss how it impacts the text:

> And the raven, never flitting, still is sitting, still is sitting
> On the pallid bust of Pallas just above my chamber door;
> And his eyes have all the seeming of a demon's that is dreaming

One **metaphor** in the excerpt from "The Raven" by Edgar Allan Poe is: 'And his eyes have all the seeming of a demon's that is dreaming' The metaphor compares the raven's eyes with a demon, which shows that the speaker thinks there is evil in the bird. This helps contribute to the overall tone of the poem and the reader's understanding of how the speaker views the bird.

POINT OF VIEW

Authors choose which character tells the story they are writing. This is called **point of view**. The point of view affects the story in many ways. There are three general types of point of view:

FIRST PERSON

- Tells a story through the eyes of one character.
- Uses the pronouns 'I,' 'me,' 'we,' and 'my.'
- The reader gets only one side of the story, without any other angles on what may have happened in the text

SECOND PERSON

- Tells a story using the pronoun 'you.'
- The least common point of view.

THIRD PERSON

- Tells a story about a character or group of characters from an outside viewpoint.
- Uses the words 'her', 'his,' 'they,' or a name to talk about a character or characters.
- A common way to show action in a story which allows the author to easily and realistically tell a story from more than one person's viewpoint.
- Gives readers a more complete view of a story as it is told from many different perspectives.

DIFFERENT FORMS OF THIRD PERSON

When an author writes in third-person point of view, there are a few options to choose from:

- **Third person omniscient** - There is an all-knowing narrator telling the story as well as interpreting events, and relating thoughts of the characters.
- **Third person limited (or closed)** - The author writes in the third person, but does so from only one character's point of view. There are two different variations of this type of narration: the narrator can either stay with the same character throughout or cycle through different characters over the course of the story.

SUBJECTIVE AND OBJECTIVE POINT OF VIEW

The point of view of a character or narrator can either be **subjective** or **objective**. When a character or narrator is describing a person, object, or idea using phrases that are based on opinions or motivated by feelings, their point of view is subjective. When they use phrases based on facts or something that can be proven, their point of view is objective. For example, if a character describes a person walking toward them and they say "Her shirt was a beautiful shade of yellow, which made her blonde hair shine even brighter" they are speaking in subjective point of view. The yellow color they think is beautiful could be someone else's least favorite color. If the same character described the situation objectively, they might say "As she walked by, I noticed her shirt was yellow and her hair was blonde." The narrator doesn't comment on his opinion of the color, just that it is factually yellow.

MULTIPLE POINTS OF VIEW

When a text has multiple important characters, the author may use multiple points of view to tell the story. This allows the author to show the reader more than one perspective. For example, if two characters are upset with each other, the author may tell the story from the point of view of each character. This will allow the reader to understand why each character is upset with the other. Alternatively, the author may use multiple points of view to give the reader a hint about what will happen later in the story. Consider a story where one section is told from the point of view of the protagonist, and the protagonist is creating a plan to defeat the antagonist. In that same story, the next section may be told from the point of view of the antagonist. Imagine that, in the next section, the antagonist is creating a plan to defeat or stop the protagonist. In this case, because they know both points of view, readers can predict conflicts and outcomes that may occur later in the story.

Style, Voice, Tone, and Mood

Style, tone, and mood all play an important role in the development of a story. The reader's impression of a story can vary based on the style, tone, and mood established by the author.

- **Style** refers to the way an author uses words, phrases, and sentence structure. The style of the text can change depending on whether the author uses short, choppy sentences, long, elaborate sentences, formal language, or informal language.
- **Voice** refers to the characteristics of a text that show the author's personality and distinguish the author from other writers. An author's voice may be recognized through the way they use words or the way they organize and present their thoughts. Voice is specific to each writer, and it can be as specific and unique as personality.
- **Tone** refers to the attitude of the writer toward the subject matter. The tone can change throughout the text or stay the same. There are many ways to describe the tone of the text, such as light, playful, questioning, humorous, serious, solemn, or tense. The reader can identify the tone by paying attention to the author's word choice.
- **Mood** refers to the overall feeling conveyed by a setting. For example, a story may be dark in terms of setting, characters, and events that occur. If a story is presented in a picturesque countryside location where the characters are content and the style of speaking is elaborate, the reader will have a different impression of the story than if the setting is in a rundown house with a pale, unhappy caretaker that rarely speaks.

Review Video: Style, Tone, and Mood
Visit mometrix.com/academy and enter code: 416961

Rhetorical Devices vs Logical Fallacies

Writers of persuasive and argumentative texts will often use strategies that may help them persuade the reader to agree with their claims. These strategies may be used to convince the reader on a logical or emotional level. The writer may also use them to prove his or her own credibility, or reliability. These strategies are called **rhetorical devices**. However, writers make statements that seem like rhetorical devices, but are not actually logical. They may sound persuasive, but they are unreasonable and may leave out part of the truth or try to prove a weak argument. These are called **logical fallacies**.

Common Rhetorical Devices

- **Direct Address**: Direct address is a strategy that authors can use to create a call to action or lead their audience to make a personal connection to the author's claim. When making a direct address, the author will make a statement or claim as if they mean to say it to each audience member, personally.
- **Analogy:** An analogy is a comparison of relationships. For example, saying that a hen is to a chick as a mare is to a colt. Both pairs include a mother animal and a baby animal, and the analogy shows a similarity between hens and mares and a similarity between colts and chicks. Authors may use analogies to explain their claims. Analogies allow authors to show how their claim is similar to a concept that the reader is more familiar with or already approves.

- **Juxtaposition:** Juxtaposition is when two contrasting ideas are presented together. Authors can use juxtaposition to make the differences between the two ideas more obvious to the reader. This may also help the author lead the reader to pay attention or prefer one idea over the other.
- **Rhetorical Question:** A rhetorical question is a question that does not need to be answered. Authors may use rhetorical questions to encourage a reader to think more deeply about an idea or apply it to their own lives. Authors may also use rhetorical questions to influence the way a reader thinks about an idea.

Common Logical Fallacies

- **Bandwagon Appeals:** Bandwagon appeals claim that everybody else agrees with the author's argument, so readers to should conform and agree, also.
- **Circular Reasoning:** When authors use circular reasoning, they use the idea they want to prove as part of their proof for the idea. People using circular arguments are actually "talking in circles." For example, someone argues, "X is illegal. Because it is illegal, one should not do it. Because one shouldn't do it, the government should prevent people from doing it. This is why it is illegal."
- **Sweeping Generalizations:** When an author makes a statement as if it is true for everyone, the author is making a sweeping generalization. For example, the statement, "Everyone loves chocolate," is a sweeping generalization. While most people do enjoy chocolate, the statement is still not true because there are people who do not like chocolate. Authors may use sweeping generalizations as evidence because they will expect the reader to ignore the fact that they are not true. Readers must be careful to consider whether statements that apply to many people are actually true.
- **Loaded Language:** An author uses loaded language when he or she makes claims that include words or phrases that lead the audience to react emotionally. While making an emotional appeal can be an effective strategy, loaded language is often used only to draw on emotions. Authors use loaded language in order to lead the audience to agree based on how the author's words have made them feel, rather than whether or not the author's words are logical and supported by evidence. Loaded language may rely on the sympathy, anger, or fear of the audience.

Chapter Quiz

1. An author's purpose in writing fiction is most often to:

a. Persuade
b. Inform
c. Entertain
d. Express

2. What is the least common point of view, that tells a story using the pronouns "you"?

a. First person
b. Second person
c. Third person
d. Narrator

3. Which of the following refers to the overall feeling conveyed by a setting?

a. Style
b. Pace
c. Tone
d. Mood

4. What type of graphic can be used to visually see the way in which two different ideas overlap?

a. Circle graph
b. Bar graph
c. Venn diagram
d. Cause and effect organizer

5. What common form of figurative language puts one idea in place of another to draw a parallel between the two ideas?

a. Metaphor
b. Simile
c. Hyperbole
d. Irony

6. What type of logical fallacy claims that everybody else agrees with the author's argument, so readers should conform and agree also?

a. Sweeping generalizations
b. Appeal to pity
c. Circular reasoning
d. Bandwagon appeals

7. What rhetorical device presents two contrasting ideas together, and can be used to make the differences between ideas more obvious to the reader?

a. Direct Address
b. Rhetorical Questions
c. Analogy
d. Juxtaposition

Chapter Quiz Answer Key

1. C: See section **Author's Purpose**

2. B: See section **Second Person**

3. D: See section **Style, Voice, Tone, and Mood**

4. C: See section **Diagrams**

5. A: See section **Metaphor**

6. D: See section **Common Logical Fallacies**

7. D: See section **Common Rhetorical Devices**

Writing

Writing Process

Brainstorming

When choosing what to write about, activities like brainstorming can help inspire new ideas or help writers see how their ideas go together. **Brainstorming** means considering a variety of topics or ideas and is mainly used to find a creative approach to a subject or problem. A good first step in brainstorming is simple **free-association** with a topic. One way of doing this is sitting down with paper and pen and writing every thought that comes to mind about the topic in a word or phrase. It does not matter how helpful or good the thought seems at first; the writer should write down everything that comes to mind about the topic. Then, the writer should read the list over a few times. Next, he or she should look for patterns, repetitions, and clusters of ideas. This allows a variety of fresh ideas to come as the writer thinks about the topic.

Free Writing

Free writing is a more organized form of brainstorming. **Free writing** means taking a limited amount of time, like 2 to 3 minutes, to write everything that comes to mind about a topic in complete sentences. When the time is up, the writer should review everything he or she has written down. Many of the sentences may not make sense, but they may contain ideas and details that help the writer organize his or her ideas and prepare to plan the composition. Usually, free writing results in more useful ideas than brainstorming because the writer's thoughts and connections are written in complete sentences. However, both methods can be used together to help the writer prepare to plan and write a composition.

Mapping

One specific way to use graphic organizers is to map an essay. There are many different types of graphic organizers. One easy method to create one is to draw a circle in the middle of the page and write a broad topic in it. Then, draw smaller circles with related topics and ideas, or with topics that fit within the broad topic, written inside and draw line to connect each circle to the main circle. This method can show ideas that fit within the broad topic and will help guide the essay, or it can show which ideas may work better as the main topic of the essay.

Once the main idea and other ideas and details for the essay have been chosen, they can be used to map the essay. Mapping is another word for using a certain type of graphic organizer. These graphic organizers look like a map and organize ideas and details as they will appear in the essay. The essay map can have the main idea at the top or in the center. If the main idea is at the top, the supporting ideas will appear below it in a row, and any additional details will appear under the supporting idea they go with. If the main idea appears in the center, the supporting ideas may appear around it, and the additional details will appear around the supporting ideas they go with.

Planning

Planning is the process of organizing a piece of writing before writing a draft. At the beginning of planning, writers should decide **why they are writing** and **who will read what they write**. The writer must also choose a **genre**, which is the **type** of composition he or she will write. There are fiction genres, such as comedy, folklore, action, and mystery. There are also nonfiction genres, such as essays, reports, poems, and journals. To plan his or her composition, a writer may create an outline or a graphic organizer, such as a Venn diagram, a spider-map, or a flowchart. These methods should help the writer choose their topic, main ideas, and how to organize the composition. If the writer needs to do research for the composition, he or she may also do so as they plan. Planning helps writers organize all of their ideas and decide if they have enough information to begin their first draft. However, writers should remember that the decisions they make during planning may change later, so their plan does not have to be perfect.

DRAFTING

Writers may then use their plan, outline, or graphic organizer to compose their first draft. They may write more drafts after the first one to improve their writing. Writing multiple drafts can help writers think of different ways to state their ideas and correct mistakes that may be hard to fix without rewriting a section of the composition, or the whole composition. There is no "right" number of drafts, so different writers may write a different number of drafts. Writing drafts also makes it easier to write freely because a writer can improve his or her composition with each draft they write.

REVISING, EDITING, AND PROOFREADING

Once a writer completes a draft, he or she can move on to revising, editing, and proofreading to improve the draft. **Revising** is making sure that the composition is right for the audience, is not missing important information, is on topic, and is well organized. The writer should also consider the composition's style when revising and ensure that it is appropriately formal or serious. Revising may happen after the first draft so that errors are not repeated in the next draft. Each draft should be revised before the next one is written so that no mistakes are missed. **Editing** comes next. Editing a composition includes steps like improving transitions between paragraphs and making sure each paragraph is on topic. While editing, the writer must pay attention to the words he or she uses and the way the information in each paragraph is organized. Writers may also fix grammar mistakes in the editing phase, since some errors will require a writer to rewrite large parts of their work. **Proofreading** means fixing misspelled words, errors in grammar, and any other small mistakes in the composition.

During the revising, editing, and proofreading steps, it can be helpful for writers to ask a peer to read their work, since he or she may notice mistakes or problems the writer missed before. A writer may also choose to read his or her own work aloud, or listen to someone else read it. Hearing a composition aloud can help writers find mistakes or opportunities for improvement in their work more easily. This happens because when something is read aloud, the person reading the text must pay closer attention to the words on the page. When a writer or a peer reads the composition, they should point out any sentence that confuses them the first time they read it. Most of these sentences can be revised in a way that makes it easier to read and understand.

ADDING AND REMOVING INFORMATION

While both revising and editing may involve changing the words in a composition, they can also involve adding or taking away words. When a writer has completed a draft and reread it, he or she may notice that something, such as a transition, important details, or an explanatory sentence, is missing. Simply changing the words to make the passage sound better will not solve this problem, so the writer must **add** whatever words and information is needed to make the passage make sense and achieve the writer's purpose.

In other cases, a writer may have words, a sentence, or sometimes an entire paragraph that gives unnecessary information or explains the information in a way that is confusing. When this happens, the extra words and information weaken the composition and must be **removed**. Sometimes, this is difficult for writers to do because it may require them to remove writing they are proud of or a fact they find interesting. Despite this, revising and editing are steps meant to improve and strengthen a composition, so the writer should change, add, or remove parts of his or her writing in a way that makes it better and achieves his or her purpose.

Revising Sentences

Sentence variety is important to consider when writing an essay. A variety of sentence lengths and types can make an essay more engaging, and different types of sentences can sometimes help readers better understand information. For example, a sentence containing a list may make more sense when written with a simple sentence structure, since writing a compound sentence containing a list may give the reader too much information at once. On the other hand, information that is closely related and can be connected with a conjunction should be written in a compound sentence, rather than a simple sentence, since a compound sentence helps the reader see that the information goes together.

Using only simple sentences often makes writing boring and bothersome to read. Writing using only compound sentences makes it difficult for writers to explain information well and difficult for readers to understand, since every sentence will include a coordinating conjunction. To check an essay for sentence variety, it is helpful to look at whether the essay contains different sentence structures and lengths. It is also important to pay attention to the way each sentence starts and avoid beginning with the same words or phrases.

Revising Vocabulary

When writing informational or argumentative texts, it is important to use **precise vocabulary**, or **word choice**, to explain your main idea and supporting details. Generalized vocabulary will not help the audience fully understand the points that you are attempting to make because it will not accurately explain your main idea and supporting details. Precise vocabulary is important to use because it will accurately describe the ideas that are central to your text. When you research a subject, make sure to familiarize yourself with any vocabulary that is involved in its explanation. Use context clues, dictionaries, or, if necessary, a technical dictionary to decode any words that you are not familiar with. Precise vocabulary also impacts the effectiveness of narrative text. Carefully choosing vocabulary to describe sensory details, or imagery, helps writers paint the best possible picture of the events they are describing through their writing.

Chapter Quiz

1. Which of the following means taking a limited amount of time, like 2 to 3 minutes, to write everything that comes to mind about a topic in complete sentences?

a. Brainstorming
b. Drafting
c. Mapping
d. Free writing

2. What is often the first step after a writer completes a draft, and involves making sure that the composition is right for the audience, it is not missing important information, is on topic, and is well organized?

a. Adapting
b. Editing
c. Proofreading
d. Revising

3. When revising sentences in an essay, which of the following is NOT good advice?

a. Avoid beginning sentences with the same words or phrases
b. Include a variety of sentence lengths
c. Improve understanding by only using compound sentences
d. Keep sentences simple when they include lists

4. In what step of the writing process does the writer decide why they are writing, who will read what they write, and what genre they want to write?

a. Brainstorming
b. Drafting
c. Mapping
d. Planning

Chapter Quiz Answer Key

1. D: See section **Free Writing**

2. D: See section **Revising, Editing, and Proofreading**

3. C: See section **Revising Sentences**

4. D: See section **Planning**

Essay Structure and Organization

Controlling Ideas and Supporting Details

In the first paragraph of a composition, writers include a sentence that explains the **controlling idea.** This sentence is also known as the **thesis**. The rest of the paragraph shows the reader why the topic of the essay is interesting and includes details that support the controlling idea. One way to understand the relationship between the controlling idea and supporting information is to think about a table: the tabletop is the controlling idea, and each of the table's legs is a supporting detail or group of details. All of the legs work together to support the tabletop and create a table, just like the supporting details work together to support the controlling idea and create a composition.

Introduction

The introduction is used to capture the reader's attention and announce the essay's controlling idea. Normally, the introduction contains about 3-5 sentences. An introduction can begin with an interesting quote, a question, a strong opinion, or something else that will **interest** the reader's and prompt them to keep reading. If the composition has a prompt, the introduction should **restate** or **summarize** some part of the prompt so that the reader will have an idea of what information will be in the essay. Finally, your introduction should include the **controlling idea**, the primary thing the essay will tell the reader.

Review Video: Introduction
Visit mometrix.com/academy and enter code: 961328

Body

In an essay's introduction, the writer states the controlling idea and prepares the reader for the information in the rest of the composition. In the body of the composition, the writer **explains**, **demonstrates**, and **gives more information about** the **controlling idea**. This is done using supporting details and examples that are relevant to the controlling idea of the composition. For example, if the composition's controlling idea is a vacation the writer took, the body will include descriptions of where the writer went, what they experienced, and what they thought of the trip. If the composition's controlling idea is the writer's opinion, the body will include examples and facts that show why he or she has formed that opinion. If composition's controlling idea is a topic and the writer wants to instruct the reader, the body will contain facts, explanations, and examples that help teach the reader about the controlling idea. A writer will use supporting details to explain the controlling idea throughout the body.

The body should also contain multiple paragraphs, and the order the writer puts these paragraphs in is important. Each paragraph should include at least one supporting detail, but a paragraph may include more than one if two or more supporting details work together to support the controlling idea. If the controlling idea is to describe something that happened, the paragraphs should match the order in which the events occurred. If the controlling idea is to present an opinion or instruct the reader, the paragraphs should be ordered in the way that would make the most sense to the reader. The order of body paragraphs is important because it can impact how easy a composition is to read.

Review Video: Drafting Body Paragraphs
Visit mometrix.com/academy and enter code: 724590

Paragraphs

After the introduction of a passage, the body paragraphs will explain and elaborate upon the controlling idea. While each paragraph should relate to the controlling idea of the composition, each paragraph should focus on one point or supporting detail. Normally, a paragraph has a good topic sentence that summarizes the paragraph's main point. A topic sentence is a sentence that gives an introduction to the paragraph and its contents. Topic sentences should contain information that is more specific than what is in the introduction and may include a supporting detail, but they should not contain explanations or examples.

Supporting Details

The next sentences in the paragraph should support the topic sentence. These sentences can contain examples, explanations, or other specific information that supports the topic sentence, which supports the controlling idea of the composition. While a paragraph may be structured in any way, as long as it logically provides information that supports the controlling idea, it can be best to use a template or pattern to make sure that each paragraph is complete and well organized. For example, a good template to follow is topic sentence, evidence, explanation, conclusion. This means that after the topic sentence, the next sentence should provide evidence, like a quote or example, that supports the paragraph's main point. Next, the paragraph should include a sentence that explains how that evidence supports the paragraph's main point. If there are multiple examples or quotes, more than one sentence may be used to explain them. Finally, there should be a concluding sentence that helps the reader understand the paragraph and prepares them for the next one.

Choosing Supporting Details and Examples

When writing an informative or argumentative text, writers must choose supporting details carefully. Including details that are irrelevant, inaccurate, or vague does not strengthen the author's writing, while relevant, accurate, provable, and specific details do strengthen the author's writing. These details can make the writer's meaning clearer or give evidence that the author's points are true or logical. Such details may include examples or facts, such as statistics, statements from others who have authority on the subject, and common events or experiences. Choosing appropriate supporting details can also help the author show that they put effort into forming their ideas. This can also make the composition more intriguing and enjoyable to read, since the writer's own interest and insight will be apparent to the reader.

Length of a Paragraph

A paragraph must contain enough information to support its main point and the composition's controlling idea. A paragraph of two or three sentences will most likely not support the main point or controlling idea because it is not likely to contain enough information, explanation, or evidence. When a paragraph does not support the main point or controlling idea, it does not help the writer achieve their purpose or goal for writing the essay. A helpful, informative paragraph will often have somewhere from three to five sentences. Also, it is important that the sentences within the paragraph lead the reader through the information. Each paragraph should flow logically and stay on topic throughout.

Starting a New Paragraph

For most forms of writing, you will need to use multiple paragraphs. This means that deciding when to start a new paragraph is very important. Reasons for starting a new paragraph include:

- To separate the introduction and conclusion from the body paragraphs
- To move from one supporting detail or point to another
- To indicate an important shift in time or place
- To show a comparison, contrast, or cause and effect relationship

Coherent Paragraphs

A smooth flow of sentences and paragraphs without gaps, shifts, or bumps will lead to paragraph **coherence**. The connections between old and new information can be shown using several methods:

- **Clearly linking ideas**, from the topic sentence to the body of the paragraph, is essential for a smooth transition. The topic sentence states the main point, and this should be followed by specific details, examples, and illustrations that support the topic sentence.
- The **repetition of key words** adds coherence to a paragraph. To avoid dull language, synonyms of the key words may be used.
- **Parallel structures** are often used within sentences to highlight the similarity of ideas and connect sentences that give similar information.
- Maintaining a **consistent verb tense** throughout the paragraph helps make paragraphs coherent. Shifting tenses affects the smooth flow of words and can disrupt the coherence of the paragraph.

Review Video: How to Write a Good Paragraph
Visit mometrix.com/academy and enter code: 682127

Transitions

Transitions between sentences and paragraphs guide readers from idea to idea and show relationships between sentences and paragraphs. Writers should use transitions carefully and only when they are truly helpful. They should also be selected to fit the author's purpose. Transitions can show relationships such as time, comparison, an order of events, and cause and effect. Transitions are often used at the beginning of a phrase, sentence, or paragraph, since this helps prepare the reader for the next piece of information.

Review Video: Transitions in Writing
Visit mometrix.com/academy and enter code: 233246

Types of Transitional Words

Time	Afterward, immediately, earlier, meanwhile, recently, lately, now, since, soon, when, then, until, before, etc.
Sequence	too, first, second, further, moreover, also, again, and, next, still, besides, finally
Comparison	similarly, in the same way, likewise, also, again, once more
Contrasting	but, although, despite, however, instead, nevertheless, on the one hand... on the other hand, regardless, yet, in contrast.
Cause and Effect	because, consequently, thus, therefore, then, to this end, since, so, as a result, if... then, accordingly
Examples	for example, for instance, such as, to illustrate, indeed, in fact, specifically
Place	near, far, here, there, to the left/right, next to, above, below, beyond, opposite, beside
Repetition, Summary, or Conclusion	as mentioned earlier, as noted, in other words, in short, on the whole, to summarize, therefore, as a result, to conclude, in conclusion
Addition	and, also, furthermore, moreover

Review Video: Transition Words
Visit mometrix.com/academy and enter code: 707563

Conclusion

The conclusion of a composition should summarize the controlling idea and show that it has been explained well. A good conclusion shows the reader why the author's controlling idea is meaningful and important and how the supporting details should help the reader understand the controlling idea. The conclusion should also give the reader something to think about that is related to the controlling idea. For example, in the conclusion, the author can invite readers to think about how they feel or what they think after reading the composition. Some things to avoid when writing conclusions include:

- Introducing a completely new idea
- Apologizing for one's opinions or writing
- Repeating the controlling idea word for word rather than summarizing them
- Using the conclusion to summarize every detail in the composition

Review Video: Drafting Conclusions
Visit mometrix.com/academy and enter code: 209408

Chapter Quiz

1. "Too," "and," "next," "still," "besides," and "finally" are all what type of transitional word?

a. Time
b. Sequence
c. Comparison
d. Contrasting

2. Which of the following should be avoided in an essay conclusion?

a. Reminding the reader of the central idea by repeating it word for word
b. Showing the reader why the author's central idea is meaningful and important
c. Showing that the central idea has been explained well
d. Giving the reader something to think about that is related to the central idea

3. A helpful, informative paragraph will often have how many sentences?

a. One to three sentences
b. Three to five sentences
c. Five to ten sentences
d. Ten to fifteen sentences

4. The body of an essay should do all of the following, EXCEPT:

a. Introduce the central idea
b. Demonstrate the central idea
c. Explain the central idea
d. Give information about the central idea

Chapter Quiz Answer Key

1. B: See section **Types of Transitional Words**

2. A: See section **Conclusion**

3. B: See section **Length of a Paragraph**

4. A: See section **Body**

Grammar

Subjects and Predicates

Subjects

Every sentence needs a subject and a predicate. The **subject** of a sentence names who or what the sentence is about. The subject may be directly stated in a sentence, or the subject may be implied. The **complete subject** includes the simple subject and any **modifiers**, such as adjectives, articles, prepositions, and adverbs, that go with it. To find the complete subject, ask *Who* or *What* before the verb to complete the question. The answer, including any modifiers, is the complete subject. To find the **simple subject**, remove all of the modifiers in the complete subject.

Examples:

simple subject: car
The small, red car is the one that he wants for Christmas.
complete subject: The small, red car

simple subject: artist
The young artist is coming over for dinner.
complete subject: The young artist

Review Video: Subjects in English
Visit mometrix.com/academy and enter code: 444771

An imperative sentence is a sentence that gives someone instructions or makes a request to someone. In **imperative** sentences, the verb's subject is understood, but is not actually present in the sentence. For example, this about the sentence *Drive to the store*. This sentence is a command, and the subject is *you*. If the subject were directly stated, the sentence would be *You, drive to the store*. Another fact to consider is that, normally, the subject comes before the verb. However, the subject comes after the verb in sentences that begin with *There are* or *There was*.

Direct:

John knows the way to the park.	Who knows the way to the park?	John
The cookies need ten more minutes.	What needs ten minutes?	The cookies
By five o'clock, Bill will need to leave.	Who needs to leave?	Bill
There are five letters on the table for him.	What is on the table?	Five letters
There were coffee and doughnuts in the house.	What was in the house?	Coffee and doughnuts

Implied:

Go to the post office for me.	Who is going to the post office?	You
Come and sit with me, please?	Who needs to come and sit?	You

Predicates

In a sentence, there is always a predicate and a subject. The subject tells what the sentence is about, and the **predicate** explains or describes the subject.

Think about the sentence *He sings*. In this sentence, we have a subject, *He*, and a predicate, *sings*. This is all that is needed for a sentence to be complete. Most sentences contain more information, but if this is all the information that is given in a sentence, then it is a complete sentence.

Now, let's look at another sentence: *John and Jane sing on Tuesday nights at the dance hall.*

subject: John and Jane — predicate: sing on Tuesday nights at the dance hall.
John and Jane sing on Tuesday nights at the dance hall.

Subject-Verb Agreement

Verbs **agree** with their subjects in number. In other words, singular subjects need singular verbs. Plural subjects need plural verbs. **Singular** is for **one** person, place, or thing. **Plural** is for **more than one** person, place, or thing. Subjects and verbs must also share the same point of view, as in first, second, or third person.

Review Video: Subject-Verb Agreement
Visit mometrix.com/academy and enter code: 479190

Number Agreement Examples:

Single Subject and Verb: Dan (singular subject) calls (singular verb) home.

Dan is one person. So, the singular verb *calls* is needed.

Plural Subject and Verb: Dan and Bob (plural subject) call (plural verb) home.

More than one person needs the plural verb *call*.

Person Agreement Examples:

First Person: I *am* walking.

Second Person: You *are* walking.

Third Person: He *is* walking.

Complications with Subject-Verb Agreement

Words Between Subject and Verb

Words that come between the simple subject and the verb do not affect subject-verb agreement.

Examples:

The joy (singular subject) of my life returns (singular verb) home tonight.

The phrase *of my life* does not affect the verb *returns*.

The question (singular subject) that still remains unanswered is (singular verb) "Who are you?"

Don't let the phrase "*that still remains…*" confuse you. The subject *question* goes with the verb *is*.

Compound Subjects

A compound subject is formed when two or more nouns joined by *and*, *or*, or *nor* act together as the subject of the sentence.

Joined by And

When a compound subject is joined by *and*, it is treated as a plural subject and requires a plural verb.

Examples:

plural subject / plural verb
You and Jon are invited to come to my house.

plural subject / plural verb
The pencil and paper belong to me.

Joined by Or/Nor

For a compound subject joined by *or* or *nor*, the verb must agree in number with the part of the subject that is closest to the verb.

Examples:

subject / verb
Today or tomorrow is the day.

subject / verb
Stan or Phil wants to read the book.

subject / verb
Neither the pen nor the book is on the desk.

subject / verb
Either the blanket or pillows arrive this afternoon.

Indefinite Pronouns as Subject

An indefinite pronoun is a pronoun that does not refer to a specific noun. Different indefinite pronouns are used as a singular noun, a plural noun, or change depending on how they are used.

Always Singular

Pronouns such as *each*, *either*, *everybody*, *anybody*, *somebody*, and *nobody* are always singular. This is because these pronouns always stand in for one person, place, or thing.

Examples:

singular subject / singular verb
Each of the runners has a different bib number.

singular verb / singular subject
Is either of you ready for the game?

Note: The words *each* and *either* can also be used as adjectives. For example, *each* person is unique. When one of these adjectives modifies the subject of a sentence, it is always a singular subject.

singular subject / singular verb
Everybody grows a day older every day.

singular subject / singular verb
Anybody is welcome to bring a tent.

ALWAYS PLURAL

Pronouns such as *both*, *several*, and *many* are always plural. This is because these pronouns always stand in for more than one person, place, thing, or idea.

Examples:

> Both (plural subject) of the siblings were (plural verb) too tired to argue.
>
> Many (plural subject) have tried (plural verb), but none have succeeded.

DEPEND ON CONTEXT

Pronouns such as *some*, *any*, *all*, *none*, *more*, and *most* can be either singular or plural depending on what they are representing in the context of the sentence.

Examples:

> All (singular subject) of my dog's food was (singular verb) still there in his bowl.
>
> By the end of the night, all (plural subject) of my guests were (plural verb) already excited about coming to my next party.

OTHER CASES INVOLVING PLURAL OR IRREGULAR FORM

Some nouns are **singular in meaning but plural in form**: news, mathematics, physics, and economics.

> The *news is* coming on now.
>
> *Mathematics is* my favorite class.

Some nouns are plural in form and meaning, and have **no singular equivalent**: scissors and pants.

> Do these *pants come* with a shirt?
>
> The *scissors are* for my project.

Note: Look to your **dictionary** for help when you aren't sure whether a noun with a plural form has a singular or plural meaning.

EXAMPLE

Which word should go in the blank?

> If Kelly is going to the party, Joan and Susan ____ going to the store.

a. Is
b. Are
c. Am
d. Was

Try using each choice in the sentence. Choice A, *is*, forms this sentence: If Kelly is going to the party, Joan and Susan is going to the store. There are two people, Joan and Susan, who are going to the store. This makes the subject of the clause plural. *Is* is a singular verb, meaning it does not agree with the subject and cannot be the answer.

Choice B, *are*, forms this sentence: If Kelly is going to the party, Joan and Susan are going to the store. The subject of the clause is still plural. But *are* is a plural verb! The subject and verb agree, so *are* is the correct answer.

Choice C, *am*, forms this sentence: If Kelly is going to the party, Joan and Susan am going to the store. *Am* is a singular verb, and it is also only used in first person, when the writer or speaker is referring to themself. The subject of the clause is plural, and the sentence is in third person, so *am* is not the correct answer.

Choice D, *was*, forms this sentence: If Kelly is going to the party, Joan and Susan was going to the store. *Was* is a singular verb, so it does not agree with the plural subject in this clause.

COMPLEMENTS

A complement is a noun, pronoun, or adjective that is used to give more information about the subject or verb in the sentence.

DIRECT OBJECTS

A direct object is a noun or pronoun that takes or receives the **action** of a verb. A complete sentence does not need a direct object, so not all sentences will have them. When you are looking for a direct object, find the verb and ask *who* or *what.*

Examples:

> I took *the blanket.*
>
> Jane read *books.*

INDIRECT OBJECTS

An indirect object is a word or group of words that show how an action had an **influence** on someone or something. If there is an indirect object in a sentence, then you always have a direct object in the sentence. When you are looking for the indirect object, find the verb and ask *to, for, whom*, or *what.*

Examples:

> We taught the old dog (indirect object) a new trick (direct object).
>
> I gave them (indirect object) a math lesson (direct object).

Review Video: Direct and Indirect Objects
Visit mometrix.com/academy and enter code: 817385

Pronoun-Antecedent Agreement

The **antecedent** is the noun that has been replaced by a pronoun. A pronoun and its antecedent **agree** when they have the same number (singular or plural) and gender (male, female, or neutral).

Examples:

Singular agreement: John (antecedent) came into town, and he (pronoun) played for us.

Plural agreement: John and Rick (antecedent) came into town, and they (pronoun) played for us.

To determine which is the correct pronoun to use in a compound subject or object, try each pronoun **alone** in place of the compound in the sentence. Your knowledge of pronouns will tell you which one is correct.

Example:

Bob and (I, me) will be going.

Test: (1) *I will be going* or (2) *Me will be going*. The second choice cannot be correct because *me* cannot be used as the subject of a sentence. Instead, *me* is used as an object.

Answer: Bob and I will be going.

When a pronoun is used with a noun immediately following (as in "we boys"), try the sentence **without the added noun**.

Example:

(We/Us) boys played football last year.

Test: (1) *We played football last ye*ar or (2) *Us played football last year*. Again, the second choice cannot be correct because *us* cannot be used as a subject of a sentence. Instead, *us* is used as an object.

Answer: We boys played football last year.

Review Video: Pronoun Usage
Visit mometrix.com/academy and enter code: 666500

Review Video: Pronoun-Antecedent Agreement
Visit mometrix.com/academy and enter code: 919704

A pronoun should point clearly to the **antecedent**. Here is how a pronoun reference can be unhelpful if it is puzzling or not directly stated.

Unhelpful: Ron and Jim (antecedent) went to the store, and he (pronoun) bought soda.

Who bought soda? Ron or Jim?

antecedent pronoun
Helpful: Jim went to the store, and he bought soda.

The sentence is clear. Jim bought the soda.

EXAMPLE

Tom printed his ticket to the concert, but he forgot ____ at home.

Which pronoun should go in the blank?

a. It
b. Them
c. Him
d. He

What is the antecedent that the missing pronoun must match? There are only four nouns in the sentence. They are *Tom*, *ticket*, *concert*, and *home*. Which one should the missing pronoun refer to? Tom is the one who forgot something, so the pronoun does not refer to Tom. The concert is not at Tom's home, so he cannot forget the concert at home. It is also not logical to say that Tom forgot his home at home The antecedent must be *ticket*.

Choice A says that the missing pronoun is *it*. The pronoun refers to *ticket*, which is a singular noun. A ticket is also a nonliving thing. The missing pronoun is also the object in the second clause. *It* is singular, refers to nonliving nouns, and can be used as the object. Choice A is correct.

Choice B says that the missing pronoun is *them*. The pronoun refers to the singular noun *ticket*. While *them* can be used to refer to nonliving nouns and can be the object of a sentence, it is a plural pronoun. Choice B is incorrect.

Choice C says that the missing pronoun is *him*. The missing pronoun refers to a nonliving thing, not a human. *Him* is an objective personal pronoun and is singular, but it only refers to living nouns. *Him* cannot represent *ticket*, so choice C is incorrect.

Choice D says that the missing pronoun is *he*. The missing pronoun refers to a nonliving noun and is the object of the second sentence. While *he* is a singular pronoun, it can only be used as the subject of a sentence and only refers to living nouns. Choice D is incorrect.

PHRASES

A phrase is a group of words that functions as a single part of speech, usually a noun, adjective, or adverb. A **phrase** is not a complete thought, and does not contain a subject, but it adds detail or explanation to a sentence, or renames something within the sentence.

CLAUSES

A clause is a group of words that contains both a subject and a predicate (verb). There are two types of clauses: independent and dependent. An **independent clause** contains a complete thought, while a **dependent (or subordinate) clause** does not. A dependent clause includes a subject and a verb, and may also contain additional information, but it cannot stand as a complete thought without being joined to an independent clause. Dependent clauses function within sentences as adjectives, adverbs, or nouns.

Example:

independent clause | dependent clause

I am running because I want to stay in shape.

The clause *I am running* is an independent clause: it has a subject and a verb, and it gives a complete thought. The clause *because I want to stay in shape* is a dependent clause: it has a subject and a verb, but it does not express a complete thought. This is due to the fact that it begins with *because*, which shows that there is more information needed to complete the thought. This dependent clause adds detail to the independent clause to which it is attached.

Review Video: Independent and Dependent Clauses
Visit mometrix.com/academy and enter code: 556903

Sentence Structure

Sentence structure is based on the type and number of clauses in the sentence. Two common sentence structures are simple sentences and compound sentences:

Simple

A simple sentence has one independent clause with no dependent clauses. A simple sentence may have a **compound subject** or a **compound verb**, or both.

Examples:

single subject | single verb

Judy watered the lawn.

compound subject | single verb

Judy and Alan watered the lawn.

single subject | compound verb | compound verb

Judy watered the lawn and pulled weeds.

compound subject | compound verb | compound verb

Judy and Alan watered the lawn and pulled weeds.

Compound

A compound sentence has two or more independent clauses with no dependent clauses. Usually, the independent clauses are joined with a comma and a coordinating conjunction or with a semicolon.

Examples:

independent clause | independent clause

The time has come, and we are ready.

independent clause | independent clause

I woke up at dawn; the sun was just coming up.

COMPLEX

A complex sentence has one independent clause and at least one dependent clause.

Examples:

dependent clause: Although he had the flu, / independent clause: Harry went to work.

independent clause: Marcia got married / dependent clause: after she finished college.

Review Video: Sentence Structure
Visit mometrix.com/academy and enter code: 700478

SENTENCE FRAGMENTS

Recall that a group of words must contain at least one **independent clause** in order to be considered a sentence. If it doesn't contain even one independent clause, it is called a **sentence fragment**.

Choosing the best steps for **repairing** a sentence fragment depends on what type of fragment it is. If the fragment is a dependent clause, it can sometimes be fixed by simply removing a subordinating word, such as *when*, *because*, or *if*, from the beginning of the fragment. Alternatively, a dependent clause can be joined to a closely related neighboring sentence. If the fragment is missing some required part, like a subject or a verb, it may be fixed by simply adding the missing part.

Examples:

Fragment: Because he wanted to sail the Mediterranean.

Removed subordinating word: He wanted to sail the Mediterranean.

Combined with another sentence: Because he wanted to sail the Mediterranean, he booked a Greek island cruise.

EXAMPLE

Which of the following changes will NOT correct this sentence fragment?

Although she had found the coin first.

a. Remove *Although*.
b. Add a comma and *she let her brother keep it* after *first*.
c. Add *She let her brother keep the coin* before *although*.
d. Remove *first*.

Choice A suggests removing the word *although* to form the following sentence: She found the coin first. This option removes the subordinating conjunction to make the clause independent. The resulting sentence is complete, so removing *although* is an acceptable way to correct the fragment. Choice A is incorrect.

Choice B forms the following sentence: Although she had found the coin first, she let her brother keep it. A comma and an independent clause have been added to the sentence fragment to form a complex sentence. The resulting sentence is complete and written correctly, so choice B is incorrect.

Choice C forms the following sentence: She let her brother keep the coin although she had found the coin first. An independent clause has been added before the sentence fragment to form a complex sentence. This sentence is correctly written and complete, so choice C is an acceptable way to correct the fragment. Choice C is incorrect.

Choice D removes the word *first*, leaving *Although she had found the coin*. This is still a sentence fragment, since it is a single dependent clause. Choice D does not correct the fragment, so D is correct.

RUN-ON SENTENCES

Run-on sentences consist of multiple independent clauses that have not been joined together properly. Run-on sentences can be corrected in several different ways:

Join clauses properly: This can be done with a comma and coordinating conjunction, with a semicolon, or with a colon or dash if the second clause is explaining something in the first clause.

Example:

> **Incorrect**: I went on the trip, we visited lots of castles.
>
> **Corrected**: I went on the trip, and we visited lots of castles.

Split into separate sentences: This correction is best to use when the independent clauses are very long or when they are not closely related.

Example:

> **Incorrect**: The drive to New York takes ten hours, my uncle lives in Boston.
>
> **Corrected**: The drive to New York takes ten hours. My uncle lives in Boston.

Make one clause dependent: This is the easiest way to make the sentence correct and more interesting at the same time. It's often as simple as adding a subordinating word between the two clauses or before the first clause.

Example:

> **Incorrect**: I finally made it to the store and I bought some eggs.
>
> **Corrected**: When I finally made it to the store, I bought some eggs.

Reduce to one clause with a compound verb: If both clauses have the same subject, remove the subject from the second clause, and you now have just one clause with a compound verb.

Example:

> **Incorrect**: The drive to New York takes ten hours, it makes me very tired.
>
> **Corrected**: The drive to New York takes ten hours and makes me very tired.

Note: While these are the simplest ways to correct a run-on sentence, often the best way is to completely reorganize the thoughts in the sentence and rewrite it.

COMMA SPLICES

A comma splice is a specific error that may appear in a run-on sentence. When a sentence has two independent clauses, but the clauses are joined with only a comma, a **comma splice** is formed. Remember that if two independent clauses are joined with a comma, a coordinating conjunction is also needed. Most of the solutions for fixing run-on sentences can also be used to correct a comma splice.

Review Video: Fragments and Run-on Sentences
Visit mometrix.com/academy and enter code: 541989

EXAMPLE

Rick wants to go see a movie tomorrow he would miss his sister's recital.

Identify the change that would NOT correct this run-on sentence.

a. Add a comma after *tomorrow*.
b. Split it into two sentences between *tomorrow* and *he*.
c. Add a comma and *but* after *tomorrow*.
d. Add a subordinating conjunction to make one of the clauses dependent.

Choice A says to add a comma after *tomorrow*. This forms the following sentence: Rick wants to go see a movie tomorrow, he would miss his sister's recital. A comma has been used to join two independent clauses, but there is no coordinating conjunction. This choice forms a comma splice, so it is not an acceptable correction for this sentence. Choice A is the correct answer.

Choice B says to split the sentence into two sentences. This forms the following two sentences: Rick wants to go see a movie tomorrow. He would miss his sister's recital. Both of these sentences are complete. This is an acceptable way to correct the run-on sentence, so choice B is incorrect.

Choice C says to add a coordinating conjunction after *tomorrow*. This forms the following sentence: Rick wants to go see a movie tomorrow, but he would miss his sister's recital. A comma and a coordinating conjunction have been added between the two independent clauses. This is an acceptable way to correct a run-on sentence. Choice C is incorrect.

Choice D says to add a subordinating conjunction to make one of the sentences dependent. There are many new sentences that could be created by adding a subordinating conjunction. For example, consider the following sentence: Although Rick wants to go see a movie tomorrow, he would miss his sister's recital. Alternatively, the following sentence could also be created: Rick wants to go see a movie tomorrow even though he would miss his sister's recital. Both of these sentences have an independent clause and a dependent clause. These sentences are both complete and written correctly, so choice D is incorrect.

EXAMPLE

Identify the sentence that has a comma splice.

a. Tom stopped at the store to buy supplies and his family met him at the campsite.
b. The ball rolled into the living room quietly, but it still startled the dog.
c. Theresa brought her mom some flowers, her mom did not have a vase.
d. Sweet potatoes, pecans, and brown sugar are all ingredients in my cousin's sweet potato casserole.

Choice A has two independent clauses joined by a coordinating conjunction. This is incorrect because there should be a comma before the coordinating conjunction. While the sentence is written incorrectly, there is no comma, so this sentence does not have a comma splice. Choice A is incorrect.

Choice B has two independent clauses joined by a comma and a coordinating conjunction. This is the correct way to write a compound sentence, so there is no error here. Choice B is incorrect.

Choice C has two independent clauses joined by a comma. This is incorrect because independent clauses should be joined together by a comma and a coordinating conjunction. When the comma is present without a coordinating conjunction between two independent clauses, a comma splice is formed. This means that choice C is correct.

Choice D is a simple sentence that contains one independent clause. The only commas used in this sentence are used to separate items in a list. There are no clauses that need to be joined or errors related to commas, so choice D does not contain a comma splice. Choice D is incorrect.

Parts of Speech

Nouns

When you talk about a person, place, thing, or idea, you are talking about a **noun**. The two main types of nouns are **common** and **proper** nouns.

Common Nouns

Common nouns are generic names for people, places, and things. Common nouns are not usually capitalized.

Examples of common nouns:

People: boy, girl, worker, manager

Places: school, bank, library, home

Things: dog, cat, truck, car

Proper Nouns

Proper nouns name specific people, places, or things. All proper nouns are capitalized.

Examples of proper nouns:

People: Abraham Lincoln, George Washington, Martin Luther King, Jr.

Places: Los Angeles, California; New York; Asia

Things: Statue of Liberty, Earth, Lincoln Memorial

Note: When referring to the planet that we live on, capitalize *Earth*. When referring to the dirt, rocks, or land, lowercase *earth*.

Singular and Plural Nouns

Singular nouns name **one** person, place, thing, or idea. **Plural nouns** name **more than one** person, place, thing, or idea. Most nouns have both a singular and plural form. Many plural nouns are spelled like the singular noun with an *-s* at the end, but this is not true for all plural nouns. Singular nouns that already end in an *s*, *o*, *ch*, *sh*, or *x* usually end in *-es* when they are in the plural form.

Singular nouns that end in a consonant followed by the letter *y* will usually lose the *y* and end in *-ies* in the plural form, and words that end with the letter *f* or *fe* will usually lose the *f* and end in *-ves*.

Some plural nouns have much different spellings than their singular form, and some plural nouns are spelled the same as their singular form. There are more rules for spelling plural nouns, but these are the most common spelling changes.

Examples of singular nouns:

> Typical nouns: dog, pencil, girl, store, hope, stingray
>
> Nouns ending in *s*, *o*, *ch*, *sh*, or *x*: mass, hero, lunch, polish, fox
>
> Nouns ending in a consonant and *y*: puppy, baby, fairy, sky
>
> Nouns ending in *f* or *fe*: self, life, calf, hoof

Examples of plural nouns:

> Typical nouns: dogs, pencils, girls, stores, hopes, stingrays
>
> Nouns ending in *s*, *o*, *ch*, *sh*, or *x*: masses, heroes, lunches, polishes, foxes
>
> Nouns ending in a consonant and *y*: puppies, babies, fairies, skies
>
> Nouns ending in a vowel and *f* or *fe*: selves, lives, calves, hooves

COLLECTIVE NOUNS

Collective nouns are the names for a group of people, places, or things that function like singular nouns. The following are examples of collective nouns: *class, company, dozen, group, herd, team,* and *public*. Collective nouns usually require an article, such as *a*, *an*, and *the*, which shows that the noun is a single unit. For example, a choir is a group of singers. Even though there are many singers in a choir, the word choir describes a single group. If we refer to the members of the group, and not the group itself, it is no longer a collective noun.

> Incorrect: The *choir are* going to compete nationally this year.
>
> Correct: The *choir is* going to compete nationally this year.
>
> Incorrect: The *members* of the choir *is* competing nationally this year.
>
> Correct: The *members* of the choir *are* competing nationally this year.

PRONOUNS

Pronouns are words that are used to stand in for nouns. There are several different types of pronouns, but the two main types are subjective and objective pronouns. **Subjective** nouns and pronouns that those that are the subject of a sentence. **Objective** nouns and pronouns are those that are an object in a sentence. Another important type of pronoun is the personal pronoun, which refers to people. Personal pronouns can be subjective or objective. **Possessive** nouns and pronouns show possession or ownership. Pronouns can also be singular or plural.

Singular

Subjective	Objective	Possessive
I	Me	My, Mine
You	You	Your, Yours
He	Him	His
She	Her	Her, hers
It	It	Its
Who	Whom	Whose

Plural

Subjective	Objective	Possessive
we	us	our, ours
you	you	your, yours
they	them	their, theirs

Reflexive: Reflexive pronouns are pronouns that function as the object of a sentence and refer to the subject. Examples of reflexive pronouns include *myself*, *yourself*, *himself*, *herself*, *itself*, *ourselves*, *yourselves*, and *themselves*.

Indefinite: Indefinite pronouns are used to refer to multiple nouns or an undefined noun. Examples of indefinite nouns include *all*, *any*, *each*, *everyone*, *either/neither*, *one*, *some*, and *several*.

Relative: Relative pronouns are used to connect relative clauses that specify or describe a noun to the rest of the sentence. Examples of relative pronouns include *which*, *who*, *whom*, and *whose*.

Review Video: Nouns and Pronouns
Visit mometrix.com/academy and enter code: 312073

VERBS

If you want to write a sentence, then you need a verb. Without a verb, you have no sentence. The verb of a sentence indicates action or being. In other words, the verb shows something's action or state of being or the action that has been done to something.

TRANSITIVE AND INTRANSITIVE VERBS

A **transitive verb** is a verb whose action (e.g., drive, run, jump) indicates a receiver (e.g., car, dog, kangaroo). **Intransitive verbs** do not indicate a receiver of an action. In other words, the action of the verb does not point to a subject or object.

> **Transitive**: He plays the piano. | The piano was played by him.
>
> **Intransitive**: He plays. | John plays well.

ACTION VERBS AND LINKING VERBS

Action verbs show what the subject is doing. In other words, an action verb shows action. **Linking verbs** link the subject of a sentence to a noun or pronoun. They can also link a subject to an adjective, so the linking verb helps create a description. You always need a verb if you want a complete sentence. However, linking verbs on their own cannot be a complete sentence. Any verb that shows a condition and connects to a noun, pronoun, or adjective that describes the subject of a sentence is a linking verb.

Action: He sings. | Run! | Go! | I talk with him every day. | She reads.

Linking:

Incorrect: I am.

Correct: I am John. | The roses smell lovely. | I feel tired.

> **Review Video: Action Verbs and Linking Verbs**
> Visit mometrix.com/academy and enter code: 743142

VOICE

Transitive verbs come in active or passive **voice**. If something does an action or is acted upon, then you will know whether a verb is active or passive. When the subject of the sentence is doing the action, the verb is in **active voice**. When the subject is acted upon, the verb is in **passive voice**.

Active: Jon drew the picture. (The subject *Jon* is doing the action of *drawing a picture*.)

Passive: The picture is drawn by Jon. (The subject *picture* is receiving the action from Jon.)

EXAMPLE

Which of the following sentences is written in passive voice?

a. The alligator quickly swam through the swamp.
b. She dug up the hidden treasure.
c. The vase was painted by an artist.
d. The bag held many apples.

In choice A, the subject is *alligator*, the verb is *swam*, and the object is *swamp*. Did the subject or the object do the action in this sentence? The alligator swam and acted upon the swamp. The subject did the action, so choice A is in active voice.

In choice B, the subject is *she*, the verb is *dug*, and the object is *hidden treasure*. Did the subject or the object do the action? She dug and acted upon the hidden treasure. The subject did the action, so choice B is in active voice.

In choice C, the subject is *vase*, the verb is *was painted*, and the object is *artist*. Did the subject or the object do the action? The vase simply existed. The painter painted and acted upon the vase. The object did the action, so choice C is in passive voice. Choice C is correct.

In choice D, the subject is *bag*, the verb is *held*, and the object is *apples*. Did the subject or the object do the action? The bag held and acted upon the apples. The subject did the action, so choice D is in active voice.

VERB TENSES

A verb **tense** shows the different form of a verb to point to the time of an action. The present and past tense are indicated by the verb's form. An action in the present, *I talk,* can change form for the past: *I talked*. However, for future tense, an auxiliary, or helping, verb is sometimes needed to show the change in form. When writing a composition, it is important to use verb tenses consistently.

Choose the best tense for the composition and do not switch to a different tense unless it is necessary or appropriate for a particular sentence or paragraph.

Present: I talk
Past: I talked
Future: I will talk

Present: The action happens at the current time.

Example: He *walks* to the store every morning.

Past: The action happened in the past.

Example: He *walked* to the store an hour ago.

Future: The action is going to happen later.

Example: I *will walk* to the store tomorrow.

Review Video: Verb Tenses
Visit mometrix.com/academy and enter code: 269472

Irregular Verbs

While most verbs gain the suffix -ed when used in the past tense, irregular verbs receive different spelling changes when they are written in the past tense. For example, *walk* is a regular verb, and it becomes *walked* when written in the past tense. However, *run* is an irregular verb because it becomes *ran* when written in the past tense.

Example

My mother _____ me about the big nest of ants near the sandbox. I thanked her for telling me!

Which of the following verbs should go in the blank?

a. Warn
b. Warned
c. Will warn
d. Warns

First, look at the sentences. The first sentence does not have enough information to show which tense it is in. However, the second sentence says that the child thanked the mother. The verb here is *thanked*, which is the past-tense form of *thank*. Because the second sentence is in the past tense, it makes sense to say that the first sentence is also in past tense.

Choice A says that the missing verb is *warn. Warn* is a present-tense verb, but it can be used in the future tense if a helping verb is present. However, this sentence is in past tense, so it needs a past-tense verb. Choice A is wrong.

Choice B says that the missing verb is *warned. Warned* is a past-tense verb, and it logically completes the sentence. Choice B is correct!

Choice C says that the missing verb is *will warn. Will warn* is a future-tense verb, meaning that it describes an action that will occur in the future. However, since the speaker already thanked his or her mother for the warning, it is not logical to use a future-tense verb in the blank. Choice C is incorrect.

Choice D says that the missing verb is *warns*. *Warn* is usually used with plural subjects, and *warns* used with single subjects. *Warns* can be used in the future or present tense, but it cannot be used in the past tense. Since the sentence is in the past tense, it needs a past-tense verb, so D is incorrect.

ADJECTIVES

An **adjective** is a word that is used to modify a noun or pronoun. An adjective answers a question: *Which one? What kind?* or *How many?* Usually, adjectives come before the words that they modify, but they may also come after a linking verb.

> Which one? The *third* suit is my favorite.
>
> What kind? This suit is *navy blue*.
>
> How many? I am going to buy *four* pairs of socks to match the suit.

Review Video: Descriptive Text
Visit mometrix.com/academy and enter code: 174903

COMPARISON WITH ADJECTIVES

Some adjectives are relative, and other adjectives are absolute. Adjectives that are **relative** can show the comparison between things. **Absolute** adjectives can also show comparison, but they do so in a different way. Let's say that you are reading two books. You think that one book is perfect, and the other book is not exactly perfect. It is not possible for one book to be more perfect than the other. Either you think that the book is perfect, or you think that the book is imperfect. In this case, perfect and imperfect are absolute adjectives.

Relative adjectives will show the different **degrees** of something or someone to something else or someone else. The three degrees of adjectives include positive, comparative, and superlative.

The **positive** degree is the normal form of an adjective.

> Example: This work is *difficult*. | She is *smart*.

The **comparative** degree compares one person or thing to another person or thing.

> Example: This work is *more difficult* than your work. | She is *smarter* than me.

The **superlative** degree compares more than two people or things.

> Example: This is the *most difficult* work of my life. | She is the *smartest* lady in school.

Review Video: Adjectives
Visit mometrix.com/academy and enter code: 470154

ADVERBS

An **adverb** is a word that is used to **modify,** or describe, a verb, adjective, or another adverb. Usually, adverbs answer one of these questions: *When? Where? How?* and *Why?* The negatives *not* and *never* are considered adverbs. Adverbs that modify adjectives or other adverbs **strengthen** or **weaken** the words that they modify.

Examples:

He walks *quickly* through the crowd.

The water flows *smoothly* on the rocks.

Note: Adverbs are usually indicated by the suffix *-ly*, which has been added to the root word. For instance, *quick* can be made into an adverb by adding *-ly* to construct *quickly*. Some words that end in *-ly* do not follow this rule and can function as other parts of speech. Examples of adjectives ending in *-ly* include: *early, friendly, holy, lonely, silly*, and *ugly*. To know if a word that ends in *-ly* is an adjective or adverb, check your dictionary. Also, while many adverbs end in *-ly*, you need to remember that not all adverbs end in *-ly*.

Examples:

He is *never* angry.

You are *too* irresponsible to travel alone.

Types of Adverbs

Different types of adverbs are used to describe particular aspects of a verb, adjective, or other adverb. The following are examples of common types of adverbs:

Time: Some adverbs show when something was done, such as *yesterday*, *today*, or *in two days*.

Manner: Some adverbs show the way something was done, such as *hurriedly*, *neatly*, *grumpily*, or *loudly*.

Frequency: Some adverbs show how often something was done, such as *seldom*, *often*, *never*, or *often*.

Degree: Some adverbs show how much or to what degree something was done, such as *completely*, *barely*, *highly*, or *halfway*.

Conjunctive: Conjunctive adverbs are used similarly to conjunctions, as they connect different ideas, but they can connect ideas from different clauses or sentences. Some examples of conjunctive adverbs are *however*, *alternatively*, *likewise*, and *then*.

Comparison with Adverbs

The rules for comparing adverbs are the same as the rules for adjectives.

The **positive** degree is the standard form of an adverb.

Example: He arrives *soon*. | She speaks *softly* to her friends.

The **comparative** degree compares one person or thing to another person or thing.

Example: He arrives *sooner* than Sarah. | She speaks *more softly* than him.

The **superlative** degree compares more than two people or things.

Example: He arrives *soonest* of the group. | She speaks the *most softly* of any of her friends.

Review Video: Adverbs
Visit mometrix.com/academy and enter code: 713951

PREPOSITIONS

A **preposition** is a word placed before a noun or pronoun that shows the relationship between an object and another word in the sentence.

Common prepositions:

about	before	during	on	under
after	beneath	for	over	until
against	between	from	past	up
among	beyond	in	through	with
around	by	of	to	within
at	down	off	toward	without

Examples:

The napkin is *in* the drawer.

The Earth rotates *around* the Sun.

The needle is *beneath* the haystack.

Can you find "me" *among* the words?

PREPOSITIONAL PHRASES

One important thing to know about prepositions is that they form special phrases, called prepositional phrases. A **prepositional phrase** begins with a preposition and ends with a noun or pronoun that is the object of the preposition. Normally, the prepositional phrase functions as an **adjective** or an **adverb** within the sentence.

Examples:

The picnic is on the blanket. (prepositional phrase: "on the blanket")

I am sick with a fever today. (prepositional phrase: "with a fever")

Among the many flowers, John found a four-leaf clover. (prepositional phrase: "Among the many flowers")

Be careful not to mistake the object in a prepositional phrase as the subject of a sentence. The subject of the sentence will not be found in a prepositional phrase because a prepositional phrase is used to describe how an object is related to the subject. Prepositional phrases do not influence subject-verb agreement.

Prepositional phrases do not influence subject-verb agreement. For example, consider the following sentence:

simple subject | prepositional phrase | verb

The basket of clothes is on the floor in the laundry room.

This sentence contains a prepositional phrase between the simple subject and the verb. The simple subject is *basket*, which is a singular noun, and the verb is *is*, which is a singular verb. They are separated by the prepositional phrase "of clothes." Even though the plural noun *clothes* comes right before the singular verb *is*, this verb shows the action of the singular noun *basket*.

Review Video: Prepositions
Visit mometrix.com/academy and enter code: 946763

EXAMPLE

Which of the following could NOT complete the sentence?

She went ____ the cave.

a. Sadly
b. Into
c. From
d. Through

Choice A says that the missing word is *sadly*. The blank is between *went* and *the cave*, meaning that the missing word will connect these pieces of the sentence. While *sadly* could be used here to show how the girl felt, there would still be missing information. A preposition is needed here to show whether she entered, exited, or stood outside of the cave. *Sadly* is an adverb, so A is the correct answer.

Choice B says that *into* would complete the sentence. Does *into* complete the sentence without leaving missing information? To say *she went into the cave* is a logical, complete sentence. Choice B is incorrect.

Choice C says that the missing word is *from*. This creates the sentence *she went from the cave*. Since she could have left the cave to go somewhere else, this is also a logical, complete sentence. Choice C is incorrect.

Choice D says that *through* would complete the sentence. The sentence would read *she went through the cave*. Since she could have explored the whole cave or found an exit on the other side of it, *through* can logically complete the sentence. Choice D is incorrect.

EXAMPLE

Identify the prepositional phrase in the following sentence.

Mable visited the store to buy some vegetables.

a. To buy
b. Visited the store
c. The store to buy
d. To buy some vegetables

Remember the pieces of a prepositional phrase. Prepositional phrases should begin with a preposition and end with a noun or pronoun. Considering these rules, can any of the answer choices be eliminated? Choice B and choice C can be eliminated because neither choice begins with a preposition!

That leaves choices A and D. Choice A says that the prepositional phrase is *to buy*. This does start with a preposition, and it does give more information about Mable's trip to the store. However, it does not end with a noun or pronoun. Choice D says that the prepositional phrase is *to buy some vegetables*. Choice D begins with a preposition and ends with a noun, and it explains why Mabel went to the store.

Choice D is the only choice that has all of the pieces of a prepositional phrase, so D is correct!

EXAMPLE

A band with 15 members _____ performing at my restaurant tonight.

Identify the verb that best completes the sentence.

a. Were
b. Is
c. Are
d. Are not

This question is asking which verb should go in the blank. There are a couple of reasons why choosing the correct verb for this sentence may be confusing. First of all, there are two nouns that appear before the verb. Second, one of these nouns is singular and one is plural.

The first step is to determine which noun goes with the verb. The two nouns are *band* and *members*. While *members* is closest to the blank, it is part of a prepositional phrase that describes *band*. The subject of the sentence is *band*, so the verb must agree with *band*.

Is *band* singular or plural? The sentence says that the band has multiple members, but there is only one band. *Band* is a collective noun, meaning that it is a singular noun. This means that the correct verb will also be singular. With this in mind, can any of the answer choices be eliminated?

Choices A, C, and D are all plural verbs. Even though the blank appears after a plural noun, this noun is part of a prepositional phrase. The verb should match the singular subject *band*. The only choice with a singular verb is choice B, so B is the correct answer.

CONJUNCTIONS

Conjunctions join words, phrases, or clauses and they show the connection between the joined pieces. **Coordinating conjunctions** connect equal parts of sentences. Coordinating conjunctions can also be used to create compound subjects and compound predicates, in addition to compound sentences.

Coordinating Conjunctions

The **coordinating conjunctions** include: *and, but, yet, or, nor, for,* and *so*

Compound Subjects:

compound subject

Terry *and* Marissa went to the movies last Saturday.

compund subject

Either pumpkin pie *or* apple pie would be a good dessert to bring to Thanksgiving dinner.

compound subject

Neither the clownfish *nor* the goldfish liked the new fish food very much.

Compound Predicates:

compound predicate

Veronica left school *and* picked up her sister from soccer practice.

compound predicate

The cat did not take a nap *or* play with the dog yesterday.

Compound Sentences:

The rock was small, *but* it was heavy.

She drove in the night, *and* he drove in the day.

Bill dressed nicely today, *for* he must give an important presentation this afternoon.

Correlative Conjunctions

Some examples of **correlative conjunctions** are: *either...or* | *neither...nor* | *not only...but also*. When one correlative conjunction is used, its matching correlative conjunction will be used later in the sentence.

Examples:

Either you are coming *or* you are staying.

He *not only* ran three miles *but also* swam 200 yards.

Review Video: Coordinating and Correlative Conjunctions
Visit mometrix.com/academy and enter code: 390329

Subordinating Conjunctions

Subordinating conjunctions link dependent clauses, clauses with either a subject or a predicate, to independent clauses, clauses with both a subject and a predicate, to form a complex sentence. The subordinating conjunction will always be at the beginning of the dependent clause. When the dependent clause is at the beginning of the sentence, it will end with a comma. When the independent clause is at the beginning of the sentence, no comma is needed.

Common **subordinating conjunctions** include:

after	since	whenever
although	so that	where
because	unless	wherever
before	until	whether
in order that	when	while

Examples:

I am hungry *because* I did not eat breakfast.

He went home *when* everyone left.

While her brother ate dinner, she played his favorite video game.

Review Video: Subordinating Conjunctions
Visit mometrix.com/academy and enter code: 958913

END PUNCTUATION

PERIODS

Use a period to end all sentences except direct questions and exclamations. Periods are also used for abbreviations.

Examples: 3 p.m. | 2 a.m. | Mr. Jones | Mrs. Stevens | Dr. Smith | Bill, Jr. | Pennsylvania Ave.

Note: An abbreviation is a shortened form of a word or phrase.

QUESTION MARKS

Question marks should be used following a **direct question**. A polite request can be followed by a period instead of a question mark.

Direct Question: What is for lunch today? | How are you? | Why is that the answer?

Polite Requests: Can you please send me the item tomorrow. | Will you please walk with me on the track.

Review Video: Question Marks
Visit mometrix.com/academy and enter code: 118471

EXCLAMATION MARKS

Exclamation marks are used after a word group or sentence that shows much feeling or has special importance. Exclamation marks should not be overused. They are saved for proper **exclamatory interjections**.

Example: We're going to the finals! | You have a beautiful car! | "That's crazy!" she yelled.

Review Video: Exclamation Points
Visit mometrix.com/academy and enter code: 199367

COMMAS

The comma is a punctuation mark that can help you understand connections in a sentence. Not every sentence needs a comma. However, if a sentence needs a comma, you need to put it in the right place. A comma in the wrong place or a missing comma will make a sentence's meaning unclear. These are some of the rules for commas:

Use Case	Example
Before a **coordinating conjunction** joining independent clauses in compound sentences	Bob caught three fish, and I caught two fish.
Between **items in a series**	I will bring the turkey, the pie, and the coffee.
After a **dependent clause** that **begins a complex sentence**	Before she left, Ashley turned off all of the lights in her house.
After **transition words**	Consequently, Joel's mother grounded him.
After an **introductory phrase**	After the final out, we went to a restaurant to celebrate.
After a **prepositional phrase** at the **beginning of a sentence**	At 10 in the evening, Georgia finally arrived home from work.
After an **adverbial clause**	Studying the stars, I was awed by the beauty of the sky.
Before and after **nonessential modifiers**	John Frank, who coaches the team, was promoted today.
Before and after **nonessential appositives**	Thomas Edison, an American inventor, was born in Ohio.
Before and after **nonrestrictive phrases** or **clauses**	His favorite movie, which premiered before he was born, is over three hours long.
After **absolute phrases**	Relieved the test was over, Leah dropped her pencil and slouched in her chair.

COMMAS FOR SETTING OFF NONESSENTIAL WORDS, PHRASES, AND CLAUSES

Identifying where to place commas for nonessential words, phrases, and clauses is sometimes tricky. If the word, phrase, or clause is necessary for the sentence to be complete or logical, then it is essential, or restrictive. Additionally, if the word, phrase, or clause cannot be removed without changing the meaning of the sentence, then it is essential. Nonessential words, phrases, and clauses are those that give unnecessary information or do not flow smoothly with the rest of the words in the sentence. These words usually can also be logically placed in more than one spot in the sentence. **Appositives** are often nonessential words or phrases. They are most often used to specify which person or thing is being discussed. An appositive is an additional name or description that may be essential or nonessential.

> **Review Video: When To Use a Comma**
> Visit mometrix.com/academy and enter code: 786797

EXAMPLE

The singer growing more exhausted with every song decided to stop dancing and stood still while singing.

Identify the nonrestrictive phrase that should be set off by commas in the above sentence.

a. The singer growing more exhausted
b. Decided to stop dancing
c. Growing more exhausted with every song
d. Stop dancing and stood still

Choice A says that *the singer growing more exhausted* is the nonrestrictive phrase. Is the sentence still a complete sentence without this phrase? No, because choice A includes the subject, *the singer*. Choice A is not the nonrestrictive phrase.

Choice B says that *decided to stop dancing* is the nonrestrictive phrase. Does the sentence make sense without this phrase? No, removing this phrase leaves the following sentence: The singer growing more exhausted with every song and stood still while singing. This is not a logical sentence, so choice B is not the nonrestrictive phrase.

Choice C says that *growing more exhausted with every song* is the nonrestrictive phrase. Removing this phrase leaves the following sentence: The singer decided to stop dancing and stood still while singing. This sentence makes sense and has the same meaning as the original sentence. This phrase gives extra information that is not essential to the sentence, so choice C is the nonrestrictive phrase. Choice C is correct.

Choice D says that *stop dancing and stood still* is the nonrestrictive phrase. Removing this phrase leaves the following sentence: The singer growing more exhausted with every song decided to while singing. This sentence is now missing important information. What did the singer decide to do while singing? The remaining sentence is now missing the verb. Removing choice D makes the sentence incomplete, so choice D is not the nonrestrictive phrase.

EXAMPLE

My friends found a stray cat, which is white and brown and brought it to my house.

Identify the best place for an additional comma in the sentence above?

a. After *friends*
b. After *white*
c. After *brown*
d. After *it*

Choice A says another comma should be added after *friends*. This would set off *found a stray cat*. Can this information be removed from the sentence? No, because the sentence would not make sense without this information. The phrase tells what the friends found. Choice A is incorrect.

Choice B says another comma should be added after *white*. This would set off *which is white*. These words cannot be removed from the sentence because the remaining sentence is not logical. Choice B is incorrect.

Choice C says another comma should be added after *brown*. This would set off the clause *which is white and brown*. Can this information be removed from the sentence? Yes, it can! This information is not necessary for the sentence to make sense, and it does not flow with the rest of the sentence. When this information is removed, the remaining sentence is logical and complete, and it flows well. Choice C is correct.

Choice D says another comma should be added after *it*. This would set off *which is white and brown and brought it*. These words cannot be removed from the sentence because the remaining words do not form a logical sentence. Choice D is incorrect.

SEMICOLONS

The semicolon is used to connect major sentence pieces of equal value. Some rules for semicolons include:

Use Case	Example
Between closely connected independent clauses **not connected with a coordinating conjunction**	You are right; we should go with your plan.
Between independent clauses **linked with a transitional word**	I think that we can agree on this; however, I am not sure about my friends.
Between items in a **series that has internal punctuation**	I have visited New York, New York; Augusta, Maine; and Baltimore, Maryland.

Review Video: How to Use Semicolons
Visit mometrix.com/academy and enter code: 370605

EXAMPLE

Which of the following sentences is NOT written correctly?

a. My sister burned the lasagna we were going to eat for dinner; we went out to eat instead of cooking something else.
b. The ball rolled into the ditch, therefore, it was muddy and wet when he retrieved it.
c. She has lived in many cities, including Nashville, Tennessee; San Diego, California; and Salt Lake City, Utah.
d. He hung the picture in the wrong spot; now there is a distracting hole in the wall.

Choice A is a compound sentence. The semicolon is used to separate two independent clauses. There is no coordinating conjunction in the sentence. This sentence correctly uses a semicolon, so choice A is incorrect.

Choice B is a compound sentence. In a compound sentence, either a coordinating conjunction or a semicolon can be used to separate the independent clauses. This sentence includes a transitional word, but it uses neither a semicolon nor a coordinating conjunction. To revise this sentence, *therefore* can be replaced by a coordinating conjunction, or the first comma can be replaced with a semicolon This sentence is written incorrectly, so choice B is the correct answer.

Choice C is a sentence that includes a list. Remember that semicolons can be used to separate items in a list when at least one of the items includes a comma. In this sentence, a list of cities is given. Since a comma is required to separate the name of a city from the name of the state it is in, each of the items in the list contain a comma. This means that each full city name must be separated by a semicolon. This sentence is written correctly, so choice C is incorrect.

Choice D is a compound sentence and does not contain a coordinating conjunction. Semicolons can be used to separate independent clauses in a compound sentence instead of a coordinating conjunction. This sentence uses a semicolon correctly, so choice D is incorrect.

COLONS

The colon is used to call attention to the words that follow it. A colon must come after a **complete independent clause**. The rules for colons are as follows:

Use Case	Example
After an independent clause to **make a list**	I want to learn many languages: Spanish, German, and Italian.
For **explanations**	There is one thing that stands out on your resume: responsibility.
To give a **quote**	He started with an idea: "We are able to do more than we imagine."
After the **greeting in a formal letter**	To Whom It May Concern:
Show **hours and minutes**	It is 3:14 p.m.
Separate a **title and subtitle**	The essay is titled "America: A Short Introduction to a Modern Country."

Review Video: Using Colons
Visit mometrix.com/academy and enter code: 868673

EXAMPLE

Which of the following sentences does NOT use a colon correctly?

a. Your reports must be submitted by 10:30 p.m.
b. Terrence: his best friend, is graduating from college on Saturday.
c. Shelly had three tasks to complete before her mother returned: empty the dishwasher, walk the dog, and tidy the living room.
d. Brian was excited to write a report over his favorite book: *Frankenstein*.

Choice A uses a colon to separate the hour from the minute. Colons are necessary when writing hours and minutes. This colon is used correctly and is in the right place, so choice A is incorrect.

Choice B uses a colon to separate a nonessential appositive. This is not an acceptable use for a colon because it is not used in a time, and it does not follow an independent clause. Also, nonessential appositives that appear in the middle of a sentence should only be set off by commas. This is an incorrect use for a colon, so choice B is the correct answer.

Choice C uses a colon to separate an independent clause from a list. This is an acceptable use for a colon. This colon is appropriately used and is in the right place, so choice C is incorrect.

Choice D uses a colon for explanation. This is an acceptable use for a colon when the word, phrase, or clause being separated follows an independent clause. The independent clause should also introduce, or describe, the information following the colon. Choice D correctly uses a colon, so it is incorrect.

PARENTHESES

Parentheses are used for additional information. Also, they can be used to put labels for letters or numbers in a series. Parentheses should be not be used very often. If they are overused, parentheses can be a distraction instead of a help.

Examples:

> **Extra Information**: The rattlesnake (see Image 2) is a dangerous snake of North and South America.
>
> **Series**: Include in the email (1) your name, (2) your address, and (3) your question for the author.

Review Video: Parentheses
Visit mometrix.com/academy and enter code: 947743

EXAMPLE

Which of the following CANNOT be set off by parentheses?

a. A short list of examples
b. A reference to a graph or chart that is relevant to the text
c. An essential phrase in a sentence
d. A number used to label an item in a series

Remember that parentheses are used to set off extra information from the rest of the sentence. Extra words set off by parentheses are often not meant to be read with the rest of the sentence in the same way as words set off by commas. Usually, the words in parenthesis do not impact the meaning of the other words in the sentence. Instead, they can include additional information that is relevant to the sentence or guide the reader to that information.

Choice A says that parentheses cannot be used to set off a short list of examples. Examples are used to elaborate on information and help the reader better understand it. Examples often do not impact the meaning of the sentence. When there are only a few examples and they do not affect the sentence's meaning, they can be set off by parentheses.

Choice B says that parentheses cannot be used to set off a reference to a graph or chart. References like these are used to lead the reader to look at a graph or chart so he or she will see important information. This keeps the writer from placing the image in between sections of text. When references are in parentheses, they are not meant to impact the meaning of the sentence. References to graphs and charts can be set off by parentheses.

Choice C says that parentheses cannot be used to set off essential phrases in a sentence. When a phrase is essential to a sentence, it should not be set off by any punctuation marks. Essential phrases cannot be set off by parentheses, so choice C is correct.

Choice D says that parentheses cannot be used to set off numbers used as labels. Sometimes, when a list appears in a sentence, the items may be referred to in a different location. In these cases, it can be helpful when the items are labeled. The labels are meant to guide the readers to the information, not to change the meaning of the sentence. Numbers used to label items in a series can be set off by parentheses.

Quotation Marks

Use quotation marks to close off **direct quotations** of a person's written or spoken words, which are also called **dialogue**. Do not use quotation marks around indirect quotations. An indirect quotation gives someone's message without using the person's exact words. Use **single quotation marks** to close off a quotation inside a quotation.

Direct Quote: Nancy said, "I am waiting for Henry to arrive."

Indirect Quote: Henry said that he is going to be late to the meeting.

Quote inside a Quote: The teacher asked, "Has everyone read Martin Luther King's 'I Have a Dream' speech?"

Quotation marks should be used around the titles of **short works**: newspaper and magazine articles, poems, short stories, songs, television episodes, and radio programs. Titles of **long works** should be italicized when they are part of a typed composition or underlined when they are part of a handwritten composition.

Examples:

"Rip Van Winkle" (short story by Washington Irving)

"O Captain! My Captain!" (poem by Walt Whitman)

Review Video: Quotation Marks
Visit mometrix.com/academy and enter code: 884918

Apostrophes

An apostrophe is used to show **possession** or the **deletion of letters in contractions**. An apostrophe is not needed with the possessive pronouns *his, hers, its, ours, theirs, whose*, and *yours*.

Singular Nouns: David's car | a book's theme | my brother's board game

Plural Nouns that end with -*s*: the scissors' handle | boys' basketball

Plural Nouns that end without -*s*: Men's department | the people's adventure

Review Video: Apostrophes
Visit mometrix.com/academy and enter code: 213068

Review Video: Punctuation Errors in Possessive Pronouns
Visit mometrix.com/academy and enter code: 221438

Apostrophes in Contractions

Contractions are combinations of words. Contractions involve taking two words, removing at least one letter from one of the words, putting an apostrophe in its place, and removing the space. For example, *does not* can be written as the contraction *doesn't*. The *o* is removed from *not* and is replaced with an apostrophe, which represents the removed letter, so it appears as *n't*. The space after does is then removed, turning *does not* into the contraction *doesn't*. Some more examples of contractions are listed below.

First Word	Second Word	Contraction
Can	Not	Can't
Do	Not	Don't
She	Will	She'll
They	Will	They'll
He	Is	He's
It	Is	It's
They	Are	They're
I	Am	I'm

Not all words can be used to form contractions, but many small, commonly used words can.

Capitalization

One important part of using correct grammar is properly capitalizing words. Usually, only nouns will be capitalized, but there are some exceptions. The most important capitalization rule is that the first word of every sentence, no matter what part of speech it is, should be capitalized. Another exception is that the pronoun *I* should always be capitalized.

Proper nouns are always capitalized, but sometimes it can be tricky to decide whether or not a noun is a proper noun. Some words that are usually common nouns may become proper nouns when used with other words or phrases. Also, when words that are not nouns are used with a noun, or when a group of words are used together as one noun, those words may also need to be capitalized.

Titles of Books, Stories, and Essays

Most of the words in titles of things like books, stories, and essays should be capitalized, but some should not. The very first word in a title should always be capitalized. Any other word in a title that is a noun, pronoun, adjective, verb or adverb should be capitalized. Articles, such as *a* or *the*, should not be capitalized. Short conjunctions and prepositions are usually not capitalized.

Abbreviations, Initials, and Acronyms

Abbreviations are shortened versions of other words. When an abbreviation shortens, or abbreviates, a word that should be capitalized, the abbreviation's first letter should also be capitalized. When the shortened word is a noun that is not capitalized, the abbreviation should be in lowercase. Initials are usually written using the first letter from multiple words. For example, John Fitzgerald Kennedy is commonly referred to by his initials, JFK. Acronyms also use the first letter from multiple words, but they are different from initials because they form words on their own. For example, NASA is an acronym for National Aeronautics and Space Administration. Some acronyms, like NASA, omit small words, such as *and*, *of*, and *for*. When initials and acronyms are used for proper nouns, each letter should be capitalized.

The types of words and phrases in the chart below are proper nouns and should always be capitalized:

	Description	Example
Historical Periods	A range of time in history that is related to specific events or circumstances	During the Romantic Period, many authors and poets wrote about their emotions.
Historical Events	Names of important events that happened in history	Napoleon Bonaparte led France after the French Revolution.
Historical Documents	Titles of important papers or compositions that are connected to historical events	The Mayflower Compact was written to create rules and expectations for the colony in Plymouth.
Languages	Names of the different languages that people speak	I want to learn to speak Cantonese, Spanish, and German.
Races and Ethnicities	Words often used to describe a person's heritage or cultural group	Malia taught her granddaughter how to hula so she could share a tradition of her Native Hawaiian heritage with her.
Nationalities	Words that describe which country a person is from	My teacher who moved to Canada last year is Romanian.
Organizations	Titles of official groups formed by people	Fewer than half of the states in America have a team in the National Basketball Association.

Review Video: Capitalization in Grammar
Visit mometrix.com/academy and enter code: 369678

EXAMPLE

Allison and Claire enjoy studying art from the beginning of the renaissance. They started a club so they and other students can learn more about it. Allison and Claire named the club Early Renaissance Art Club, which can be abbreviated to ERA Club. The students that joined elected Claire as the president and Allison as the vice president. The club's first meeting will take place after Christmas vacation.

Which of the following changes should be made in the passage?

a. In the first sentence, *Renaissance* should be capitalized.
b. In the third sentence, *ERA* should be written as *Era*.
c. In the fourth sentence, *president* and *vice president* should be capitalized.
d. In the last sentence, *Christmas* should be in lowercase.

Choice A says that *Renaissance* should be capitalized in the first sentence of the passage. The Renaissance is a historical period, so *Renaissance* is a proper noun that should always be capitalized. Choice A is correct.

Choice B says that *ERA* should be written as *Era*. In the third sentence of the passage, the word *era* is used as an acronym. Remember that all letters in an acronym should be capitalized. The correct capitalization is *ERA*, so choice B is incorrect.

Choice C says that *president* and *vice president* should be capitalized. Titles for people are capitalized when they are used as part of a person's name or in the place of a person's name. In this passage, these titles are not used as part of anyone's name or in place of anyone's name, so they should be in lowercase. Choice C is incorrect.

Choice D says that *Christmas* should be in lowercase. The passage says that the first meeting will be held after Christmas break. Even though *Christmas* is used to describe when the students are getting a vacation from school, it is the name of a holiday. Names of holidays are always capitalized, so choice D is incorrect.

Word Confusion

To, Too, and Two

To can be an adverb or a preposition for showing direction, purpose, and relationship. A dictionary can also be used to see the many other ways to use *to* in a sentence.

Examples: I went to the store. | I want to go with you.

Too is an adverb that means *also, as well, very,* or *in excess.*

Examples: I can walk a mile too. | You have eaten too much.

Two is a number.

Example: You have two minutes left.

There, Their, and They're

There can be an adjective, adverb, or pronoun. Often, *there* is used to show a place or to start a sentence.

Examples: I went there yesterday. | There is something in his pocket.

Their is a pronoun that is used to show ownership.

Examples: He is their father. | This is their fourth apology this week.

They're is a contraction of *they are.*

Example: Did you know that they're in town?

Its and It's

Its is a possessive pronoun that shows ownership.

Example: The guitar is in its case.

It's is a contraction of *it is.*

Example: It's an honor and a privilege to meet you.

AFFECT AND EFFECT

There are two main reasons that *affect* and *effect* are so often confused: 1) both words can be used as either a noun or a verb, and 2) unlike most homophones, their usage and meanings are closely related to each other. Here is a quick explanation of the four usage options:

Affect (n): feeling, emotion, or mood that is displayed

Example: The patient had a flat *affect.* (i.e., his face showed little or no emotion)

Affect (v): to alter, to change, to influence

Example: The sunshine *affects* the plant's growth.

Effect (n): a result, a consequence

Example: What *effect* will this weather have on our schedule?

Effect (v): to bring about, to cause to be

Example: These new rules will *effect* order in the office.

EXAMPLE

Choose the correct spelling from each pair of homophones in the following passage.

> I found a unique tree in the forest. (It's/Its) trunk is blue, and it has (two/too) many branches to count. I brought some of my friends to see it, but the tree did not seem to (affect/effect) them. While (their/they're) not fascinated by the strange tree, I am!

The first pair of homophones is *it's* and *its*. Remember that the contraction *it's* is used in place of *it is*. *Its* is a possessive pronoun that shows a thing's ownership or possession. An easy way to decide whether *it's* or *its* is correct is to see how the sentence sounds with *it is*, instead. *It is trunk is blue* does not make sense. *Its trunk is blue* means that the tree has a blue trunk, so *its* is the correct choice.

The next pair of homophones is *two* and *too*. *Two* only means the number two. *Too* can mean *also* or *in excess*. Which of these makes the most sense in this sentence? *Two many branches to count* or *too many branches to count*? The correct meaning is that there is an abundance of branches, so *too* is the correct choice for this pair.

The third pair of homophones is *affect* and *effect*. Since both of these words can be used as a noun or verb, identifying the correct part of speech is a helpful first step. The part of speech is a verb, since the correct word will show what *the tree* does to *them*. *Affect* as a verb means to change or influence. *Effect* as a verb means to lead to or cause something to happen. Replace the homophone with these synonyms. Seeing the tree cannot cause or lead the speaker's friends to exist, but it can change them or influence them. *Affect* is the correct choice for this pair.

The last pair of homophones is *their* and *they're*. *Their* is a possessive pronoun used to show that multiple people or things own something. *They're* is a contraction used in place of *they are*. Replace the homophone with *they are*. Does the sentence make sense? It does because they, the speaker's friends, are not fascinated by the tree. Saying *their not fascinated* does not make sense. *They're* is the correct choice for this pair.

Chapter Quiz

1. Every sentence always has a subject and a/an:

a. Imperative
b. Preposition
c. Predicate
d. Modifier

2. Which of the following sentences does NOT have an implied subject?

a. Take John on a quick walk.
b. Don't get lost.
c. John knows the way to the park.
d. Bring me back some flowers.

3. Which pronoun can be either singular or plural depending on what it is representing in the context of the sentence?

a. Nobody
b. Either
c. Several
d. All

4. Which of the following is written in third person perspective?

a. I am walking
b. He is walking
c. You are walking
d. We are walking

5. Which of the following best describes the function of an indirect object?

a. Shows how an action had an influence
b. Takes or receives the action of a verb
c. Explains or describes the subject
d. Shows that there is more information needed

6. What sentence has correct pronoun use?

a. Bob and I will be going.
b. Us all love eating ice cream.
c. You and me should go shopping.
d. Us boys played football last year.

7. Which of the following is a group of words that contains both a subject and a verb, and can be either independent or dependent?

a. Antecedent
b. Fragment
c. Phrase
d. Clause

8. Which of the following is an example of a complex sentence (as opposed to a simple or compound sentence)?

a. The time has come, and we are ready.
b. Judy and Alan watered the lawn and pulled weeds.
c. Marcia got married after she finished college.
d. I woke up at dawn; the sun was just coming up.

9. What method of correcting run-on sentences is the easiest way to make the sentence correct and more interesting at the same time?

a. Split into separate sentences
b. Join clauses properly
c. Reduce to one clause with a compound verb
d. Make one clause dependent

10. Which of the following is a word placed before a noun or pronoun that shows the relationship between an object and another word in the sentence?

a. Adjective
b. Adverb
c. Preposition
d. Conjunction

11. What punctuation mark(s) should be added to the following sentence to make it grammatically correct?

Relieved the test was over Leah dropped her pencil and slouched in her chair

a. Relieved the test was over Leah dropped her pencil and slouched in her chair.
b. Relieved the test was over, Leah dropped her pencil and slouched in her chair.
c. Relieved the test was over: Leah dropped her pencil and, slouched in her chair.
d. Relieved, the test was "over" Leah dropped her pencil and slouched in her chair.

12. Which of the following is specifically used to connect major sentence pieces of equal value?

a. Comma
b. Semicolon
c. Colon
d. Hyphen

13. Which of the following should be put in single quotation marks?

a. Quote inside a quote
b. Indirect quote
c. Direct quote
d. All of the above

Chapter Quiz Answer Key

1. C: See section **Predicates**

2. C: See section **Subjects**

3. D: See section **Depend on Context**

4. B: See section **Person Agreement Examples**

5. A: See section **Indirect Objects**

6. A: See section **Pronoun-Antecedent Agreement**

7. D: See section **Clauses**

8. C: See section **Complex**

9. D: See section **Run-on Sentences**

10. C: See section **Prepositions**

11. B: See section **Commas**

12. B: See section **Semicolons**

13. A: See section **Quotation Marks**

Extended Constructed Response

Essays

Essays usually focus on one topic, subject, or goal. There are several types of essays, including informative, persuasive, and narrative. An essay's structure and formality depend on the type of essay and its goal. While narrative essays typically do not include outside sources, other types of essays often require some research and the use of primary and secondary sources.

The basic format of an essay typically has three major parts: the introduction, the body, and the conclusion. The body is further divided into the writer's main points. Most essays will have at least three main points, but essays that go into more depth can have almost any number of main points.

An essay's introduction should answer three questions:

1. What is the **subject** of the essay?

   If an essay is about a book, the answer would include the title and author of the book, as well as any additional information needed, such as the subject or argument of the book.

2. How does the essay **discuss** the subject?

   To answer this, the writer briefly summarizes the main points and the evidence supporting them to let readers know how the essay is organized and what information they can expect to read.

3. What will the essay **prove**?

   This information is in the thesis statement, usually the opening paragraph's last sentence, which clearly states the writer's message.

The body elaborates on all the main points related to the thesis, introducing one main point at a time, and includes supporting evidence with each main point. Each body paragraph should state the point in a topic sentence, which is usually the first sentence in the paragraph. The paragraph should then explain the point's meaning, support it with quotations or other evidence, and then explain how this point and the evidence are related to the thesis. The writer should then repeat this procedure in a new paragraph for each additional main point.

The conclusion restates the content of the introduction, including the thesis, to remind the reader of the essay's main argument or subject. The essay writer may also summarize the highlights of the argument or description contained in the body of the essay, following the same organization originally used in the body. For example, a conclusion might look like: Point 1 + Point 2 + Point 3 = Thesis, or Point 1 → Point 2 → Point 3 → Thesis Proof. Good organization makes essays easier for writers to compose and provides a guide for readers to follow. Well-organized essays hold attention better and are more likely to get readers to believe or agree with the writer.

Using Sources in Essays

Sometimes writers use information from others in their work. This is most common in expository and persuasive writing. For an expository essay, a writer may not know all of the information that he or she needs to finish the composition. The writer may use other people's work to find the missing information and complete the composition. Persuasive writers may do research to find facts or statements from others that support their own beliefs and make their writing more persuasive. In both cases, research helps the writer find information that **supports** his or her **original work**.

Outside information must be relevant, true, and helpful to be appropriate for a composition. Writers must also be careful not to use too much outside information, since this can make the composition unoriginal. If a writer does use outside information, it is extremely important that the writer mention in the composition where the information came from. If the writer forgets or chooses not to say where the information came from, he or she has stolen someone else's work and presented it as their own. Doing this is called **plagiarism**.

Informational Texts

Informational texts, also called instructional or expository texts, are compositions written to inform the reader about a specific topic. An informational essay can inform readers in a variety of ways, such as giving them instructions, telling them facts about the topic, or teaching them why something happens. Informational texts should be logical, meaning that they should present information in an order that the reader can easily understand, and they should include the right amount of information so the writer successfully informs his or her audience of new information.

Informational texts should also focus on a **controlling idea**. In the introduction of an informational text, there may be a sentence or two that clearly state the essay's controlling idea. This sentence, or sentences, is called a **thesis statement**. The controlling idea should be clear throughout the composition. By emphasizing the controlling idea in the introduction, body, and conclusion, the writer can ensure that the controlling idea is clear. One way to make sure that the controlling idea is emphasized is to think about the purpose of each part of the essay. The introduction prepares the reader by telling them what the rest of the essay is about, so the controlling idea should be **introduced** in this section. The body tells the reader the information the writer wants to tell the audience, so this **explains** the controlling idea and facts about it to the reader. The conclusion is used to **remind** the reader of how the information in the body is related and **restates** the controlling idea one final time.

Review Video: Informational Text Visit mometrix.com/academy and enter code: 924964

Structures or Organizational Patterns in Informational Texts

Informational text can be **descriptive**, meaning that it gives information that can be experienced through the five senses, or it answers the questions what, who, when, where, and why. One common method of organizing informational text is to put it in a certain sequence, or order. **Chronological** texts include events in the order that they occurred, from start to finish. **How-to**, or **instructional**, texts organize information into a series of instructions in the order in which the steps should be followed. **Comparison-contrast** structures of informational text describe different ideas to their readers by pointing out how things or ideas are similar and how they are different. **Cause and effect** structures of informational text describe events that occurred and the causes or reasons for those events. **Problem and solution** structures of informational texts introduce and describe problems and offer one or more solutions for each problem described.

Argumentative Writing

In argumentative writing, the writer expresses a belief or opinion that he or she wants to lead readers to agree with. When writing an argumentative composition, the writer should first identify the **topic** his or her opinion is about. The topic may be serious or fun, as long as there is one clear topic in the composition. The next step is for the writer to determine his or her opinion on the topic and determine why he or she holds that opinion. In order to persuade others to agree with their opinion, the writer must be able to give readers reasons to support the opinion. If the writer does not know why he or she has an opinion, it will be difficult to convince readers to agree. In addition to having reasons that support their opinion, writers should prepare examples that support each of these reasons in order to strengthen their composition.

Once the writer has determined his or her topic, opinion, and reasons for having the opinion, he or she is ready to begin writing an argumentative essay. In the introduction, the writer should capture the reader's interest, introduce the topic, and reveal his or her opinion about the topic. In the body of the composition, the writer should remind the reader of the opinion and give his or her reasons for holding the opinion. If the writer has any examples, facts, or other information that supports his or her opinion or reasons for believing it, these should also be included in the body. Writers may also use a body paragraph to mention opposing opinions or beliefs and explain why they disagree with them. As in other compositions, the conclusion should remind the reader of the essay's topic and purpose, as well as remind the reader how the opinion has been explained and supported. The conclusion should also invite the reader to continue thinking about the topic and writer's opinion. This can be done through questions or statements that lead readers to consider whether or not they agree with the author's opinion or what their own opinions are.

Review Video: Argumentative Writing
Visit mometrix.com/academy and enter code: 561544

Informative vs. Persuasive Writing

Informative writing, also called explanatory or expository writing, is written to show that something is true or factual, while **persuasive** writing is written to lead the reader to agree with something that may or may not be true or factual. While persuasive text is written to **persuade** readers to agree with the author's position, informative text simply **provides information** to readers. Informative writing **informs** readers about why or how something is as it is. This can include offering new information, explaining how a process works, or describing a concept for readers.

Facts and Opinions

Writers and readers must always be aware of the difference between fact and opinion. A **fact** can be tested and proven to be true. An **opinion**, on the other hand, is someone's personal thoughts or feelings. Opinions are often not changed by information. If an author writes that a newborn elephant is about five times taller than a newborn giraffe, then he or she is stating a fact. If the author writes that giraffes are more interesting than elephants, then he or she is giving an opinion because this cannot be proven to be true or false. Opinions are often supported by facts. For instance, the author might use a comparison between the way that giraffes eat and the way elephants eat as evidence of how giraffes are more interesting. An opinion supported by facts tends to be more convincing. On the other hand, when authors support their opinions with other opinions, readers should seriously think about and read the argument carefully to see whether it is logical and trustworthy.

Review Video: Distinguishing Fact and Opinion
Visit mometrix.com/academy and enter code: 870899

Responding to a Text

An essay prompt may require writers to write about a text they have read. When writing an essay like this, writers should show that they understand the text they have read. They may mention their own thoughts, ideas, and opinions in the essay. However, the main idea of the essay should be about the text mentioned in the prompt.

When planning the essay, writers should consider what the text is about and how it is written. Writers should identify the purpose, main idea, and structure of the text. For informational and persuasive texts, they should also think about the supporting details the author used in the text. All of these facts about the text will help writers understand the text well and allow the writer to create a response to the text.

Responding to Multiple Texts

Essay prompts may ask writers to write about more than one text. In this case, writers should identify the purpose, main idea, and structure of each text. They should also look at the kinds of supporting details that the author of each text uses. Once writers know these details, they should think about the differences and similarities between the texts. The main ideas of each text may oppose each other, or one may support the other. Writers will need to write about both texts in the essay, so they must understand both texts and the connection between the texts.

Correspondence

Letters are written using a different format than an essay or book. A letter should begin with a greeting that names the person or group that is meant to receive the letter. Consider the following examples of greetings:

- Dear Mr. Johnson,
- To whom it may concern:
- To Bernard,
- Hello Grandma,

The greeting used at the beginning of the letter depends on the writer's purpose for writing the letter. If the letter is being written to a business, an owner or manager of a company, or someone who has a higher rank than the writer, the letter should be **formal**. A formal greeting should begin with "Dear" followed by the name of the recipient. For formal greetings, never address the recipient by their first name only. If the letter is being written to a friend or a family member, it may be **informal**. For informal letters, the greeting may start with a word other than *dear* and may name the recipient by their first name only or by a nickname.

Word Choice and Tone in Letters

The **purpose** of a letter also influences the way the body of the letter is written. For formal letters, the writer should use **formal, professional language**. The purpose of the letter should be clearly stated in the introduction. Whether the letter is written to give a complaint or share an opinion, the writer should keep a formal tone and write in a way that is **respectful** to the recipient. The writer should also be specific and provide any information that the recipient may need to respond appropriately. If a letter is informal, the writer can use **casual, friendly language**. The writer should think about their own relationship with the recipient and use a tone that fits the relationship and purpose for the letter.

Closing Letters

All letters should end with a **closing**, as well. The closing will include a word or phrase that signals that the body of the letter has ended, such as *sincerely*, *best wishes*, *until later*, or *with love*. The word or phrase should be followed by a comma, and the writer's name should be written underneath this on the next line. Formal letters should include closing words like *sincerely* or *thank you*.

Chapter Quiz

1. What type of essay does NOT typically include outside sources?

a. Expository
b. Informative
c. Persuasive
d. Narrative

2. Which of the following is NOT true of informational texts?

a. Informational texts are also called instructional or expository texts
b. Informational texts should be logical
c. Informational texts should focus on a central idea
d. Informational texts can only be structured chronologically

3. In an argumentative essay, which of the following should be included in the body?

a. A reminder of the writer's opinion and his or her reasons for holding the opinion
b. Examples, facts, or other information that supports the writer's opinion
c. Opposing opinions or beliefs and explanations of why the writer disagrees with them
d. All of the above

4. A letter that requires a formal greeting should always start with:

a. Dear
b. To whom it may concern
c. Greetings
d. Hello

5. At the end of a letter the closing is followed by:

a. A period and the writer's name
b. A comma and the writer's name
c. A colon and the writer's name
d. A semicolon and the writer's name

CHAPTER QUIZ ANSWER KEY

1. D: See section **Essays**

2. D: See section **Structures or Organizational Patterns in Informational Texts**

3. D: See section **Argumentative Writing**

4. A: See section **Correspondence**

5. B: See section **Closing Letters**

Informational Text Example

Below is a prompt for an informational text. There is also an example of an essay that addresses the prompt. There are multiple drafts of this essay to show what kinds of changes a writer may make during the writing process to improve his or her work.

PROMPT:

Do you ever dream of going to a new city, state, or even country? Write about one place you want to travel to on vacation. Be sure to share why you would like to visit that place.

Rough Draft

Imagine traveling into the city or the beach and being transported back in time. This is what it must be like to live in Greece. The old buildings, beautiful beaches, and Greek foods are reasons I want to visit Greece.

Several buildings from ancient Greece are still standing, and they can easily be enjoyed by visitors and the people of Greece today. Some of the most famous ones, like the Parthenon, are located throughout the capital. This means that even when you are sitting in an air-conditioned restaurant in Athens, you can still see what is left of history. There are also tours that teach visitors more about these structures and the events that happened at each one. Though seeing these structures is not the only reason I would like to visit Greece, they would be enough of a reason for me to visit.

In addition to the scenery, another reason to visit Greece is to try real Greek and Mediterranean foods. I have tried a few Greek foods, like baklava and pita bread, and I enjoyed them. While these foods are available in America, I think they are probably made a little differently in Greece. I am interested in seeing what the differences are and trying new things. I hope I can visit Greece soon, because I am getting hungry just thinking about the food there!

Greece has a variety of beaches, as some are small with rocky structures and some look like normal beaches. The water is also different from some American waters because Greece is next to the Mediterranean Sea. Also, many historical events and myths took place on some of the beaches. I would love to sit on one of those beaches and try to imagine ships or characters from myths coming to the shore! The beaches in Greece are beautiful, but I think they also sound fun and interesting!

Walking through historical structures, visiting unique beaches, and eating new foods there is my dream. If I only ever have the chance to go on one vacation, I hope it is to Greece!

Revised Draft

Imagine traveling into the city or the beach and being transported back in time. This is what it must be like to live in Greece. The remaining historical sites that are still there allow visitors to see two cultures side by side. The old buildings, beautiful beaches, and Greek foods are reasons I want to visit Greece.

Several buildings from ancient Greece are still standing, and they can easily be enjoyed by visitors and the people of Greece today. Some of the most famous ones, like the Parthenon, are located throughout the capital. This means that even when you are sitting in an air-conditioned restaurant in Athens, you can still see what is left of history. There are also tours that teach visitors more about these structures and the events that happened at each one. Though seeing these structures is not the only reason I would like to visit Greece, they would be enough of a reason for me to visit.

Greece has a variety of beaches, as some are small with rocky structures and some look like normal beaches. The water is also different from some American waters because Greece is next to the Mediterranean Sea. Also, many historical events and myths took place on some of the beaches. I would love to sit on one of those beaches and try to imagine ships or characters from myths coming to the shore! The beaches in Greece are beautiful, but I think they also sound fun and interesting!

In addition to the scenery, a third reason to visit Greece is to try real Greek and Mediterranean foods. I have tried a few Greek foods, like baklava and pita bread, and I enjoyed them. While these foods are available in America, I think they are probably made a little differently in Greece. I am interested in seeing what the differences are and trying new things. I hope I can visit Greece soon, because I am getting hungry just thinking about the food there!

Greece is a special place where the old and the new come together. Walking through historical structures, visiting unique beaches, and eating new foods there is my dream. If I only ever have the chance to go on one vacation, I hope it is to Greece!

Revised Draft Notes

Remember the purpose of the revising stage of the writing process. When revising, it is important to look at the whole composition. Do all of the paragraphs strengthen the composition? Do the introduction and conclusion help the reader understand the controlling idea and main points?

In this revision, nothing has been removed, but there are some additions. Look at the underlined words. In the introduction, a sentence has been added. Why? Previously, the introduction had only a hook and a thesis. The sentences were well written, but the writer did not provide a connection between the hook and the thesis. The new sentence connects the ideas in both sentences and introduces some of the main points the writer will discuss in the essay.

In the conclusion, another sentence has been added. This sentence strengthens the composition by creating a transition from the body to the conclusion. Before, the conclusion began abruptly by listing the three main points from the body of the essay. This sentence makes the essay flow better by giving the reader a transition from the body to the conclusion. This sentence reminds the reader of composition's controlling idea before repeating the writer's main points and sharing his or her hopes.

Finally, the third and fourth paragraphs have been switched. Why is that? Before, the writer discussed ancient buildings, then food, then the beaches. This revised draft discusses buildings, then beaches, then food. This new order puts the more closely related points, the scenery of the buildings and beaches, closer together in the essay. This helps the reader by making the organization of the essay more logical.

EDITED DRAFT

Imagine traveling into the city or the beach and being transported back in time. This is what it must be like to live in <u>Greece, since the remaining</u> historical sites ~~that are still there~~ allow visitors to see two cultures side by side. The ~~old~~ <u>ancient</u> buildings, beautiful beaches, and Greek foods are reasons I want to visit Greece.

Several buildings from ancient Greece are still standing, and they can easily be enjoyed by visitors and the people of Greece today. Some of the most famous ones, like the Parthenon, are located throughout the capital. This means that even when you are sitting in an air-conditioned restaurant in Athens, you can still see ~~what is left~~ <u>glimpses</u> of history. There are also tours that teach visitors more about these structures and the events that happened at each one. ~~Though seeing these structures is not the only reason I would like to visit Greece, they would be enough of a reason for me to visit.~~ <u>Seeing these structures alone is enough of a reason for me to visit Greece!</u>

<u>Another reason I want to travel to Greece is to see the beaches there. There are</u> a variety of beaches, as some are small with rocky structures and some look like ~~normal~~ <u>typical</u> beaches. The water is also different from some American waters because Greece is next to the Mediterranean Sea. Also, many historical events and myths took place on some of the beaches. I would love to sit on one of those beaches and try to imagine ships or characters from myths coming to the shore! The beaches in Greece are beautiful, but I think they also sound fun and interesting!

In addition to the scenery, a third reason to visit Greece is to try ~~real~~ <u>authentic</u> Greek and Mediterranean foods. I have tried a few Greek foods, like baklava and pita bread, and I enjoyed them. While these foods are available in America, I think they are probably made a little differently in Greece<u>, so</u> I am interested in seeing what the differences are and trying new things. I hope I can visit Greece soon, because I am getting hungry just thinking about the food there!

Greece is a special place where the old and the new come together. Walking through historical structures, visiting unique beaches, and eating new foods there is my dream. If I only ever have the chance to go on one vacation, I hope it is to Greece!

Edited Draft Notes

Since the writer has revised his or her work, the next step is to edit the composition. Remember that editing is very similar to revising, but editing usually includes paying attention to each paragraph, instead of the whole composition. Look at the changes that were made to each paragraph.

There are small changes throughout this draft. First, look at the introduction. Before, the introduction had four sentences that were about the same length. In this draft, the second and third sentences have been combined to make a longer sentence. This creates more sentence variety in the introduction, which makes the composition more entertaining for the writer's audience. A few words have been crossed out, as well. *That are still there* has been replaced with *remaining*. This change makes the writing more concise and formal. Also, *old* has been replaced with *ancient*. This clarifies what kind of buildings the writer is describing by using a word that more specifically describes the age of the buildings.

In the next paragraph, *what is left* has been replaced with *glimpses*. This change makes the writing more concise by using one word instead of three. Furthermore, this change makes the writing more interesting and entertaining by using a better vocabulary word. At the end of the paragraph, the last sentence has been condensed. Most of the sentences in this paragraph are long. Shortening this sentence adds sentence variety to this paragraph and makes the concluding sentence more concise. Overall, these changes make the paragraph easier to read by eliminating unnecessary words and using better vocabulary.

There are a few more changes left in the third and fourth paragraphs. A transition has been added to the beginning of the third paragraph. Now, the writer introduces the next main point before describing the beaches. This makes the essay flow better overall and making it easier for the writer's audience to read. *Normal* has been replaced with *typical*. Since there are so many different beaches in the world, there are not really any normal beaches. *Typical* is a much clearer word. Now, the reader knows that the writer is trying to distinguish the beaches in Greece from the type of beaches that he or she sees most often.

In the next paragraph, *real* has been replaced with *authentic*. The food the writer has tried in America has been real food, not fake food, so this is poor word choice. Now, *authentic* clarifies the writer's meaning that the food will be closer to its original Greek or Mediterranean style. These changes in word choice improve the clarity of the essay by using specific words that better communicate the writer's points. Finally, the third and fourth sentences have been joined together. This increases sentence variety by adding a longer sentence to this paragraph.

Final Draft

Imagine traveling into the city or the beach and being transported back in time. This is what it must be like to live in Greece, since the remaining historical sites allow visitors to see two cultures side by side. The ancient buildings, beautiful beaches, and Greek foods are reasons I want to visit Greece.

Several buildings from ancient Greece are still standing, and they can easily be enjoyed by visitors and the people of Greece today. Some of the most famous ones, like the Parthenon, are located throughout the capital. This means that even when you are sitting in an air-conditioned restaurant in Athens, you can still see glimpses of history. There are also tours that teach visitors more about these structures and the events that happened at each one. Seeing these structures alone is enough of a reason for me to visit Greece!

Another reason I want to travel to Greece is to see the beaches there. There are a variety of beaches, as some are small with rocky structures and some look like typical beaches. The water is also different from some American waters because Greece is next to the Mediterranean Sea. Also, many historical events and myths took place on some of the beaches. I would love to sit on one of those beaches and try to imagine ships or characters from myths coming to the shore! The beaches in Greece are beautiful, but I think they also sound fun and interesting!

In addition to the scenery, a third reason to visit Greece is to try authentic Greek and Mediterranean foods. I have tried a few Greek foods, like baklava and pita bread, and I enjoyed them. While these foods are available in America, I think they are probably made a little differently in Greece, so I am interested in seeing what the differences are and trying new things. I hope I can visit Greece soon, because I am getting hungry just thinking about the food there!

Greece is a special place where the old and the new come together. Walking through historical structures, visiting unique beaches, and eating new foods there is my dream. If I only ever have the chance to go on one vacation, I hope it is to Greece!

FINAL DRAFT EVALUATION

The essay answers the prompt and is on topic throughout the composition. The controlling idea is clear and is stated in the introduction, supported in the body, and restated in the conclusion. The thesis statement restates parts of the prompt and gives the reader a preview of the rest of the essay. The body uses well-structured paragraphs to explain the supporting details and examples and connects them to the controlling idea. The conclusion also emphasizes the controlling idea and supporting details and invites the reader to consider what they have read.

The essay is also interesting and written with a variety of sentence types. It uses transitions and good paragraph structure to make the essay easy for the reader to understand. The introduction also uses a hook to get the reader's attention and help him or her relate to the information in the essay. Not only does this essay answer the prompt and have appropriate structure, but it also makes use of good, engaging, and interesting details.

Practice Test #1

Reading

"The Boy Musician"

by Kate Dickinson Sweetser

(1) Johannes Chrysostemus Wolfgangus Theophilus Mozart—what a burden to be put upon a baby's tiny shoulders!

(2) If there is any truth underlying the belief that a name can in some measure foreshadow a child's future, then surely Wolfgang Mozart, who was born in Salzburg in 1756, came honestly by his heritage of greatness. When he was only a day old, he received the five-part name, to which was later added his confirmation name of Sigismundus. But as soon as he could choose for himself, the little son of Marianne and Leopold Mozart from his store of names, selected Wolfgang, to which he added Amadeus, by which combination he was always known, and the name is forever linked with the memory of a great genius.

(3) Almost before he could talk plainly the little fellow showed himself to be a musical prodigy, and when he was scarcely three years old, he would steal into the room where his father was giving a lesson on the harpsichord to Anna (or "Nannerl," as she was called), the sister five years older than himself. While she was being taught, Wolfgang would listen and watch with breathless attention.

(4) One day when the lesson was over, he begged his father to teach him too, but Leopold Mozart only laughed as he answered, glancing down into the child's serious face looking so intently into his:

(5) "Wait, my little man, thou art but a baby yet. Wait awhile, my Wolferl!" and the disappointed little musician crept away, but as soon as Nannerl and his father had left the room, the tiny fellow crept back again, went to the harpsichord and standing on tiptoe, touched the keys with his chubby fingers stretched wide apart until he reached and played *a perfect chord*! Leopold Mozart was in another part of the house, but his sensitive ear caught the sound, and he rushed back to find his baby on tiptoe before the harpsichord, giving the first hint of his marvelous ability.

(6) At once the proud and excited father began to give him lessons, and always, too, from that day, whenever Nannerl had her lesson, Wolfgang perched on his father's knee, and listened with rapt absorption, and often when the lesson was over, he would repeat what she had played in exact imitation of her manner of playing.

(7) Leopold Mozart, who was himself a talented musician, saw with pride almost beyond expression, that both of his children inherited his musical ability, and soon felt that Wolfgang was a genius. When the boy was only four, his father, to test his powers, tried to teach him some minuets. To his perfect astonishment, Wolfgang played after him in a most extraordinary manner, not merely striking the notes correctly, but marking the rhythm with accurate expression, and to learn and play each minuet the little fellow required only half an hour.

(8) When he was five years old, one day his father entered the sitting-room of their home and found Wolfgang bending over a table, writing so busily that he did not hear his father enter, or see that he was standing beside him. Wolfgang's chubby little hand held the pen awkwardly, but held it with firm determination while it travelled back and forth across a large sheet of paper on which he was scribbling a strange collection of hieroglyphics, with here and there a huge blot, testifying to his haste and inexperience in the use of ink.

(9) What was he trying to do? His father's curiosity finally overcame him and he asked:

(10) "What are you doing, Wolfgang?" The curly head was raised with an impatient gesture.

(11) "I am composing a concerto for the harpsichord. I have nearly finished the first part."

(12) "Let me see it."

(13) "No, please, I have not yet finished."

(14) But even as he spoke, the eager father had taken up the paper and carried it over to where a friend stood, and they looked it over together, exchanging amused glances at the queer characters on it. Presently Leopold Mozart, after looking carefully at it, said:

(15) "Why it really seems to be composed by rule! But it is so difficult that no one could ever play it."

(16) "Oh, yes, they could, but it must be studied first," exclaimed little Wolfgang eagerly, and running to the harpsichord, he added:

(17) "See, this is the way it begins," and he was able to play enough of it, to show what his idea in writing it had been, and his father and the friend who had before exchanged glances of amusement, now looked at each other with wonder not untouched with awe.

Refer to the passage "'The Boy Musician'" to answer questions 1-8.

1. What theme is developed in the passage based on the interaction between Wolfgang Mozart and his father Leopold?

a. The qualities of a genius can surprise even their parents.
b. Children may work very hard to receive their parents' approval.
c. Siblings often battle for their parents' attention.
d. Children avoid disobeying their parents for fear of punishment.

2. How does the author's use of a third-person omniscient point of view impact the reader's understanding of the events in the story?

a. The reader understands how the author of the passage has been inspired by Wolfgang Mozart.
b. The reader knows how both Wolfgang Mozart and his father feel about the concerto Wolfgang has written.
c. The reader understands why Leopold Mozart thinks that three-year-olds are too young to learn music.
d. The reader knows how the historical time period the passage is set in creates conflict.

3. What can the reader infer about Leopold Mozart based on the passage?

a. Leopold Mozart was only proud of Wolfgang and not of Nannerl.
b. Leopold Mozart thought his children should be of a certain age before learning music.
c. Leopold Mozart felt upset that his son was a better musician than he was.
d. Leopold Mozart taught Wolfgang how to write musical compositions.

4. Which best explains how the story's setting influenced Wolfgang Mozart's value of music?

a. The story is set in a time period that took place before music was recorded.
b. The story is set in a household where Wolfgang Mozart could only speak to his family.
c. The story is set in a time period where children were commonly given lengthy names.
d. The story is set in a household where Wolfgang Mozart observed his talented father.

5. Which sentence from the passage best demonstrates that the passage is historical fiction?

a. Leopold Mozart was in another part of the house, but his sensitive ear caught the sound, and he rushed back to find his baby on tiptoe before the harpsichord, giving the first hint of his marvelous ability.
b. When he was five years old, one day his father entered the sitting-room of their home and found Wolfgang bending over a table, writing so busily that he did not hear his father enter, or see that he was standing beside him.
c. If there is any truth underlying the belief that a name can in some measure foreshadow a child's future, then surely Wolfgang Mozart, who was born in Salzburg in 1756, came honestly by his heritage of greatness.
d. While she was being taught, Wolfgang would listen and watch with breathless attention.

6. Read the dictionary entry (adapted from Merriam-Webster) for the word *chord*.

chord \ [kawrd] \ noun 1. a feeling or emotion 2. a line segment that connects two points on a curve 3. a group of three or more tones that produce harmony 4. a thin rope made of interwoven strands

Which definition is the best match for how chord is used in paragraph 5?

a. Definition 1
b. Definition 2
c. Definition 3
d. Definition 4

7. What is the most likely reason that the author included the information in paragraphs 4 and 5?

a. To highlight how much Wolfgang Mozart wanted to learn music
b. To show that Wolfgang Mozart could never have made great music without his father's influence
c. To detail the inspirations for Wolfgang Mozart's earliest musical compositions
d. To suggest that Wolfgang Mozart was motivated to be a better musician than his sister

8. How does the author's use of terms like "my little man" and "my Wolferl" contribute to the tone in paragraph 5?

a. It creates a warning tone.
b. It creates a hopeful tone.
c. It creates an affectionate tone.
d. It creates a friendly tone.

The Trouble with Tests

(1) Lisa was a good student. She studied hard, diligently did her homework, and turned in assignments on time. Whenever she had to take a test, however, Lisa had a problem. Her hands began to sweat, and her stomach began to churn. She felt dizzy and breathless and sick. As a result, Lisa couldn't focus and always did poorly on tests. Her grades suffered, and so did her confidence level.

(2) Lisa's problem is a common one. Often called test anxiety, it includes any unusual stress symptoms that occur during tests. Symptoms can be as mild as light nausea or a headache or as severe as vomiting or uncontrollable shaking. Millions of students deal with test anxiety every year, but few realize it can be improved through three simple steps.

(3) The first step to improving test anxiety is practicing better study habits. Proper preparation is an important step to overcoming test anxiety. It is important to develop regular study times and avoid last minute "cramming" for a test. Studying heavily on the day of or night before a test can actually increase test anxiety in most students. The better option is to devote at least a half-hour block of time to reviewing class materials each day. This can help embed information in the brain, making it more accessible at test time.

(4) Using memory games and tools is another way to improve study habits. Using these tools and games can help students better retain information. It also makes learning more fun, which can reduce stress levels. Flashcards with key points or ideas can be very helpful when used alone or with a study partner. Mnemonic devices—silly sayings to help students recall complex concepts—are also helpful tools for reducing stress and improving test performance. An example of a mnemonic device is "Every Good Boy Deserves Fudge" to help music students remember the note names for the lines of the treble clef staff (EGBDF).

(5) The second step to reducing test anxiety is to use relaxation techniques. The first relaxation technique that is useful for test anxiety is visualization. This involves choosing a favorite place or event. When test anxiety symptoms appear, students can close their eyes and visualize themselves in that favorite place or at that favorite event. The students should focus on sensory information—sights, sounds, smells, etc. This refocuses the attention of the brain and reduces anxiety.

(6) Another relaxation technique that works well for test anxiety is deep breathing. When the body is under stress, breathing becomes shallower, causing the heart rate to increase and the blood pressure to rise. Conscious deep breathing helps increase oxygen flow to the body, reducing the heart rate and blood pressure. To practice deep breathing, simply draw air in through the nose for five seconds, and then release the air through the mouth, blowing out steadily for five seconds. Done with eyes open or closed, deep breathing exercises reduce stress and relax the body.

(7) The third step to reducing test anxiety is positive self-talk. Often, test anxiety is the result of or is compounded by a lack of faith in abilities. Students can overcome this through positive self-talk and self-affirmation. Before each test, a student should repeat, "I can do this"—or some similar positive mantra—over and over. This can be

done out loud or silently; either way, it creates a positive attitude and outlook that can reduce anxiety.

(8) The self-affirmation of celebrating success is key to overcoming test anxiety. Students should share test-taking victories with friends and loved ones. Students should also feel proud when they do well on a test. Every success is a blow to the obstacle of test anxiety. As with anything else, practice makes perfect, and celebrating success helps a student practice triumph over test anxiety.

(9) Test anxiety is a real problem, not an imagined issue or an excuse. It can be overcome, however, through three basic steps. First, students must use study tools and good habits for proper preparation. Second, students must use relaxation techniques—such as visualization and deep breathing—to help release stress from the body. Finally, students must engage in positive self-talk and celebrate successes to create an atmosphere of triumph. When all three of these steps are consistently practiced, test anxiety will become a thing of the past.

Refer to the passage "The Trouble with Tests" to answer questions 9-16.

9. Which of the following gives the best summary of "The Trouble with Tests"?

a. Lisa is an example of a student with test anxiety. She had distressing symptoms but was able to reduce her test anxiety after trying three simple steps consistently. As a result, she was able to do well on tests.
b. Many students suffer from test anxiety, and the main cause is poor study habits. Rather than "cramming," students should study a half-hour each day by using flashcards, memory games, and tools. These make learning more fun and distract from anxious thoughts of upcoming tests.
c. Some symptoms of test anxiety include sweating, nausea, headache, and dizziness. It's important to consider using relaxation techniques like deep breathing, as these can slow the heart rate and help reduce the body's stress response, relieving the symptoms of test anxiety.
d. Although test anxiety is common, there are simple strategies that can reduce it. These strategies include forming better study habits through preparation, tools, and games; using relaxation techniques like visualization and deep breathing; and using positive self-talk and celebrating successes.

10. Reread paragraph 7 in "The Trouble with Tests." What does *mantra* mean?

a. A deep breathing technique
b. A good-luck charm
c. A type of criticism
d. A repeated phrase

11. Which sentence from "The Trouble with Tests" best shows that, though test anxiety is common, students may feel alone in their experiences?

a. As a result, Lisa couldn't focus and always did poorly on tests.
b. Millions of students deal with test anxiety every year, but few realize it can be improved through three simple steps.
c. Studying heavily on the day of or night before a test can actually increase test anxiety in most students.
d. When test anxiety symptoms appear, students can close their eyes and visualize themselves in that favorite place or at that favorite event.

12. Paragraphs 4 and 8 support which key idea?

a. Other people can play a role in helping with test anxiety.
b. Games and tools can aid in remembering important concepts.
c. Doing well on a test confirms that a student is improving at managing their test anxiety.
d. It's important to share even small successes on tests.

13. Which sentence best states the controlling idea of "The Trouble with Tests"?

a. Test anxiety is common, but it can be reduced or eliminated by using specific strategies.
b. Students like Lisa are not just imagining the stressful symptoms that tests cause.
c. Having better study habits can significantly improve test anxiety.
d. A student with test anxiety should use the help of other people rather than suffering alone.

14. The passage "The Trouble with Tests" uses an organizational structure that:

a. Convinces the reader to try improving their study habits
b. Shows a cause-and-effect relationship between test anxiety and grades
c. Outlines a step-by-step process to overcome test anxiety
d. Reveals why some students do not experience test anxiety

15. Based on the information in "The Trouble with Tests," what can the reader conclude?

a. Forming good study habits is the most important way to reduce test anxiety.
b. Test anxiety is unlikely to go away on its own.
c. Teachers don't always understand test anxiety in their students.
d. The stress symptoms of test anxiety might indicate a bigger health problem.

16. What is the most likely reason that the author opens the passage with a brief narrative describing Lisa's experience? Write your answer on the lines below and support it with evidence from the passage.

Just Trying to Help

(1) One afternoon, Sharon was making a short film for a school project. She had worked all week to create costumes and props that would make the film stand out. She was excited to put everything in place and get started. However, just as she was about to start filming, she realized that she did not have a place to put the camera.

(2) "Oh gosh, how am I going to film anything?" Sharon said to herself just as her little sister, Emma, walked past her room.

(3) "What's wrong, Sharon?" Emma asked, concerned.

(4) Sharon chuckled and answered, "Oh, it's not a big deal. I have to make a video for school, and I just realized that I don't have a good place to put the camera." She paused, thinking. "I don't think mom and dad have a tripod, and I don't want to ask them to buy one."

(5) "Oh," Emma frowned. She looked around the room and saw Sharon's bookshelf. "You could take the books off and make a tower and put the camera on top!"

(6) Sharon laughed again. "No, I need to be able to point the camera up and down at different angles, and I can't do that if I put it on the stack of books."

(7) Emma frowned again, but then smiled. "Oh, I know! I can hold the camera!"

(8) "Oh, I wish you could, but I don't think you can hold it up high enough for some of the scenes. And I don't have a chair that would be safe for you to stand on. I'm sorry, Emma. But thank you for trying to help."

(9) Tears filled Emma's eyes and she began to walk away.

(10) "Hey, come back!" Sharon called. Emma turned around and began to sniffle. "What's wrong?" Sharon asked her.

(11) "I want to be able to help you!" Emma explained. "But I'm too little and I don't know how."

(12) "Oh, Emma." Sharon crouched down to hug her. "I'm glad you want to help me. Maybe there's a way you can. Let me think for a minute."

(13) Sharon and Emma sat on the floor, both looking at the props and costumes that were waiting to be used. Sharon sat up, looked at Emma, and smiled. "I think I've got it! What if you are the one in the video? Then I can hold the camera! What do you think about that?"

(14) Emma walked over to the costumes and put one on over her outfit. It was very loose, and she hung her head. "All of the costumes are too big. And I don't know what I'm supposed to do or say."

(15) At that moment, Sharon and Emma's dad walked by. "What are you two up to?" he asked. Sharon explained the problem, and he said, "Hm, yeah, you would have to remake all of the costumes. But here's an idea! What if I hold the camera? Then you can use the costumes you already have."

(16) "But then Emma can't help," Sharon said.

(17) "That's alright, Sharon," Emma said as she sat next to her. "But can I watch? Can I be your audience?"

(18) "Of course you can! Wow, I think this will work. Thanks, Dad!"

(19) They spent the afternoon filming scenes for the project. Sharon and Emma's dad held the video camera, and they brought Sharon's ideas to life. Emma sat and watched Sharon, laughing at the funny scenes and encouraging Sharon when she made mistakes.

(20) When they were done, Emma said to Sharon, "That was fun! Thank you for letting me stay and watch, even though I couldn't help."

(21) "You're very welcome," Sharon answered. "Thank you for laughing at some of the scenes. That let me know that they were actually funny. And thanks for cheering me on when I messed up. That helped me stay confident in what I was doing." She paused and added, "In the end, you were a huge help after all!"

Deeds of Kindness

by Epes Sargent

Suppose the little Cowslip
—Should hang its golden cup
And say, "I'm such a little flower
—I'd better not grow up!"
How many a weary traveller
—Would miss its fragrant smell,
How many a little child would grieve
—To lose it from the dell!

Suppose the glistening Dewdrop
—Upon the grass should say,
"What can a little dewdrop do?
—I'd better roll away!"
The blade on which it rested,
—Before the day was done,
Without a drop to moisten it,
—Would wither in the sun.

Suppose the little Breezes,
—Upon a summer's day,
Should think themselves too small to cool
—The traveller on his way:
Who would not miss the smallest
—And softest ones that blow,
And think they made a great mistake
—If they were acting so?

How many deeds of kindness
—A little child can do,
Although it has but little strength
—And little wisdom too!
It wants a loving spirit
—Much more than strength, to prove
How many things a child may do
—For others by its love.

Refer to the passage "Just Trying to Help" to answer questions 17-20.

17.Which two inferences can the reader make about Sharon and Emma's relationship based on the passage? Select all that apply.

a. Sharon and Emma compete for their father's attention.
b. Emma wants to be like Sharon when she is older.
c. Sharon and Emma have a close and supportive relationship.
d. Sharon is frustrated with Emma's lack of help.
e. Sharon and Emma are considerate of each other's feelings.

18. How does Emma's desire to help Sharon affect the resolution of the conflict?

a. It causes Emma to come up with other ideas on how she can help Sharon.
b. It demonstrates Emma's sadness when she realizes she is too little to help.
c. It allows Emma to still be involved and help her sister as she watches the filming.
d. It highlights that Emma felt discouraged once she put the costume on and saw it was too big.

19. Which piece of Emma's dialogue from the passage most clearly shows the conflict Emma experiences?

a. "What's wrong, Sharon?"
b. "But can I watch? Can I be your audience?"
c. "Oh, I know! I can hold the camera!"
d. "But I'm too little and I don't know how."

20. Which of the following gives the best summary of "Just Trying to Help"?

a. Emma was upset that she couldn't help her big sister, Sharon, with a video project. Once Emma and Sharon's dad asks what's going on, he is able to help, and Emma enjoys watching Sharon film scenes for the project.
b. Emma, Sharon, and their dad spend the afternoon filming scenes for Sharon's school project. Sharon had worked hard on costumes and props. After the filming, she tells Emma how thankful she is that Emma could be her audience for the project.
c. Sharon encounters problems with where to put the camera when trying to make a video for school. Her little sister, Emma, wants to help, but neither Sharon nor Emma's ideas are achievable. The girls' dad steps in to help hold the camera and Emma is finally able to help Sharon by being the audience.
d. Sharon was trying to make a video for school. She had costumes and props but needed a place to put the camera. Sharon wished that her little sister Emma could help, but neither of them could think of a solution for where to put the camera to successfully film the scenes.

Refer to the passage "Deeds of Kindness" to answer questions 21-24.

21.Based on the poem "Deeds of Kindness," which of the following statements would the poet most likely agree with?

a. Every act of kindness is significant.
b. Doing a kind deed with a friend is a good way to help others.
c. Being kind can help you succeed in reaching your goals.
d. Kind actions can bring people together for a common cause.

22. How do the rhyme scheme, meter, and short line lengths contribute to the effect of this poem?

a. They are consistent throughout the poem, so the poem is easy for children to memorize.
b. They make it read similarly to poetry for children, which highlights the poem's message.
c. They are unique and make the poem special, so people are likely to remember its message.
d. They make the poem sound the way the images described in it sound in real life.

23. What is the most likely reason that the author includes the last stanza in the poem "Deeds of Kindness"?

a. To contrast the characteristics of a child to items found in nature
b. To suggest that children are not yet wise enough to help others
c. To convince the reader that appreciating nature starts in childhood
d. To highlight that even small children can make a difference

24. What purpose does the use of extended metaphor serve in the poem "Deeds of Kindness"?

a. It explains what it is like to be a part of nature by comparing the reader to flowers.
b. It shows the value of children by comparing them to small delights in nature.
c. It exaggerates the meaning of what it is to be kind by comparing actions to objects.
d. It provides the point of view of nature by comparing people to plants.

Refer to the passages "Just Trying to Help" and "Deeds of Kindness" to answer questions 25-27.

25. Which of the following ideas is supported by both "Just Trying to Help" and "Deeds of Kindness"?

a. No person or thing is too little to be helpful.
b. Doing kind deeds for your family members is rewarding.
c. A problem can be solved when multiple people step in to help.
d. Ignoring things that seem small and insignificant can have a cost.

26. How is the depiction of the items in nature in "Deeds of Kindness" different from the depiction of Emma in "Just Trying to Help"?

a. In "Deeds of Kindness," there is a focus on how the items in nature feel, while in "Just Trying to Help," there is not a focus on Emma's feelings.
b. In "Deeds of Kindness," there is no mention of family, while in "Just Trying to Help," a family disagreement is described.
c. In "Deeds of Kindness," the items in nature are described along with their purposes, while "Just Trying to Help" shows Emma as she tries to find a purpose.
d. In "Deeds of Kindness," the items in nature make many attempts to be helpful, but in "Just Trying to Help," Emma only tries to help once.

27. Read the following from "Deeds of Kindness."

Suppose the little Breezes
---Upon a summer's day
Should think themselves too small to cool
---The traveler on his way

Which sentence from "Just Trying to Help" shows the same idea as this excerpt?

a. When they were done, Emma said to Sharon, "That was fun! Thank you for letting me stay and watch, even though I couldn't help."
b. Emma frowned again, but then smiled. "Oh, I know! I can hold the camera!"
c. "I want to be able to help you!" Emma explained. "But I'm too little and I don't know how."
d. Tears filled Emma's eyes and she began to walk away.

Extended Response

Your STAAR test will include the following instructions for your extended response question. The response prompts used here are similar to the prompts you will see on the STAAR test.

28. Read the passage "Just Trying to Help." Based on the passage, write a response to the following:

Explain how Sharon and Emma displayed selflessness.

Write a well-organized informational composition that uses specific evidence from the article to support your answer.

Remember to —

- clearly state your thesis
- organize your writing
- develop your ideas in detail
- use evidence from the selection in your response
- use correct spelling, capitalization, punctuation, and grammar

Manage your time carefully so that you can —

- review the selection
- plan your response
- write your response
- revise and edit your response

Revising

Camden wrote the following paper about his brother's first birthday party. Read the following paper and note the revisions that Camden should make. Once you have read his paper, answer the questions that follow it.

First Party

(1) Today, my brother turned one year old. (2) We had a big party to celebrate, and a lot of people came. (3) My aunt came to the house early to help my mom hang streamers. (4) My cousin helped me make party favors for both the big kids and the babies. (5) We packed the little bags with candy, pencils, whistles, and noisemakers. (6) The people my parents invited started to arrive just after we finished. (7)

(7) My dad lit the barbeque in the backyard and took orders from the guests. (8) He made hamburgers, turkey burgers, hot dogs, chicken wings, and sausages. (9) My aunt sliced strips of onion, tomato, pickles, and lettuce. (10) She also cut up an avocado because she knows that it is my favorite thing to put on my hamburger. (11) I usually can only have avocado on my hamburger at restaurants. (12) My cousins, friends, and I all played in the backyard after we ate.

(13) My brother slept through most of the party (14) He was awake when it was time for cake. (15) He didn't know he was missing his party by napping. (16) My mom put him in his high chair, and we all sang "Happy birthday" to him. (17) There was one, and my mom blew it out, candle in the center of the large cake, since he was too little to do it himself.

(18) My brother sat in his chair and ate cake. (19) Soon there was cake everywhere! (20) It was all over his hands, his face, his tabletop, and his chair. (21) There was blue icing all over the place. (22) He even lifted up his arms and grabbed pieces of his hair, which spread the icing even farther. (23) His big, blue eyes looked at everyone as they smiled and laughed. (24) He stuffed some more cake into his mouth and smiled. (25) I think he knew he had a good first birthday.

29. Where in paragraph 1 should the sentence below be added?

My grandparents on my dad's side even flew in from California the day before to help.

a. After sentence 1
b. After sentence 2
c. After sentence 4
d. After sentence 5

30. On the lines below, write a new sentence that correctly combines sentences 13 and 14.

____

____

____

31. Which of the following is the best sentence to add after sentence 6 to improve the introduction of this paper?

a. My family members that were already there to help were not in the group of people that arrived at that time.
b. I recognized many of the people that came in since they were either family members or close friends of my parents.
c. I was afraid that there would not be one left over for me to keep, but we ended up with plenty of leftover bags.
d. Soon the house was filled with family, friends, and even some babies for my brother to play with.

32. Sentence 17 is unclear. Which of the following shows the best way to rewrite sentence 17?

a. My mom blew it out, and there was one candle in the center of the large cake, since he was too little to do it himself.
b. There was one candle in the center of the large cake, and my mom blew it out since he was too little to do it himself.
c. Since he was too little to do it himself, there was one candle in the center of the large cake, and my mom blew it out.
d. In the center of the large cake, since he was too little to do it himself, there was one candle, and my mom blew it out.

33. Which transition word would be best to add to the beginning of sentence 21?

a. Later
b. Conversely
c. Additionally
d. However

Kaianna wrote the following paper about her experience at a new restaurant. Read the following paper and note the revisions that Kaianna should make. Once you have read her paper, answer the questions that follow it.

Dinner is Served

(1) Every year, my friend and I celebrate each other's birthdays by going out to dinner. (2) On my birthday, my family took us to Aribba, my favorite Mexican food restaurant. (3) For Annmae's birthday, she chose a Japanese restaurant called Tomo, where the food is cooked at the table.

(4) I had never eaten Japanese food before, so I did not know what to expect because I had never eaten it before. (5) When the hostess brought us to our table, I was surprised to see that there were four extra seats. (6) That was not the only thing that was new to me. (7) The table was not a regular restaurant dinner table. (8) It was a half circle, and there was a giant sheet of metal in the center. (9) The hostess came back with other people and sat them with us at our table.

(10) We filled out cards to show what kind of food we wanted. (11) We had to pick between chicken, beef, shrimp, and pork. (12) A man then came to our table and lit the metal sheet. (13) I was not sure what kind of metal it was, but it must have been metal with a high melting point. (14) He laid out rice and vegetables, and he started cutting and cooking them. (15) He worked so fast that it was almost hard for me to see his hands. (16) After he cooked the rice, he cooked each of the different meats and started plating the food. (17) While things were cooking, he would take his spatula and fling a piece of bell pepper or carrot at someone there. (18) He tossed the most to Annmae since it was her birthday, but they all hit her chin and fell on the table.

(19) It was really exciting to watch our food be cooked right in front of us. (20) The chef was nice, and the food was delicious. (21) I even liked having other people sit at our table because it was like being at a dinner party. (22) I am really glad that my friend chose Tomo, and I can't wait to see what new restaurant we try next year!

34. Sentence 4 is repetitive. On the lines below, rewrite sentence 4 so that it is no longer repetitive.

____

____

____

35. What sentence could BEST follow and support sentence 9?

a. When that happened, I understood why there were extra seats.
b. The hostess smiled at us as she left.
c. The woman wore a blue dress, and her hair was tied back.
d. I wondered how many times she was going to come back.

36. Which sentence from the third paragraph is unneeded and should be removed?

a. Sentence 12
b. Sentence 13
c. Sentence 15
d. Sentence 16

37. Sentence 17 uses unclear wording. Which of the following phrases should replace the word *there* in sentence 17?

a. near the spatula
b. behind him
c. across the restaurant
d. at the table

Editing

Lexi is writing an essay about sculptors. Read the following paragraph from the body of Lexi's essay and look for errors that she needs to correct. Once you have read the paragraph, answer the questions that follow them.

Before Their Time

(1) Although daumier was one of the first modern sculptors, his work did not influence later artists. (2) This is because most of the other artists at the time hardly ever got to see any of his work. (3) This is also true of the work of Degas, who was known as a painter rather than a sculptor. (4) And yet, Degas was clearly the one of the greatest sculptors of the era. (5) A large number of his sculpted works can been found in museums today. (6) His bronze sculptures of dancers and horses have a similar look to the wax models that he created when first designing it. (7) His more complex scenes seem like a combination of sculpture and painting. (8) However, when looked at more closely they have qualities that cannot be created on only a painted canvas.

38. Which change would correct the mistake in sentence 1?

a. Add a comma after *Although*.
b. Change *daumier* to *Daumier*.
c. Change *did* to *does*.
d. Change *later* to *latest*.

39. Select the verb or verb phrase that should be used in sentence 5.

A large number of his sculpted works ________ found in museums today.

can been
will be
can be
have been

40. Which change would correct the mistake in sentence 6?

a. Change *have* to *has*.
b. Add a semicolon after *look*.
c. Change *that* to *which*.
d. Change *it* to *them*.

41. Which of the following shows the best way to write sentence 8?

a. However, when looked at more closely they have qualities that cannot be created on only a painted canvas.
b. However, when looked at more closely; they have qualities that cannot be created on only a painted canvas.
c. However, when looked at more closely, they have qualities that cannot be created on only a painted canvas.
d. However, when looked at. More closely, they have qualities that cannot be created on only a painted canvas.

Carmen is writing an essay about preparing one's car for driving in the winter. Read the following paragraph from the body of Carmen's essay and look for errors that she needs to correct. Once you have read the paragraphs, answer the questions that follow them.

Preparing Your Car for Winter

(1) Anyone who lives in a place that receives snow during the winter months know how important it is to have a working vehicle. (2) Before winter begins; get the car or truck serviced. (3) In addition to this, consider taking the following steps. (4) First, check and make sure that the windshield wipers work properly. (5) Few things our worse than being unable to see in snow or sleet. (6) Most wiper blades do not last longer than a year. (7) While you are at it, be sure that the windshield washer reservoir has fluid. (8) If it does not, do not fill it with water, as plain water will freeze in the winter.

42. Which change would correct the mistake in sentence 1?

a. Change *lives* to *lived.*
b. Change *winter* to *Winter.*
c. Change *know* to *knows.*
d. Add a comma after *is.*

43. Which of the following shows the best way to write sentence 2?

a. Before winter begins; get the car or truck serviced.
b. Before winter begins. Get the car or truck serviced.
c. (Before winter begins) get the car or truck serviced.
d. Before winter begins, get the car or truck serviced.

44. Which change would correct the mistake in sentence 5?

a. Change *our* to *are.*
b. Change *worse* to *worst.*
c. Change *being* to *been.*
d. Add a comma after *snow.*

45. Which change would correct the mistake in sentence 6?

a. Change *do* to *would.*
b. Add a comma after *longer.*
c. Change *than* to *for.*
d. No change is needed in sentence 6.

Answer Key and Explanations for Test #1

Reading

1. A: TEKS Standard (8.7)(A)

Throughout the passage, Wolfgang surprises his father with his abilities multiple times, such as when he plays a perfect chord at age three, plays minuets correctly after learning them in only a half hour, and creates a difficult harpsichord concerto at the age of five. These instances bring Leopold astonishment, wonder, and awe. This supports choice A, which is the correct answer. The passage does not suggest that Wolfgang had to work hard to receive Leopold's approval. In fact, Leopold was very proud of his son and recognized his talent, so choice B is incorrect. The passage does not support the idea that Wolfgang and his sister Nannerl had to battle for their parents' attention. The brother and sister receive music lessons together and their father is proud of both of them, so choice C is incorrect. The passage does not include any description of Wolfgang avoiding disobeying his father or fearing punishment from him, so choice D is incorrect.

2. B: TEKS Standard (8.9)(E)

Because of the third-person narration, the reader knows how both Wolfgang Mozart and his father, Leopold Mozart, feel about Wolfgang's concerto. For example, Wolfgang Mozart is "impatient" when his father interrupts him but then "eagerly" plays the first part of his composition. Leopold Mozart is at first "amused" and then is full of "wonder" and "awe" after seeing and hearing his young son's concerto. Knowing the thoughts and feelings of more than one character without them being stated in dialogue is common of a third-person omniscient point of view. Choice A is incorrect, as the author would use a first-person point of view with words such as "I" or "me" if she were describing how she had been inspired by Wolfgang Mozart. The passage does not clearly explain why Leopold Mozart thinks his son's age is too young to learn music, so choice C is incorrect. The passage does not include evidence that supports the idea that conflict is created because of the historical time period, so choice D is incorrect.

3. B: TEKS Standard (8.5)(F)

The passage reveals that Leopold Mozart gave lessons to Wolfgang's older sister, Nannerl, but told Wolfgang to wait when Wolfgang asked for lessons at age three. Based on this, the reader can infer that Leopold Mozart felt that three years old was too young to learn music. He only gave his young son lessons once he heard Wolfgang's talent. Although the passage is mainly about Wolfgang and describes him as a "genius," paragraph 7 states that Leopold saw "with pride almost beyond expression, that both of his children inherited his musical ability." This means that the reader cannot infer that Leopold was not also proud of Nannerl, so choice A is incorrect. The passage does not support the idea that Leopold was upset about his son Wolfgang's musical ability. There is only evidence of Leopold being proud of Wolfgang, so choice C is incorrect. Initially, Leopold is curious and amused when his son composes a piece of music. He is later filled with "wonder" and "awe" upon hearing Wolfgang play it. From Leopold's reactions, the reader cannot infer that he taught his son to write compositions, so choice D is incorrect.

4. D: TEKS Standard (8.7)(D)

The story is set in a household where Wolfgang Mozart spends time around his father, who is a talented musician. It is evident that Leopold Mozart values music since he teaches lessons to

Nannerl, and later to Mozart. Since Wolfgang Mozart grew up surrounded by music, it is logical to assume that this influenced his appreciation of music, so choice D is correct. The time period of the story and the fact that music was not yet recorded did not directly influence Wolfgang Mozart's value for music. Someone can value music regardless of a given time period or how they listen to it, so choice A is incorrect. Although the passage mainly features Wolfgang Mozart and his family members, there is no evidence that he did not talk to other people besides his family, so choice B is incorrect. The fact that Wolfgang Mozart was given multiple names did not influence his beliefs on music, so choice C is incorrect.

5. C: TEKS Standard (8.8)(A)

Historical fiction stories take place in the past. They have characteristics that are appropriate for the given time period and include both historically accurate events and fictional events. Choice C tells the reader where (Salzburg) and when (1756) Wolfgang Mozart was born, which is a historically accurate event. It also tells the reader the setting of the passage, which shows the reader that this is a work of historical fiction. Choice A describes a character's reaction to an event, which is not unique to historical fiction, so this choice is incorrect. Choice B describes a scene that could happen in any type of fiction, not just historical fiction, so this choice is incorrect. Choice D describes a character's behavior that could occur in any genre of fiction or nonfiction, making this choice incorrect.

6. C: TEKS Standard (8.2)(A)

Paragraph 5 says that young Mozart touched the keys of the harpsichord to play "a perfect chord," which shows that *chord* is a musical term. This means that definition 3—three or more tones that produce harmony—is the best fit. Based on the way the word is used in paragraph 5, it would not make sense to say that Mozart played a feeling or emotion, so choice A is incorrect. The word *chord* is not used in the paragraph to describe a shape or line segment, so choice B is incorrect. Definition 4 describes a cord rather than a chord, and it does not describe something Mozart's father could have heard him playing musically, so choice D is incorrect.

7. A: TEKS Standard (8.9)(A)

In paragraph 5, Wolfgang Mozart's father tells him to wait to learn music, as he is "but a baby." However, Wolfgang Mozart creeps back into the room and plays a chord even though his father has told him no and he can only reach the keyboard by "standing on tiptoe." The paragraph highlights the fact that multiple challenges were standing in young Wolfgang Mozart's way, but he wanted to learn music anyway, so choice A is correct. Paragraphs 4 and 5 do not suggest that Wolfgang Mozart could have only made great music with his father's influence. In fact, the passage shows that his father initially told him he must wait to learn music because he was too young, so choice B is incorrect. The information in paragraphs 4 and 5 does not explain what inspired his earliest compositions, so choice C is incorrect. Paragraphs 4 and 5 do not suggest that Wolfgang Mozart wanted to be a better musician than his sister, so choice D is incorrect.

8. C: TEKS Standard (8.9)(F)

The language in paragraph 5 creates an affectionate tone. Leopold Mozart refers to his son, Wolfgang, as "my little man" and calls him by a nickname, "my Wolferl." This shows that even though Leopold Mozart told his son he was too young to learn music yet, he was doing so in a warm and loving manner, so choice C is correct. Although Leopold Mozart denied his son's request, he did so lovingly, not by giving a warning or using stern words, so choice A is incorrect. In this paragraph, Mozart is told that he must wait to learn music because he is so young. This disappoints Wolfgang rather than giving him hope, so choice B is incorrect. The warm and loving language in paragraph 5 is used by a father giving guidance to his son. His word choice is more personal and emotional than language used by friends, so choice D is incorrect.

9. D: TEKS Standard (8.6)(D)

This summary captures all the key ideas of the passage. It states that test anxiety is common but can be reduced with simple strategies, and it gives a list of the strategies given in the article. The passage opens with an example of a student with test anxiety, Lisa. However, the passage is not about Lisa. Also, this summary includes information that is not provided by the passage, so choice A is incorrect. Choice B leaves out key ideas and suggests that poor study habits are the main cause of test anxiety, so it is incorrect. Choice C leaves out key ideas in the passage since it only talks about relaxation techniques. It leaves out the other strategies and the main idea that test anxiety is common but can be managed, so choice C is incorrect.

10. D: TEKS Standard (8.2)(B)

"I can do this" is an example of a mantra, or a phrase that is repeated to benefit the speaker. In the context of the passage, a mantra can be used to reinforce that a student believes in his or her own abilities to do well on tests. Since a mantra is something with words that a student would repeat, it is not likely to be a deep breathing technique, so choice A is incorrect. A good-luck charm would be something a student would hold or carry for test anxiety, not something he or she would say, so choice B is incorrect. Choice C is incorrect because a mantra is described as something positive, and criticism is often negative.

11. B: TEKS Standard (8.6)(C)

Test anxiety is common. This is shown by the passage through the statement that millions of students deal with it. However, the fact that "few realize it can be improved" suggests that students still feel alone in dealing with their test anxiety. If students knew others shared their anxiety, they would be more likely to know about and share solutions, so choice B is correct. Choice A describes one student with test anxiety; it does not show that test anxiety is common or that students may feel alone, so it is incorrect. Choice C simply describes a common study habit that can increase test anxiety, so this choice is incorrect. Choice D describes a step that students can take to reduce test anxiety. This choice does not show that test anxiety is common or that students may feel alone in dealing with it, so it is incorrect.

12. A: TEKS Standard (8.5)(G)

Paragraphs 4 and 8 explain ways that other people can help a person manage test anxiety, such as using flashcards together and sharing test-taking victories, so choice A is correct. The use of games and tools is only supported by paragraph 4, so choice B is incorrect. Only paragraph 8 suggests that doing well on a test confirms an improvement in test anxiety management, not paragraph 4, so choice C is incorrect. The importance of sharing small successes is not supported by paragraph 4, only paragraph 8, so choice D is incorrect.

13. A: TEKS Standard (8.8)(Di)

Choice A captures the controlling idea of the passage, which is that test anxiety is common but can be improved through the use of specific strategies. The use of Lisa as an example helps illustrate what it can be like for students who experience test anxiety. However, the idea that Lisa and others are experiencing a genuine type of anxiety is not the entire passage's controlling idea, so choice B is incorrect. Forming good study habits is just one specific strategy. Choice C gives a supporting detail from the passage, not the controlling idea, so it is incorrect. Going to other people for help with test anxiety is a supporting detail mentioned in the passage. Choice D leaves out important aspects of the controlling idea, so it is incorrect.

14. C: TEKS Standard (8.9)(B)

The passage is organized in a way that outlines a step-by-step process to overcome test anxiety. It does this by stating that there are three simple steps to achieve this and giving details that show how to do each step, so choice C is correct. The passage does discuss the value of improving study habits when aiming to improve test anxiety, but study habits are not the main topic of the passage, so choice A is incorrect. The passage does note that test anxiety can make a student's grades suffer, as illustrated with the example of Lisa, but the passage does not focus on the cause-and-effect relationship between test anxiety and students' grades, so choice B is incorrect. The passage does not reveal why some students do not experience test anxiety. It only highlights the ways that test anxiety can be overcome, so choice D is incorrect.

15. B: TEKS Standard (8.5)(H)

The passage provides three steps that can help a person overcome test anxiety when they are practiced consistently. This shows the reader that test anxiety is not likely to go away on its own, so choice B is correct. Forming good study habits is one of the steps, but it is not described as the most important way to reduce test anxiety, so choice A is incorrect. The passage does not explain text anxiety from a teacher's perspective, so choice C is incorrect. The symptoms of test anxiety are described, but the possibility that they could point to a bigger health problem is not discussed, so choice D is incorrect.

16. TEKS Standard (8.8)(Diii)

The author most likely includes the description of Lisa's experience with test anxiety to illustrate that it is a real and distressing problem. Lisa is described as a good student who studies hard and turns in assignments on time, but she still experiences stress symptoms during tests that then affect her grades and confidence. This example shows the reader why test anxiety is an important topic. This response is supported by the sentences "Lisa's problem is a common one." and "Millions of students deal with test anxiety every year, but few realize it can be improved through three simple steps."

17. C, E: TEKS Standard (8.5)(F)

Based on the passage, the reader can infer that Sharon and Emma have a close and supportive relationship and consider each other's feelings. Emma offered to help Sharon in multiple ways when she gets frustrated. Sharon comforted Emma when Emma was sad about not being able to help. Emma was also eager to be Sharon's audience even though Emma couldn't help directly with the camera or by being in the video, and Sharon was thankful for Emma's help. The reader cannot infer that Sharon and Emma compete for their father's attention, as the passage does not give any evidence that supports this, so choice A is incorrect. While Emma wanted to help and support Sharon, the reader cannot infer that Emma wants to be like Sharon when she is older. None of Emma's dialogue or actions shows this, so choice B is incorrect. Sharon did not get frustrated with Emma not being able to help. In fact, Sharon tried to think of another way that Emma could help when Emma was sad about being too little to help, so choice D is incorrect.

18. C: TEKS Standard (8.7)(B)

Emma is motivated to help Sharon and tries to come up with ways to help. When her ideas do not work, she decides that she is okay with simply watching and being Sharon's audience. Emma's involvement ends up being very helpful to Sharon after all. So, even though Sharon would have been able to complete her project without Emma, Emma's desire to help causes the resolution to the conflict to be more helpful to Sharon than she expected. Emma does come up with different ideas for helping Sharon. However, since those ideas do not work, they add to the conflict rather than resolving it, so choice A is incorrect. Emma becomes sad in response to her developing conflict, wanting to help but being unable to. This is not part of the conflict resolution, so choice B is incorrect. Emma's discouragement upon finding that the costume is too big is part of the rising action rather than the conflict resolution, so choice D is incorrect.

19. D: TEKS Standard (8.6)(C)

Emma wanted to help Sharon, but she was too little to hold the camera or fit into the costumes. She did not know how else she could help, which made her feel upset. A conflict is a struggle that must be overcome. However, Emma asking Sharon what is wrong does not show what Emma is struggling with, so choice A is incorrect. Emma asking Sharon if she can watch and be the audience does not show the conflict Emma is experiencing, so choice B is incorrect. In choice C, Emma tries to provide a solution. Though this solution is not the best one for the problem at hand, this dialogue does not show a conflict that Emma is experiencing. It shows Sharon's conflict more clearly, as it shows that she needs someone to hold the camera. Choice C is incorrect.

20. C: TEKS Standard (8.6)(D)

Choice C is the most accurate summary of the events and conflict in the passage. The key concepts of the story's conflict and resolution are all present: Sharon's problem, Emma's desire to help, Emma's struggle to find a way to help, the girls' dad helping solve the problem, and Emma being able to help after all by being the audience. Choice A is incorrect, as it does not clearly describe the key ideas, conflict, and resolution of the passage and leaves out the fact that Emma was able to help after all. Choice B leaves out the story's conflict, which is that Emma wants to help Sharon but can't, so this choice is incorrect. Choice D is incorrect because it leaves out the resolution of the story.

21. A: TEKS Standard (8.5)(C)

The poet would most likely agree that every act of kindness is significant since the poem describes things that seem insignificant but highlights the difference they can make in the lives of others. While the poem highlights the value of deeds of kindness, it does not discuss doing kind deeds with a friend. The reader cannot predict that the poet would agree with the statement in choice B, so it is incorrect. The poem does not provide any evidence that being kind can help someone succeed in their goals, so the reader cannot predict that the poet would agree with this statement and choice C is incorrect. The poem does not support the idea that kind deeds unite people and bring them together for a cause, so choice D is incorrect.

22. B: TEKS Standard (8.8)(B)

This poem has a consistent rhythm and rhyme scheme, and it uses short lines. It also has a sing-song quality. These characteristics make this poem similar to many other poems written for children. This quality of the poem brings the reader's attention to the group that the poem is about: children. By doing this, the meter, structure, and rhyme highlight the poem's message, so choice B is correct. Choice A is incorrect because the consistency of the poem does not guarantee that it is easy to memorize. Choice C is incorrect because the rhyme scheme, meter, and line lengths used in this poem are not unique. They are commonly used in poetry. Choice D is incorrect because the rhyme scheme, meter, and line lengths do not cause the poem to sound like the elements of nature that the poem describes. The poem's sound is consistent, but the natural elements it describes are different from one another.

23. D: TEKS Standard (8.9)(A)

The last stanza highlights the fact that even small children can make a difference. It says that they can do deeds of kindness with a "loving spirit," even if they may have "little strength" or "little wisdom," so choice D is correct. It is not accurate to say that the poem contrasts children to things found in nature. Instead, it shows that though the cowslip, dewdrop, breezes, and little child may all seem small or insignificant, they can make a difference, so choice A is incorrect. While the last stanza states that a child may have "little wisdom," this is a detail that is used to contrast the fact that a child can still do loving and kind things for others. Therefore, the stanza is not suggesting that children are not wise enough to help others, so choice B is incorrect. The last stanza of the poem does not describe the value of appreciating nature or suggest that this starts in childhood, so choice C is incorrect.

24. B: TEKS Standard (8.9)(D)

A metaphor is a type of figurative language that compares two things. An extended metaphor continues throughout a work and uses more details than a standard metaphor. The purpose of the extended metaphor, which compares children to small delights in nature, is to show the value of children and how they can be helpful despite their age and experience. The extended metaphor is not used to explain what it is like to be a part of nature, and it does not compare the reader to the flowers mentioned in the poem, so choice A is incorrect. The extended metaphor does not use exaggeration; its language is literal and factual, so choice C is incorrect. The extended metaphor does not provide nature's point of view, and this is not the purpose of the poem, so choice D is incorrect.

25. A: TEKS Standard (8.5)(E)

Both passages suggest that no person or thing is too little to be helpful. In "Just Trying to Help," Emma was too little to help Sharon by holding the camera or wearing the costumes, but she was ultimately very helpful to Sharon by acting as an audience member. In "Deeds of Kindness," each of the four stanzas describes something that is small or little but is still helpful despite its size. While "Deeds of Kindness" does focus on kind deeds, it does not focus on kind deeds done for family members, so choice B is incorrect. Only "Just Trying to Help" shows multiple people working together to solve a problem, where "Deeds of Kindness" does not focus on solving problems or working together, so choice C is incorrect. Neither passage suggests that ignoring things that seem small can result in a cost. Instead, the passages suggest that things that seem small can be helpful, so choice D is incorrect.

26. C: TEKS Standard (8.5)(E)

In "Deeds of Kindness," the purpose of the items in nature are stated as each item is described. In "Just Trying to Help," Emma's purpose in the situation is not made clear until the end of the story. This makes choice C correct. "Just Trying to Help" does focus on Emma's feelings, as it shows that she felt sad and disappointed when she could not find a way to help, so choice A is incorrect. While family is only mentioned in "Just Trying to Help," the story does not center around a family disagreement, so choice B is incorrect. The items in nature do not make many attempts to be helpful. On the other hand, Emma came up with multiple ways to try to help Sharon in "Just Trying to Help," not just one, so choice D is incorrect.

27. C: TEKS Standard (8.5)(E)

Both the excerpt from the poem and choice C show something or someone thinking they are too small to help. Choice A shows how Emma feels after being a part of the activity. It does not show that she feels too small or little to help, so this choice is incorrect. Choice B shows one of Emma's ideas for helping, not her decision that she is too small to help, so this choice is incorrect. Choice D shows Emma's emotions upon not being able to help, but it does not make it clear that she felt she was too little to help, so this choice is incorrect.

Extended Response

28. TEKS Standard (8.6)(B)

Please use the rubric below to make sure your response meets these criteria. Try to have a friend or family member grade your response for you or take a break after writing your response and return to grade it yourself with fresh eyes.

Below is an excerpt of the STAAR Grades 6-EII Informational Writing Rubric.

Score Point	Organization and Development of Ideas
3	• **Controlling idea/Thesis is clear and fully developed** The controlling idea/thesis is clearly identifiable. The focus is consistent throughout, creating a response that is unified and easy to follow. • **Organization is effective** A purposeful structure that includes an effective introduction and conclusion is evident. The organizational structure is appropriate and effectively supports the development of the controlling idea/thesis. The sentences, paragraphs, or ideas are logically connected in purposeful and highly effective ways. • **Evidence is specific, well chosen, and relevant** The response includes relevant text-based evidence that is clearly explained and consistently supports and develops the controlling idea/thesis. For pairs in grades 6 through EII, evidence is drawn from both texts. The response reflects a thorough understanding of the writing purpose. • **Expression of ideas is clear and effective** The writer's word choice is specific, purposeful, and enhances the response. Almost all sentences and phrases are effectively crafted to convey the writer's ideas and contribute to the overall quality of the response and the clarity of the message.

Score Point	Conventions
2	Student writing demonstrates **consistent command** of grade-level-appropriate conventions, including correct: • sentence construction • punctuation • capitalization • grammar • spelling The response has few errors, but those errors do not impact the clarity of the writing.

Revising

29. B: TEKS Standard (8.10)(Bi)

This sentence should be added after sentence 2. The sentence states that the grandparents traveled from California to help with the party, so it should be placed after the sentence that tells the reader that many people came to the party. Additionally, sentence 3 explains that the author's aunt came to help the next day. This sentence leads into sentence 3 by telling what happened before the aunt came over to help. This sentence would not make sense after sentence 1. Adding it there would make it seem like the grandparents flew in to help the author's brother turn one, so choice A is incorrect. Sentences 4 and 5 happen on the day of the party, so this sentence should not come after either of these sentences. That would put the events out of order, so choices C and D are incorrect.

30. TEKS Standard (8.10)(C)

Sentence 13 states that the author's brother slept through most of the party. Sentence 14 states that the author's brother was awake when it was time for cake. Since the author's brother was asleep in sentence 13 but is awake in sentence 14, the new sentence should show that something has changed. One way to combine these sentences is to make them into one compound sentence by adding a comma and the coordinating conjunction *but*. This would result in the sentence "My brother slept through most of the party, but he was awake when it was time for cake." This sentence includes all of the information that is in sentences 13 and 14. Also, the use of the conjunction *but* shows that a change occurred. A correct sentence may be slightly different, but it must include the information from the original sentences and show the relationship between the ideas. It must also be concise, grammatically correct, and complete.

31. D: TEKS Standard (8.10)(Bi)

Choice D is the correct answer because it creates an effective end for the introductory paragraph and is a good transition from sentence 6 to sentence 7. It shows the type of people that arrived and helps show the reader what the party was like. Choice A is incorrect because it gives the reader information that can easily be inferred from the information that is already present. It is unnecessary and does not improve the introduction. Choice B is incorrect because this information can be inferred, and it does not give as many helpful details as choice D. Choice C is incorrect because it does not give relevant information, effectively end the introduction, or provide a transition into the next sentence and paragraph.

32. B: TEKS Standard (8.10)(C)

Choice B is correct because it is the clearest way to write the sentence. It clearly states that the cake has one candle in its center and that the author's mother blew the candle out because the author's brother was too little to reach it. Choice A is incorrect because it does not make clear what *it* is. It also suggests that the reason there was one candle is that the author's brother is too little to blow it out. Choices C and D are incorrect because they also suggest that the author's brother's size is the reason that there is one candle on the cake.

33. C: TEKS Standard (8.10)(Bi)

Sentences 19 and 20 explain that there was cake everywhere, including all over the author's brother. Sentence 21 explains that there was blue icing all over the place. Since the icing came from the cake, and both the cake and icing are everywhere, the transition word should show that sentence 21 is also describing the mess that the young boy is making. *Additionally* is the best choice, so choice C is correct. Later is not an appropriate transition word because it suggests that the events in sentence 21 happen a while after the events in sentence 20. These events are happening at the same time, so choice A is incorrect. *Conversely* is not an appropriate transition word because it would suggest that sentences 20 and 21 are describing contradictory events. This is not true, so choice B is incorrect. *However* is not an appropriate transition word because sentence 21 does not contradict sentence 20, so choice D is incorrect.

34. TEKS Standard (8.10)(C)

Sentence 4 currently tells the reader twice that the author has never eaten Japanese food. The sentence should be rewritten to state that the author has never eaten Japanese food and does not know what to expect of the experience. The sentence should not repeat any of this information. One example of a way to properly rewrite this sentence is "I had never eaten Japanese food before, so I did not know what to expect." The sentence may also be rewritten to say "Because I had never eaten Japanese food before, I did not know what to expect." A correct revision may be slightly different from these examples, but it should have the same meaning as the original sentence, avoid repetition, and be free of any grammatical or spelling errors.

35. A: TEKS Standard (8.10)(Bii)

Choice A is correct because this sentence elaborates on the information in sentence 9. It shows that the reason that there were four extra seats is that more people would be sitting at that table. Choices B, C, and D are incorrect because they give details that are unneeded and do not support the reader's understanding of the events that are described in the passage.

36. B: TEKS Standard (8.10)(Bii)

Sentence 13 can be removed from the third paragraph because it gives the reader unnecessary information. It also does not support the reader's understanding of the rest of the paragraph. Choice A is incorrect because sentence 12 is necessary. Without sentence 12, the reader would not understand what is happening in the rest of the paragraph. Choice C is incorrect because it includes a supporting detail that helps the reader better understand the event being described. This detail helps show what made this event memorable for the author. Choice D is incorrect because sentence 16 includes information that the reader needs in order to understand sentence 17.

37. D: TEKS Standard (8.10)(C)

Sentence 17 says that the man is flinging food to people. Sentence 18 says that the man tossed most of the food to Annmae. The phrase that is used to replace *there* in sentence 18 should describe where Annmae is since she is one of the people to whom the man is flinging the food. Annmae is at the table, so choice D is correct. Annmae is not near the spatula, since the spatula is on or above the metal sheet, so choice A is incorrect. Annmae is somewhere in front of the man, so choice B is incorrect. Annmae is at the same table that the man is cooking at. She is not somewhere across the restaurant, so choice C is incorrect.

Editing

38. B: TEKS Standard (8.10)(Dv)

Daumier is the name of an artist, so it is a proper noun. Proper nouns must always be capitalized, so choice B is correct. Choice A is incorrect because *although* is part of the dependent clause "Although daumier was one of the first modern sculptors." This word should not be separated from the rest of the clause, so a comma should not be placed after it. Choice B is incorrect because *does* is a present-tense verb, but sentence 1 is written in the past tense. *Did* is a past-tense verb, so it is used correctly in sentence 1. The adjective *later* is a comparative adjective, so it should be used when comparing two nouns. The adjective *latest* is a superlative adjective, so it should be used when comparing three or more nouns. In sentence 1, Daumier is being compared to the group of artists who came after him. This means that two nouns are being compared, so the comparative adjective *later* is the correct word to use, and choice D is incorrect.

39. can be: TEKS Standard (8.10)(Dii)

Degas's works are still in museums today, so the verb that goes in the blank should show that his works are presently in museums. The verb phrase *can be* shows this, so it is the correct choice. The verb phrase *can been* is incorrect because it does not make sense. *Can* means that something is currently able to happen, but *been* means that something happened or existed in the past. These words cannot be used together to create a verb phrase. The verb phrase *will be* is used to show that something will exist in the future. This does not fit the meaning of the sentence, so this phrase is not the correct answer. The verb phrase *have been* shows that something has happened or has existed in the past. It does not show that something currently exists or happens, so it is incorrect.

40. D: TEKS Standard (8.10)(Div)

Both *it* and *them* are pronouns. When used to represent an object or group of objects, *it* can be used in place of a singular noun and *them* can be used in place of a plural noun. In sentence 6, the pronoun is used to represent "his bronze sculptures of dancers and horses." Since this is a group of objects, the pronoun *them* must be used, so choice D is correct. The verb *have* is used to show the action of the bronze sculptures. Since the verb is used with a plural noun, it must also be plural. *Have* is a plural verb, and *has* is a singular verb, so choice A is incorrect. Choice B is incorrect because there is no need for a semicolon after *look* in sentence 8. *That* is used to introduce essential information, while *which* is used to introduce nonessential information. In sentence 8, *that* comes before essential information, so choice C is incorrect.

41. C: TEKS Standard (8.10)(Dvi)

Sentence 8 contains a transition word, a dependent clause, an independent clause, a second dependent clause, and a prepositional phrase. When a dependent clause comes before an independent clause, a comma must be used after the dependent clause. In sentence 8, the dependent clause "when looked at more closely" comes before the independent clause "they have qualities." This means that a comma should be placed after the word *closely*. Only choice C correctly punctuates the sentence this way, so it is correct. While choice D does include a comma after *closely*, it also splits the sentence into two and creates the sentence fragment "However, when looked at." This makes it incorrect. Choice A is incorrect because it does not include any punctuation after the word *closely*. Choice B is incorrect because a semicolon cannot be used to connect a dependent clause to an independent clause.

42. C: TEKS Standard (8.10)(Diii)

While the verb *know* comes right after the plural noun *months* in sentence 1, it describes the action of the singular pronoun *anyone*. Because it shows the action of a singular verb, it should be changed to *knows*, a singular verb. Choice C is correct. Choice A is incorrect because *lived* is a past-tense verb, but sentence 1 is in the present tense. Choice B is incorrect because seasons are not proper nouns, so they do not need to be capitalized. Choice D is incorrect because there is no need for a comma after *is*. The clause "to have a working vehicle" does not need to be set apart from the rest of the sentence.

43. D: TEKS Standard (8.10)(Di)

Sentence 2 is a complex sentence. It begins with a dependent clause, "Before winter begins," and ends with an independent clause, "get the car or truck serviced." In complex sentences, when the sentence begins with a dependent clause, a comma must be placed between the dependent clause and the independent clause. This makes choice D the correct answer. Choice A is incorrect because a semicolon cannot be used to connect a dependent clause to an independent clause. Choice B is incorrect because "Before winter begins" is not a complete sentence, so it cannot be punctuated with a period. Choice C is incorrect because parentheses are used to set apart nonessential, or extra, information. The information in parentheses in choice C is needed, it is not extra information, so it should not be placed within parentheses.

44. A: TEKS Standard (8.10)(Dvii)

The word *our* is a possessive pronoun that is used to show that multiple owners possess something. The word *are* is a plural verb that is used to show that two nouns are doing the same thing or are in the same state of being or location. In sentence 5, the sentence is saying that there are only a few things worse than not being able to see when driving in snow or sleet. The word *worse* is the state of being for the few things, so *are* is the correct word to use in this sentence, and choice A is correct. The word *worse* is a comparative noun, so it is used to compare two nouns. The word *worst* is a superlative adjective, so it is used to compare three or more nouns. In sentence 5, only two things are being compared: being unable to see in snow and sleet and all other driving conditions. Since only two things are being compared, the comparative adjective *worse* is used correctly, and choice B is incorrect. Choice C is incorrect because *been* is a past-tense verb, but sentence 5 is written in the present tense. Choice D is incorrect because a comma is not needed between *snow* and *or*. In lists with more than two items, a comma is usually added before *and* or *or*. However, this list only includes two items, so it does not need to include a comma.

45. D: TEKS Standard (8.10)(D)

There are no grammatical or spelling errors in sentence 6, so choice D is correct. The word *would* is used to show that something will only happen in certain circumstances. Sentence 6 states that the majority of wiper blades wear out in a year. This is not only true in certain circumstances, so *do* is the correct word to use, and choice A is incorrect. Choice B is incorrect because there is no need for a comma after *longer*. The phrase *than a year* does not need to be set apart by commas. Choice C is incorrect because changing *than* to *for* would make the meaning of the sentence incorrect. Stating that the wiper blades will not last longer for a year means that the period of time that the wiper blades can be used for will be extended and that they will only last longer after one year. This does not make sense. Stating that the wiper blades do not last longer than a year means that the period of time that the wiper blades can be used is close to one year. This makes sense, and it is the intended meaning of the sentence.

Practice Test #2

Reading

Like Riding a Kite

(1) Imagine soaring high above the earth. There is no engine, no fuselage beneath you. There is only you, your glider, the wind, and the sky. It's like riding a kite with no strings attached, rising and falling on the breeze like a bird. It is freedom and thrill and ultimate pleasure. This is the world of hang gliding.

(2) While many people have a general idea of what hang gliding is all about, few really understand the sport. Most people don't realize a majestic glider can be collapsed to the size of a duffel bag. Few people know that gliders can stay aloft for hours and that the world distance record for a single glider flight is nearly 190 miles. Even fewer people realize that a hang glider can actually climb in the sky, even without an engine. In California, in the 1980s, one expert glider pilot gained more than 14,000 feet of altitude after takeoff! Hang gliders have mind-boggling capabilities.

(3) The amazing sport of hang gliding has a rich history dating back to the 1890s. In 1891, the first hang glider was invented by Otto Lilienthal in Germany. It was made of wood and cloth, weighed 40 pounds, was 23 feet wide, and could go about 35 miles per hour (mph) at an altitude of 100 feet. British inventor Percy Picher also built gliders with similar features in the late 1890s. Unfortunately, both inventors were killed in glider crashes before their designs were perfected. With the element of danger involved in early hang gliding—and with the advent of airplane flight by the Wright brothers in 1903—many people lost interest in hang gliding.

(4) After the end of World War II, however, many military-trained pilots wanted to keep flying. Airplanes were too expensive for most people, so the sport of hang gliding was reborn. Through invention and innovation, new designs for hang gliders began to emerge. These included new materials and designs for glider construction and the addition of a control bar to improve safety. The basic design for today's hang gliders premiered at a meet in California in 1971. It included a broad, flexible wing on a sturdy frame with a control bar and a seat or safety harness.

(5) Since 1971, few major design changes have been made to hang gliders, although as new materials for construction become available, minor changes are made to improve flight. Modern sails range from 13 to 28 feet across. They are made of durable, lightweight, manmade fabric—such as nylon—and are designed to flex in shape and tension based on the wind. The sail is attached to a frame made from aluminum tubing. The frame includes a control bar that is shaped like a rounded triangle and used for steering. Suspended from the frame is a harness or seat to improve pilot comfort and safety.

(6) Another way pilots improve comfort and safety is through the use of proper gear and equipment. Pilots should wear light, protective clothing and gloves designed for hang gliding. A helmet is also an important safety component. In addition, pilots need special instruments that are used during flight. These tools help measure thermals, the warm air currents used to lift and propel gliders through the air.

(7) Thermals are important to both taking off and staying aloft, but they aren't the only factor in flight. Modern gliders weigh about 35 pounds and are specially balanced to a pilot's weight and preferences. To take off, the pilot is secured in the glider and then runs off the edge of a large hill or cliff, where thermals catch the glider and lift it into the air. If the wind is sustained at 12 mph or above, the pilot may even be able to take off without running. Once the glider is airborne, the pilot steers by shifting his or her weight and using the control bar. Each glider has its own unique feel, and a pilot must know the glider well to achieve a safe takeoff, flight, and landing.

(8) In addition to knowing the unique feel of the glider, a pilot must know the safety rules of the sky to have a safe flight. Pilots of hang gliders do not need to be licensed, but they must obey all rules and laws for flying. Hang glider pilots should never fly in bad weather or high winds. They must yield the right of way to any aircraft in distress and all hot air balloons. They must never intentionally fly into a cloud or a flock of birds. Finally, hang glider pilots should stay at least five miles away from airports during flight and at least 100 feet from buildings, telephone wires and poles, populated places, and crowds.

(9) Throughout history, mankind has looked for a way to soar with the birds across the canvas of the sky. Hang gliding offers that opportunity. With modern features and equipment, and with proper training in techniques and the rules of the sky, hang glider pilots can safely experience the thrill of flight. In a glider, the pilot is one with the breeze, the sunlight, and the world itself. Hang gliding is truly like riding a kite through the expanse of the heavens.

Refer to the passage "Like Riding a Kite" to answer questions 1-9.

1. Read this sentence from paragraph 2.

> Few people know that gliders can stay aloft for hours and that the world distance record for a single glider flight is nearly 190 miles.

Based on this text evidence from the passage, what is the meaning of *aloft*?

a. Motor powered
b. Suspended in the air
c. In one piece
d. Collapsible

2. Read the following sentences from paragraph 1:

> Imagine soaring high above the earth. There is no engine, no fuselage beneath you. There is only you, your glider, the wind, and the sky. It's like riding a kite with no strings attached, rising and falling on the breeze like a bird.

What is the effect of the figurative language used in these sentences?

a. They help the reader understand where the inspiration for hang gliding came from.
b. They show the reader the reason for the many concerns about the safety of hang gliding.
c. They allow the reader to understand what hang gliding is like and why people enjoy it.
d. They interest the reader by presenting facts and historical events in a poetic way.

3. Paragraph 3 states "With the element of danger involved in early hang gliding—and with the advent of airplane flight by the Wright brothers in 1903—many people lost interest in hang gliding." What is the most likely reason for this change?

a. The Wright brothers did well publicizing their invention.
b. Most people had already experienced hang gliding.
c. Both were dangerous, but planes were new and exciting.
d. Planes were a safer way to fulfil the desire for flight.

4. Which sentence from the passage shows that advances in technology have made hang gliding safer?

a. Thermals are important to both taking off and staying aloft, but they aren't the only factor in flight.
b. In addition to knowing the unique feel of the glider, a pilot must know the safety rules of the sky to have a safe flight.
c. These included new materials and designs for glider construction and the addition of a control bar to improve safety.
d. It was made of wood and cloth, weighed 40 pounds, was 23 feet wide, and could go about 35 miles per hour (mph) at an altitude of 100 feet.

5. What is the most likely reason the author of this passage uses a chronological structure for paragraphs 3 through 5?

a. To help the reader create a mental image of hang gliding
b. To explain the changes in popularity and safety of hang gliding
c. To give step by step instructions for the process of hang gliding
d. To persuade readers to give hang gliding a try on their own

6. Read this summary of the passage "Like Riding a Kite":

> Hang gliding is a freeing and exciting sport that allows participants to glide with the birds and accomplish new feats. It got its start in the late 19th century. However, due to safety issues and the invention of the plane, many people lost interest in it. After World War II, hang gliding became popular again, and changes were made to hang gliding equipment and procedures to make the sport safer.

Which idea should be included in this paragraph to create a complete summary of the passage?

a. Now, pilots who follow safe practices can enjoy the sport of hang gliding.
b. Some rigs are small enough to pack down into a duffel bag.
c. The Wright Brothers can be blamed for the demise of the glider.
d. Hang gliding allows participants to get closer to nature.

7. In paragraph 3, what does *advent* mean?

a. End
b. Beginning
c. Expansion
d. Popularity

8. Which of the following statements are key ideas from the passage, and which are simply supporting details? Mark your answer for each statement below.

Statement	Key Idea	Supporting Detail
Modern glider sails are 13 to 28 feet wide.		
Glider pilots must know the rules of the sky.		
All glider pilots should wear helmets for safety.		
Modern glider design premiered in 1971.		
Hang gliding involves more than meets the eye.		

9. What was the author's main purpose in writing this article?

a. To inform readers about the sport of hang gliding
b. To entertain readers with a description of hang gliding
c. To help readers analyze the development of hang gliding
d. To persuade readers to try hang gliding

Annabel Lee

by Edgar Allan Poe

It was many and many a year ago,
 In a kingdom by the sea,
That a maiden there lived whom you may know
 By the name of Annabel Lee;
And this maiden she lived with no other thought
 Than to love and be loved by me.

I was a child and she was a child,
 In this kingdom by the sea,
But we loved with a love that was more than love—
 I and my Annabel Lee—
With a love that the wingèd seraphs of Heaven
 Coveted her and me.

And this was the reason that, long ago,
 In this kingdom by the sea,
A wind blew out of a cloud, chilling
 My beautiful Annabel Lee;
So that her highborn kinsmen came
 And bore her away from me,
To shut her up in a sepulchre
 In this kingdom by the sea.

The angels, not half so happy in Heaven,
 Went envying her and me—
Yes!—that was the reason (as all men know,
 In this kingdom by the sea)
That the wind came out of the cloud by night,
 Chilling and killing my Annabel Lee.

But our love it was stronger by far than the love
 Of those who were older than we—
 Of many far wiser than we—
And neither the angels in Heaven above
 Nor the demons down under the sea
Can ever dissever my soul from the soul
 Of the beautiful Annabel Lee;

For the moon never beams, without bringing me dreams
 Of the beautiful Annabel Lee;
And the stars never rise, but I feel the bright eyes
 Of the beautiful Annabel Lee;
And so, all the night-tide, I lie down by the side
 Of my darling—my darling—my life and my bride,
 In her sepulchre there by the sea—
 In her tomb by the sounding sea.

Refer to the passage "Annabel Lee" to answer questions 10-17.

10. Read lines 26-33 of the poem.

> But our love it was stronger by far than the love
> Of those who were older than we—
> Of many far wiser than we—
> And neither the angels in Heaven above
> Nor the demons down under the sea
> Can ever dissever my soul from the soul
> Of the beautiful Annabel Lee;

Based on these lines, what can the reader predict?

a. The narrator will act rationally in laying Annabel to rest.
b. The narrator will continue to love Annabel as he did before she passed.
c. The angels will see her death was wrong and return Annabel to the narrator.
d. The angels will kill the narrator in order to reunite him with Annabel.

11. This question has two parts. After you answer Part A, answer Part B:

Part A: Read this information about the word sepulchre.

> From the Latin sepulcrum, which means "burial place"

Based on this information, which of the following is a synonym for sepulchre?

a. Garden
b. Shack
c. Storage
d. Crypt

Part B: Which line from the poem supports the answer to part A?

a. In this kingdom by the sea
b. In her tomb by the sounding sea
c. And bore her away from me
d. Can ever dissever my soul from the soul

12. What can be concluded from lines 21-26?

a. The angels in heaven are responsible for Annabel's death.
b. The narrator is being challenged to find Annabel.
c. All men on the sea quickly knew of the passing of Annabel.
d. Annabel was killed by men of the sea on a cold night.

13. What is the most likely reason the narrator uses dashes at the end of some lines?

a. To create a break so the next line can begin
b. To emphasize the information between the dashes
c. To fully replace the use of commas
d. To make the rhythm of the poem clearer

14. How does the author's word choice impact the tone of this poem?

a. By describing the "kingdom of the sea," he creates a fantastical tone.
b. By mentioning the moon, stars, and night sky, he creates a dark tone.
c. By using words like "killing" and "tomb," he creates a sorrowful tone.
d. By conveying actions like "bore" and "shut," he creates an urgent tone.

15. Which lines from the poem best support the idea that Annabel returned the narrator's love?

a. That a maiden there lived whom you may know
By the name of Annabel Lee;
And this maiden she lived with no other thought
Than to love and be loved by me.
b. For the moon never beams, without bringing me dreams
Of the beautiful Annabel Lee;
And the stars never rise, but I feel the bright eyes
Of the beautiful Annabel Lee;
c. So that her highborn kinsmen came
And bore her away from me,
To shut her up in a sepulchre
In this kingdom by the sea.
d. And neither the angels in Heaven above
Nor the demons down under the sea
Can ever dissever my soul from the soul
Of the beautiful Annabel Lee;

16. Which of the following is the best summary of "Annabel Lee"?

a. A young couple living in a seaside kingdom loved one another with great intensity. Their love was so enviable that even the angels in heaven were jealous. Because of their jealousy, the angels killed the girl. The narrator lived on feeling forever attached to Annabel.
b. A female child in a seaside town must be married away to a royal. However, she is in love with another child in the town. In her attempt to run away with the person she loves, Annabel passes away tragically in the cold.
c. A young man who works on the sea loves Annabel deeply. He cares for her so much that he wants her to live on a ship with him. As such, he prays to angels in heaven to have her brought to him.
d. A young maiden feels as though her love for the narrator is one sided. As such, she begins to behave carelessly. One night, she is killed in a chilling wind. It is only at this point that the narrator confesses his love for the girl.

17. What is the most likely reason the narrator wrote this poem?

a. To warn others against falling too deeply in love
b. To accuse the heavens of taking his love
c. To send a final message to his love
d. To show the nature of everlasting love

More than Video Games

(1) The school bell rang, and it took all the self-control Reggie had not to jump up and run out of the classroom. He hurriedly swung his backpack onto his back, made his way outside to his dad's car, and got in.

(2) "Hey, Bud," Reggie's dad said with a laugh. "What are you in such a hurry for?"

(3) "Dad, remember? Alien Quest 3 came out today! And I have a whole weekend to play it."

(4) "Oh, that's right! Well, we'll start downloading it when we get home, and that should give you plenty of time to finish your homework."

(5) "I already finished all of my homework. And we preordered it, remember? It should already be downloaded."

(6) "Oh wow, alrighty then. Well, until we get home, tell me about your day. Surely there's more going on in your life than video game releases."

(7) Reggie talked about school for a few minutes, but soon began telling his dad all about Alien Quest 3. As soon as they got home, Reggie bolted inside. He yelled a quick hello to his mom and younger brother as he shut the door to his room. He turned on the game and could hardly wait as it loaded and the words "Alien Quest 3" slowly appeared on the screen.

(8) Reggie hardly noticed the first hour and a half go by. He had gotten used to the new features of the game in no time and was flying through the quests. He only stopped when his stomach began growling, and he glanced at his watch. *Oh wow*, he thought, *it's past dinner time*. Reggie paused the game and walked to the kitchen.

(9) "We saved some pizza for you," Reggie's mom called out from the living room.

(10) Reggie piled some pizza slices on a plate, but as he walked back to his room, he heard a familiar sound. He looked at his family and realized that they were all watching one of his favorite movies. He hesitated, and his dad looked up at him.

(11) "Oh, sorry, your brother wanted to watch a movie, and I didn't want to interrupt your game. I forgot how much you like this one," he explained. He turned to Reggie's brother, John, and said, "Maybe we should save this one for another day. Reggie wouldn't want us to watch it without him, and he's been waiting to play his new game today."

(12) "Okay," John said quietly, disappointed.

(13) "Wait," Reggie said. He turned toward his room, then back toward his family. He pivoted between the two for a few seconds before he finally said, "Give me a second, and I'll come watch it with you. I just need to save my progress."

(14) "Are you sure, Bud?" Reggie's mom asked. "You've been looking forward to that game for a while."

(15) "Yeah, I'm sure. I do have all weekend to play it." He looked at John and added, "After all, there's more to life than video games."

The Top Five Reasons Video Games Are Good for Your Health

(1) Too many people think video games are just time-wasters. They say video games are for weak-minded imbeciles. They insist that no good can come from this electronic entertainment. In contrast to these common theories, I believe video games offer numerous benefits. Let me share with you the top five reasons that video games are good for your health.

(2) First, video games improve overall coordination. Response times are quicker, attention is more focused, and awareness is heightened. When I play video games, I find myself focused and intent on my mission. Since I began playing video games, my coordination—particularly my hand-eye coordination—has improved immensely. Even my handwriting has improved! The advent of motion sensor systems, such as Nintendo's Wii, Microsoft's Xbox 360 Kinect, and Sony's PlayStation 3 Move, has further enhanced users' coordination and reaction times.

(3) In addition to improving coordination and reaction times, many games also enhance logic and reasoning abilities. Most games employ some sort of strategy, whether in sporting competitions, driving pursuits, fantasy quests, or military battles. Winning a game—even just playing a game—requires a plan and the ability to adjust that plan and adapt to changing conditions. The ability to use logic and reason to solve problems leads to the ability to think on your feet. These are all important life skills, making video games beneficial for personal development.

(4) Sometimes, however, you are not concerned about developing new skills—you just want to have fun. Video games are a great way to fill empty hours productively. They focus mental energies and allow unbridled relaxation. They entertain small children and keep older ones out of trouble. Finally, video games allow safe and fun experimentation in a variety of environments, with a plethora of tools, at a relatively low cost.

(5) Beyond creating skills and filling the hours with fun, video games also create a sense of passion and excitement. They encourage goal setting and persistence. They develop a healthy spirit of competition. When you play a game often, you develop a deep desire to accomplish a little more or go a little further each time you play. This breeds excitement, anticipation, and a constant hope for success. Setting incremental goals and working passionately toward those goals leads to achievement in video games and in life.

(6) Finally, the skills and attitudes gained playing video games often open the door for development of deep social bonds. There is a unique camaraderie among those who play games together, almost as if they were teammates. These bonds tend to be strongest when a common game is played or when individuals are members of an online community. Even without these commonalities, however, the shared universe of video games provides the foundation for social interaction, conversation, and friendship.

(7) Are video games without pitfalls? Certainly not. But many games offer life-improving benefits that are often overlooked. They improve coordination and response time, enhance logic and reasoning, fill empty hours productively, create a sense of passion and excitement, and foster a variety of social bonds among players

of all types, skill levels, and backgrounds. With so many positive aspects, video games are worth checking out. Try them—you might find you like them!

Refer to the passage "More than Video Games" to answer questions 18-21.

18. Which of the following statements best represents the theme of this passage?

a. You can't choose family.
b. Life is about balance.
c. Gaming is harmful.
d. New isn't always better.

19. In paragraph 7, the author explains that "Reggie bolted inside." What is the most likely reason the author used this hyperbole?

a. To demonstrate how quickly Reggie could run
b. To explain how the game was supposed to be played
c. To make the reader feel eager about the game
d. To help show how excited Reggie was

20. Read this excerpt from the passage.

> (3) "Dad, remember? Alien Quest 3 came out today! And I have a whole weekend to play it."
> (4) "Oh, that's right! Well, we'll start downloading it when we get home, and that should give you plenty of time to finish your homework."
> (5) "I already finished all of my homework. And we preordered it, remember? It should already be downloaded."
> (6) "Oh wow, alrighty then. Well, until we get home, tell me about your day. Surely there's more going on in your life than video game releases."
> (7) Reggie talked about school for a few minutes, but soon began telling his dad all about Alien Quest 3. As soon as they got home, Reggie bolted inside. He yelled a quick hello to his mom and younger brother as he shut the door to his room. He turned on the game and could hardly wait as it loaded and the words "Alien Quest 3" slowly appeared on the screen.

What event is foreshadowed by this scene?

a. Reggie will not be able to play the entire weekend because he will beat the video game before then.
b. Reggie's father will want to join him and play along, but Reggie will not let him.
c. Something important will prevent Reggie from spending the entire weekend playing the video game.
d. The mother and younger brother will be upset that Reggie blew by them, and they won't speak to him.

21. Which of the following characteristics of the story help the reader identify it as realistic fiction?

a. The events are possible.
b. It is written in the past tense.
c. The setting is a modern home.
d. It focuses on a small family.

Refer to the passage "The Top Five Reasons Video Games Are Good for Your Health" to answer questions 22-25.

22. How does the information from paragraph 3 support the author's argument?

a. By outlining the physical benefits of playing video games
b. By detailing how video games make players smarter
c. By portraying video games as an affordable form of entertainment
d. By explaining how playing games supports personal development

23. Why did the author use a rhetorical question in paragraph 7?

a. To ask the reader to consider something
b. To bring attention to a point he will refute
c. To force the reader to pause while reading
d. To provoke the reader's desire to play games

24. Why does the author present a counter argument in paragraph 7?

a. To give the reader both sides of the argument so they can make their own decision about playing video games
b. To convince readers to play fewer video games once they have developed the skills listed in the passage
c. To acknowledge the negative side of video games and explain that the good aspects outweigh the bad
d. To explain to readers that they should monitor how much time they play and make sure they are taking breaks

25. Who is likely the intended audience for this passage?

a. People who view games negatively
b. Avid and passionate gamers
c. Board of Education members
d. Video game developers

Refer to the passages "More than Video Games" and "The Top Five Reasons Video Games Are Good for Your Health" to answer questions 26-28.

26. How is the conclusion of "More Than Video Games" different than the conclusion of "The Top Five Reasons Video Games are Good for Your Health"?

a. It addresses a need for balance in gaming and other aspects of life.
b. It addresses the opposing view of the topic of video games.
c. It portrays playing video games negatively.
d. It uses an extended metaphor to make the same point.

27. How might the opinions of Reggie from "More Than Video Games" and the author of "The Top Five Reasons Video Games are Good for Your Health" be different?

a. The author of "The Top Five Reasons Video Games are Good for Your Health" would find family time more valuable than Reggie would.
b. Reggie would prioritize video games over school while the author of "The Top Five Reasons Video Games are Good for Your Health" would be eager to use his or her gaming skills to complete schoolwork.
c. The author of "The Top Five Reasons Video Games are Good for Your Health" would likely feel video games were a solution to many problems while Reggie would likely seek help from his family.
d. Reggie would feel it is important that people are educated about the benefits of video games while the author of "The Top Five Reasons Video Games are Good for Your Health" would want them to form their own opinions.

28. What is one similarity between the passages?

a. Both explain the benefits of playing video games.
b. Both portray video games as a small part of life.
c. Both depict characters that are indifferent to gaming.
d. Both discuss the enjoyment of playing video games.

Extended Response

Your STAAR test will include the following instructions for your extended response question. The response prompts used here are similar to the prompts you will see on the STAAR test.

29. Read the passages "More Than Video Games" and "The Top Five Reasons Video Games Are Good for Your Health." Based on the passages, write a response to the following:

Explain whether or not playing video games is a healthy hobby to practice.

Write a well-organized argumentative composition that uses specific evidence from the article to support your answer.

Remember to —

- clearly state your thesis
- organize your writing
- develop your ideas in detail
- use evidence from the selection in your response
- use correct spelling, capitalization, punctuation, and grammar

Manage your time carefully so that you can —

- review the selection
- plan your response
- write your response
- revise and edit your response

Revising

Richard wrote the following paper about a memorable vacation. Read the following paper and note the revisions that Richard should make. Once you have read his paper, answer the questions that follow it.

A Grand Family Road Trip

(1) Nothing says summer like a family road trip. (2) There's just something about the hours in a crowded car that makes each road trip a memorable—if misguided—adventure. (3) I've been on several road trips in my life, and each one had its own special charm. (4) However, above all other road trips, I will always remember my family's trip to the Grand Canyon.

(5) The day we left was bright and cloudless. (6) I squeezed into the backseat between my little brother, Ronnie, and my big sister, Rebecca. (7) We piled the ingredients of a successful road trip around us: sodas, snacks, music, and games. (8) By the time we hit the freeway, Ronnie and I had each already downed a whole soda and were halfway through a party-size bag of chips. (9) Needless to say, we begged to stop at every rest area along the route, driving my father crazy.

(10) Another thing that drove my father memorably crazy was our road games. (11) Twenty minutes into our drive, Rebecca began the alphabet game. (12) We started with the letter A, and each time one of us saw the next letter of the alphabet somewhere outside, we shouted it out. (13) There were long periods of silence as we watched road signs and license plates intently. (14) Then, when it appeared, we would all burst out shouting, and my startled father would sit up in surprise and yell at us to keep the noise down. (15) The alphabet game was a source of great amusement during that never-ending trip.

(16) The trip wasn't all fun and games, however. (17) In fact, we had several disasters on our journey. (18) In retrospect, our challenges seem almost funny. (19) At the time, they seemed tragic. (20) We blew a tire on a lonely, dusty stretch of highway in triple-digit temperatures. (21) We caught some fish in a tiny, lakeside campground just across the Arizona border, but Mom turned our fish to charcoal over the campfire. (22) When we finally made it to the Grand Canyon, Rebecca fell on a rocky trail and broke her ankle. (23) We spent the rest of the trip in a dimly-lit hotel room, playing cards and watching movies so Rebecca wouldn't feel left out.

(24) Looking back, I'm sure it wasn't the trip my parents had planned for it to be. (25) But it was a trip I will never forget. (26) It was the imperfections that made the trip so memorable.

30. Which of the following sentences is a supporting detail that can be added after sentence 5?

a. The forecast said that we would see the same conditions at the Grand Canyon, and that they would last throughout our trip.
b. My brother and sister were taking too long to get ready, so I was grumpy with them by the time they got to the car.
c. I asked my parents how long the drive would take, but they said that it would depend on the traffic.
d. While Mom and Dad were focused on making sure all of our luggage fit in the car, my siblings and I were eagerly waiting to pile in the car.

31. Sentence 14 uses unclear wording. Which of the following phrases should be used to replace the word *it* in sentence 14?

a. the next letter
b. the alphabet game
c. the Grand Canyon
d. the next road sign

32. Sentences 18 and 19 can be combined. On the lines below, write a new sentence that correctly combines sentences 18 and 19.

____

____

____

33. Which of the following sentences should be used to replace sentence 26 and conclude this paper?

a. Even though it happened at the beginning, the alphabet game was the best part of the entire trip.
b. In the end, it would have been more enjoyable if we had not blown a tire and Rebecca had not broken her ankle.
c. The challenges we faced and the unexpected experiences made our Grand Canyon adventure the most memorable trip ever.
d. I feel blessed to have such an adventurous family, even if we get frustrated with one another sometimes.

Marley wrote the following paper about the history of painting. Read the following paper and note the revisions that Marley should make. Once you have read her paper, answer the questions that follow it.

The History of Paint

(1) From the earliest days of humanity, people have expressed themselves through painting. (2) While techniques and materials have changed, some ancient knowledge is still used today. (3) The cave paintings from the past are still used for our education and enjoyment because of the various materials used to make them. (4) The paint itself was made from a variety of materials but was usually made from dirt or charcoal blended with various liquids to make a paste.

(5) To create paint colors, like shades of red, yellow, and brown, ancient people used other materials that could be found in the earth. (6) Charcoal or burned bones were used to create a black paint. (7) Calcite rock was ground to make white paint. (8) To find deposits of the different minerals, people may have walked as far as 25 miles. (9) The liquids used to make paint included various animal parts and saliva. (10) These binding materials sealed the paintings to the cave walls, and the pigment soaked into the stone, creating a permanent art gallery.

(11) While nearly all of the ancient pigments remain in use today, many new paint sources have been discovered or developed over the years. (12) Ancient Egyptians began using plants to create new shades, adding yellow, green, and blue to their color options. (13) They were the first to create a white powder base, apply dyes to it, and create different shades of paint. (14) They also were the first to coat finished paintings with a thin layer of resin or varnish to protect them and allow them to survive through the years.

(15) Ancient Rome also made contributions to painting. (16) Artists developed a process known as wax emulsion. (17) During this process, they heated beeswax and mixed in salt water and potassium carbonate to make a paste. (18) Romans utilized many of the paint colors of the Egyptians and added a few of their own. (19) They were particularly fond of vermilion, a vibrant red made from a stone called cinnabar. (20) This form of vermilion is still used today, but with great caution, as it contains mercury and is highly toxic.

(21) Medieval art saw the rise of egg tempera painting, which involved mixing the color with egg and water. (22) The protein in the egg sealed the pigment to the surface and gave it a shiny, slightly crackled look that can still be seen in art from this period. (23) The medieval age was also known for its use of mineral pigments. (24) Just as ancient humans dug colored minerals from the earth for their cave paintings, medieval artists dug them up and shaped them into chalks to create their red, brown, and yellow tones. (25) Green earth was particularly useful in achieving various flesh tones. (26) The famed works of Michelangelo, Rembrandt, and others were created using these mineral pigments.

(27) Many of the pigments and painting methods developed centuries ago are still used, in some form, today. (28) Modern developments allow artists to use wider range of shades and paint types. (29) Painting has changed drastically since the time of artists like Michelangelo and Rembrandt.

34. Which sentence in paragraph 2 should be removed?

a. Sentence 5
b. Sentence 6
c. Sentence 8
d. Sentence 9

35. Sentence 13 is a bit unclear. Which of the following is the best revision of sentence 13?

a. They were the first to create white powder base and dyes to apply to it to create different shades of paint.
b. They were the first to create a white powder base, applying dyes to it to create different shades of paint.
c. They were the first to create a white powder base and apply dyes to it, creating different shades of paint.
d. They were the first to create a white powder base. They applied dyes to it. This created different shades of paint.

36. Which of the following should replace sentence 15 to create a more effective and engaging introductory sentence for paragraph 4?

a. The Ancient Romans created a new process called wax emulsion.
b. The Ancient Romans also made unique contributions to the art of painting.
c. The Ancient Romans made their own contributions to painting.
d. The Ancient Romans used the developments of others and their own methods when painting.

37. Which of the following is an effective conclusion for the paper and should be used to replace sentence 29?

a. Modern paint usually includes more ingredients than the paint used in ancient cultures, so paint has continued to change over time.
b. While many ancient cultures used different techniques, methods, and styles, paintings from all over the world look very similar today.
c. Modern painters often still study the methods and techniques of ancient artists, even though they have modern materials available to them.
d. However, when an artist picks up a paint brush, he or she is still following the traditions and methods of ancient artists.

Editing

Claire is writing an essay about the US Coast Guard. Read the following paragraph from the body of Claire's essay and look for errors that she needs to correct. Once you have read the paragraphs, answer the questions that follow them.

The United States Coast Guard

(1) The United States Coast Guard was founded in 1790. (2) It is the branch of the military that is responsible for protecting the country's sea-related interests. (3) The branch was originally created to defend the US from smugglers and to enforce tariff and trade laws. (4) While this may have seemed like a job for the Navy, the Navy's purpose is very different from the Coast Guard's. (5) The Navy's job is to engage in combat and defend the seas from threats too the US and its interests worldwide. (6) As part of the Department of Homeland Security, the United States Coast Guard is considered a federal law enforcement agency. (7) The mission of the department is to protect the US coastlines and american waters by enforcing US and international laws.

38. Which change would correct the mistake in sentence 2?

a. Change *military* to *Military.*
b. Change *is responsible* to *are responsible.*
c. Change *country's* to *countrys'.*
d. No change is needed in sentence 2.

39. Which change would correct the mistake in sentence 4?

a. Change *this* to *these.*
b. Change *have seemed* to *seem.*
c. Change the comma to a semicolon.
d. Change *from* to *for.*

40. Which change would correct the mistake in sentence 5?

a. Change *is* to *are.*
b. Add a comma after *combat.*
c. Change *seas* to *Seas.*
d. Change *too* to *to.*

41. Which change would correct the mistake in sentence 7?

a. Change *mission* to *mishion.*
b. Change *american* to *American.*
c. Add a comma after *waters.*
d. Change *US* to *US's*

August is writing an essay about King James I of England. Read the first two paragraphs of August's essay and look for errors that he needs to correct. Once you have read the paragraphs, answer the questions that follow them.

King James I

(1) In 1603, Queen Elizabeth I of England died. (2) She had never married and had no heir, so the throne passed to a distant relative: James Stuart. (3) James was the son of Elizabeth's cousin and former rival for the throne Mary, Queen of Scots. (4) James was crowned King James I of England. (5) At the time, he was also King James VI of Scotland. (6) The combination of his two roles creates conflict that haunted the two nations for generations to come.

(7) The conflict developed from rising tensions among the people within the nations, as well as between it. (8) While some scholars dismisses religion as a cause, it undoubtedly played a role in the problems that faced England and Scotland.

42. Which change would correct the mistake in sentence 3?

a. Change *was* to *is.*
b. Change *Elizabeth's* to *Elizabeths.*
c. Add a comma after *throne.*
d. Change *Queen* to *queen.*

43. Select the correct verb to use in sentence 6.

The combination of his two roles ___________ conflict that haunted the two nations for generations to come.

creates
will create
created
create

44. Which change would correct the mistake in sentence 7?

a. Add a semicolon after *developed.*
b. Change *from* to *into.*
c. Change *within* to *with in.*
d. Change *it* to *them.*

45. Which change would correct the mistake in sentence 8?

a. Change *While* to *Since.*
b. Change *scholars* to *Scholars.*
c. Change *dismisses* to *dismiss.*
d. Remove the comma after *cause.*

Answer Key and Explanations for Test #2

Reading

1. B: TEKS Standard (8.2)(B)

In the context of this sentence, *aloft* means "suspended in the sky," so choice B is correct. The sentence from paragraph 2 says that a glider can "stay aloft," so the reader knows that *aloft* is a state that the glider can be in or out of. This sentence also discusses the world record for a single glider flight, which shows that *aloft* must be related to the glider's flight. Choice A is incorrect because gliders are not motor powered, and being motor powered is not a state they can be in and then out of. Choice C is incorrect because this sentence does not discuss the glider being split into pieces, and neither does the rest of the passage. Choice D is incorrect because the glider is always collapsible. It does not stay collapsible for just a few hours at a time.

2. C: TEKS Standard (8.9)(E)

The imagery and similes used in paragraph 1 allow the reader to understand the appeal of hang gliding. They show that the sport allows pilots to soar through the air and experience the freedom and excitement of flying. Though readers most likely have not experienced hang gliding, this figurative language helps them understand how it feels and highlights its most attractive effects. Choice C is correct. Choice A is incorrect because the passage does not make it clear that the experience of flying like a bird or freely soaring through the air inspired the first inventors of hang gliders. Choice B is incorrect because the unsafe parts of hang gliding are not described in paragraph 1. Choice D is incorrect because this excerpt does not give the reader facts or describe events from the past. It only describes a positive hang-gliding experience.

3. D: TEKS Standard (8.5)(F)

Because of the death of early hang gliders, hang gliding was not seen as safe. These hang gliders' deaths occurred during the same time that airplane flight was becoming possible. After both of these factors came into play, people lost interest in hang gliding. From this, it can be inferred that the general public felt planes were a safer alternative for those who wanted to experience flight. The sentence does not suggest that the Wright Brothers publicizing their invention made people less interested in hang gliding and more interested in flight by planes, so choice A is incorrect. Choice B is incorrect because very few people had experienced hang gliding at this time. While it is mentioned that hang gliding had an element of danger, the passage does not suggest that planes were also dangerous. Furthermore, hang gliders were also new at this time, so choice C is incorrect.

4. C: TEKS Standard (8.6)(C)

Choice C explains that new technology and changes to the design of hang gliders increased safety for people who hang glide. Choice A only addresses the use of thermals, currents of warm air, in flying. Because choice A does not refer to safety, it is incorrect. Choice B is incorrect because it mentions safety as it relates to knowing rules, not changes in technology. Choice D explains the build of early gilders, not advanced ones, so it is incorrect.

5. B: TEKS Standard (8.9)(B)

The chronological organization of these paragraphs helps readers understand when hang gliders first became popular, why the interest in the sport later declined, and how their popularity grew again along with their safety. It provides a timeline of the progression of hang gliding and the public's interest in it. Paragraph 1 helps provide readers with a mental image of hang gliding, but does so with descriptive writing that is only used in this paragraph, so choice A is incorrect. While a chronological order could be used to give step by step instructions, no instructions are given in these paragraphs, so choice C is incorrect. Choice D is incorrect because this passage is not written to persuade readers, as the passage does not present an argument or a call to action.

6. A: TEKS Standard (8.6)(D)

The summary includes ideas about the start of hang gliding and its growth in popularity and safety. Adding choice A after the last sentence would best complete the summary by showing that, with safe practices, hang gliding can be enjoyed as a sport today. Choice B explains how small hang gliders can break down, but this is a small detail from the passage. It does not make the summary more effective, so it is incorrect. Adding choice C would be redundant, so it is incorrect. The summary already explains that the invention of the plane contributed to the loss of interest in hang gliding. Choice D is incorrect as this idea is given in the first sentence of the summary.

7. B: TEKS Standard (8.2)(B)

Paragraph 3 mentions "the advent of airplane flight by the Wright brothers in 1903." The Wright brothers created the first successful motored airplane. This means that the Wright brothers brought on airplane flight and allowed it to begin. The word *advent* means "beginning," so choice B is correct. The passage supports the idea that airplane flight was an available option for those who wanted to fly. This means that airplane flight was occurring, not ending, so choice A is incorrect. The passage does not support the idea that airplane flight was clearly increasing in 1903, only that it was made possible, so choice C is incorrect. In paragraph 4, the passage states that airplanes were expensive and used during World War II. This does not show that airplane flight would have been popular in 1903 or soon after, so choice D is incorrect.

8. TEKS Standard (8.5)(G)

Statement	Key Idea	Supporting Detail
Modern glider sails are 13 to 28 feet wide.		X
Glider pilots must know the rules of the sky.	X	
All glider pilots should wear helmets for safety.		X
Modern glider design premiered in 1971.		X
Hang gliding has had a dynamic history.	X	

The passage mentions the safety concerns involved in hang gliding many times. It also supports the idea that the sport is popular today because it is safer now, but only when pilots know and follow the rules. The passage's description of the many events and challenges that occurred throughout the history of the sport show that it has had a dynamic history. These are both key ideas. The passage does not focus on the specific physical characteristics of gliders. The size of glider sails today is just a supporting detail. The passage also does not focus on specific safety rules, so each rule is a supporting detail. While a large portion of the passage explains the history of hang gliding, specific events are supporting details for the larger key idea.

9. A: TEKS Standard (8.9)(A)

The author's main purpose for writing this passage is to tell the reader about hang gliding. The author explains how long hang gliding has been taking place, how it got started, how it works, and some rules and safety guidelines pilots must follow. The author does not describe hang gliding throughout the passage, so choice B is incorrect. The author does not provide an analysis of the development of hang gliding. He or she instead uses a few paragraphs to give the reader a brief history of hang gliding, so choice C is incorrect. The author does not write in a persuasive manner or use persuasive methods, so choice D is incorrect.

10. B: TEKS Standard (8.5)(C)

In these lines, the speaker explains that their love was strong and that his soul cannot be separated from Annabel's. Based on these ideas, the reader can predict that the narrator will continue to love Annabel as he did before she died. Because of the intensity of the narrator's feelings, the reader cannot predict that the speaker will behave rationally when laying Annabel to rest, so choice A is incorrect. In these lines, the narrator explains that the angels cannot make him stop loving Annabel. In lines before this, it is suggested that the angels caused her death. There is no suggestion that the angels will decide that separating them wrong, so the reader cannot predict that they will return her to him. This makes choice C incorrect. Similarly, these lines do not suggest that the angels will kill the narrator to reunite them, so choice D is incorrect.

11. TEKS Standard (8.2)(C)

Part A: D: *Sepulchre* is used twice in this poem. It is first used to name a place where Annabel is "shut up" in line 19 and is later used to describe her "tomb" in line 41. Knowing that information as well as the fact that *sepulcher* comes from a word meaning "burial place," *crypt* is the best synonym, as it also means a burial place or vault. This makes choice D correct. Gardens, shacks, and storage rooms are not typical places where bodies are laid to rest, so choices A, B, and C are incorrect.

Part B: B: The last line of the poem, "In her tomb by the sounding sea," repeats and gives more information about line 40, "In her sepulchre there by the sea." Line 41 clarifies that the sepulchre is a tomb, which supports the correct answer to Part A. Choice A is incorrect because it is repeated throughout the poem to show the reader the larger setting. It does not show the meaning of *sepulchre*. Choice C is incorrect because, while Annabel was taken from the speaker and laid in her sepulchre, this line does not show the reader what kind of place a sepulchre is. This line does not eliminate the incorrect answer choices in Part A. Choice D is incorrect because it only describes the speaker's view of his love for Annabel. It does not show what kind of place she has gone to.

12. A: TEKS Standard (8.5)(H)

The narrator portrays the angels in heaven as being unhappy and envious of the love he and Annabel share. He implies that they caused the "chilling wind" that killed Annabel, so choice A is correct. Lines 17-20 say "that her highborn kinsmen came and bore her away from me, to shut her up in a sepulchre in this kingdom by the sea." The highborn kinsmen, who can be interpreted as literal relatives or as angels, have separated Annabel from the narrator. However, there is no mention or evidence of this being a challenge for the narrator, so choice B is incorrect. Lines 23 and

24 explain that all men of the sea are aware that the angels' envy is the reason for Annabel's death. However, this does not mean that they quickly knew of Annabel's passing. In fact, the beginning of the poem shows that her death could have occurred long ago, so choice C is incorrect. Line 26 explains that a wind sent by the angels was responsible for "chilling and killing" Annabel, not a person, so choice D is incorrect.

13. B: TEKS Standard (8.8)(B)

The dashes used in this poem emphasize certain statements from the narrator. They create a visual break that highlights the writing between them. For example, in lines 9 through 11, the dashes are used to draw attention to "I and my Annabel Lee" to emphasize that it was the two of them that loved so intensely. They are also used in lines 22 and 23 to emphasize the author saying "yes!" as though he had an epiphany that the angels killed Annabel. Choice A is incorrect because these dashes are not meant to create a break. This is not necessary, and a new line can begin without the use of a dash, as most of the lines in the poem do. While commas can be used where the dashes are, there are commas throughout the poem, so choice C is incorrect. Because dashes are read like commas, they do not change the rhythm or make it clearer, so choice D is incorrect.

14. C: TEKS Standard (8.9)(F)

The author uses words like *killing* and *tomb*, along with *chilling* and *sepulchre*, to create a sad and sorrowful tone as he morns the loss of his love. The use of kingdom of the sea tells the reader the setting of the poem. It is not used as an element of fantasy, so choice A is incorrect. The way the moon, stars, and night sky are used in the poem does not create a dark tone. The author uses them in the last stanza to explain how he mourns at night, so choice B is incorrect. *Bore* and *shut* are not used to create an urgent tone. They are only used to describe the separating of Annabel from the narrator, so choice D is incorrect.

15. A: TEKS Standard (8.6)(C)

The last two lines in choice A show Annabel's love for the narrator. She could not think of anything other than loving and being loved by the narrator. The lines in choice B explain that the narrator cannot go a night without seeing Annabel in his dreams. This shows the narrator's never-ending love for Annabel, but not Annabel's love for the narrator, so choice B is incorrect. The lines in choice C explain Annabel's separation from the narrator, not her love for him, so it is incorrect. The lines in choice D explain how the narrator feels his soul can never be disconnected from Annabel. This reflects his love for her, not her love for him, so choice D is incorrect.

16. A: TEKS Standard (8.6)(D)

Choice A summarizes the poem most accurately. The narrator and Annabel were young lovers, and their love made the angels jealous. The narrator explains that the angels killed Annabel for this reason. He also explains that he will continue to love and feel attached to Annabel. Choice B says that Annabel was to be married to a royal. This is not true, so choice B is incorrect. Choice C claims that the narrator worked on the sea and wanted Annabel on the ship with him. The poem does not suggest that the narrator worked on a ship. It only shows that they were in a seaside kingdom. The narrator also blames the angels for killing Annabel. He does not pray to them, so choice C is incorrect. Choice D is incorrect because Annabel and the narrator are in love throughout the poem, and they return each other's love.

17. D: TEKS Standard (8.9)(A)

This poem shows an example of everlasting love as the author continually mourns the death of his love and portrays their love as eternal, so choice D is correct. Even after her death, the narrator has not stopped loving or forgotten Annabel. Choice A is incorrect because this poem is not a cautionary tale. It does not explain the downside of falling in love. It only recounts the narrator's story. While the narrator is certain the angels killed Annabel because they were jealous, the poem only focuses on this briefly. The primary focus is on the way her death made the narrator feel, so choice B is incorrect. The poem is not written as a message or letter to Annabel, so choice D is incorrect.

18. B: TEKS Standard (8.7)(A)

Reggie was incredibly excited about playing his new game and became so engrossed that he missed dinner and was going to miss a movie with his family. He realized that the game was taking up all his time and that there were other important things, like family time, that he could be doing. This caused him to recognize that there was more to life than games and that he needed to balance how he spent his time, so choice B is correct. Choice A is incorrect because Reggie does not express frustration with his family or the desire to choose different family members. Even though Reggie missed family dinner while playing, games are not portrayed as harmful in his passage. Reggie saw that he needed to play less so he could spend time with family, not give up video games altogether, so choice C is incorrect. Reggie was excited about the new game, but the passage does not include any comparison between this new game and an old one, so choice D is incorrect.

19. D: TEKS Standard (8.9)(D)

By saying that Reggie "bolted inside," the author demonstrates that Reggie ran into the house very quickly so he could play the game. This demonstrates his excitement, making choice D correct. As his quick pace was due to excitement, not necessarily his usual running speed, the statement is not meant to show how quickly Reggie can run, so choice A is incorrect. Reggie was running so he could start playing the game. He was not yet playing it, so choice B is incorrect. The hyperbole is used to show Reggie's excitement, not to make the reader excited. This would be done with descriptive writing that explained the details of the game in an enticing way, so choice C is incorrect.

20. C: TEKS Standard (8.7)(C)

Reggie tells his father that he has all weekend to play his new game, to which his dad says "there's more going on in your life than video game releases." This foreshadows, or hints at, Reggie's later realization that there is more to life than video games and his decision to prioritize time with his family. While the passage does suggest that Reggie will play through the game quickly, this is not foreshadowed, especially by this excerpt, so choice A is incorrect. Reggie's father does not show or mention that he wants to play the game himself. Instead, he suggests the opposite in this conversation by explaining that he thinks there is more to life than games, so choice C is incorrect. Choice D is incorrect. There is a brief mention of Reggie quickly greeting his mother and brother, but neither of them acts in a way that suggests that they are upset by his behavior.

21. A: TEKS Standard (8.8)(A)

The events that occur in this story, such as Reggie being excited to play and being so interested in his game he forgets about dinner, are very possible. Being picked up from school and spending time with family are parts of many people's days. This makes the story an example of realistic fiction. Though the story is written in past tense, the tense does not make it realistic. Many genres can be written in past tense, so choice B is incorrect. Similarly, stories within other genres can be written with modern homes as the setting, so choice C is incorrect. Though the story does focus on a small family, this is not an element that is specific to realistic fiction. Stories in many genres could focus on a family, making choice D incorrect.

22. D: TEKS Standard (8.8)(Ei)

Paragraph 3 focuses on the benefits of video game play that relate to strategy, logic, and reasoning. It also refers to these as important life skills, so choice D is correct. Choice A is incorrect because the physical benefits, such as coordination, of video game play are outlined in paragraph 2. Though paragraph 3 focuses on the mental aspect of games, the author does not claim that video games make an individual smarter, so choice B is incorrect. The author does not discuss the affordability of games, so choice C is incorrect.

23. B: TEKS Standard (8.9)(G)

In paragraph 7, the author poses the question "are video games without pitfalls?" and acknowledges that they are not. The author then explains why video games are still beneficial, in spite of this fact. The rhetorical question is used to bring attention to an argument that others may make before going on to prove that the benefits outweigh the pitfalls. Choice A is incorrect because, since the author immediately answers the question, he or she is not really asking the reader to ponder whether or not video games have pitfalls. There are many ways to force a reader to pause while reading, such as using punctuation. Question marks are not the only form of punctuation that would cause a reader to pause, so choice C is incorrect. Because the question brings attention to the downside of video games, the author is most likely not using it to make the reader want to play. This makes choice D incorrect.

24. C: TEKS Standard (8.8)(Eii)

In paragraph 7, the author states that playing video games comes with pitfalls. However, the author also explains that the positive effect of the aspects mentioned in the passage is greater than the negative effect of those pitfalls. This passage is persuasive, so it is meant to convince readers that video games are beneficial and should be played. This means that the counterargument is not included in order to give readers information to make their own decision. The writer still wants readers to support the playing of video games and try it themselves. This makes choice A incorrect. The passage does not suggest that the number of games played should be reduced once the reader has developed the skills mentioned in the essay, so choice B is incorrect. The author of the passage does not mention time limits or playing in moderation, so choice D is incorrect.

25. A: TEKS Standard (8.8)(Eiii)

This passage is persuasive and written to convince people that there are benefits to playing video games. This means that it is most likely written for people who view games negatively, as the author wants to change their minds. Avid gamers are people that play video games often and enthusiastically, so they would not need to be convinced to play, and choice B is incorrect. The passage does not mention how gaming impacts learning in schools, so it is unlikely that this passage is written for members on the Board of Education. This means that choice C is incorrect. Choice D is incorrect because the passage neither suggests improvements for games nor praises game developers, so it is unlikely that they are the intended audience.

26. A: TEKS Standard (8.5)(E)

"More Than Video Games" highlights the importance of doing things outside of playing video games. "The Top Five Reasons Video Games are Good for Your Health" does not. These conclusions differ, so choice A is correct. The conclusion of "More Than Video Games" does not address an opposing view or counterargument. "The Top Five Reasons Video Games are Good for Your Health" does, so choice B is incorrect. Neither passage portrays playing video games as something negative, so choice C is incorrect. The conclusion of "More Than Video Games" does not make the same point as "The Top Five Reasons Video Games are Good for Your Health," so choice D is incorrect.

27. C: TEKS Standard (8.5)(E)

The author of "The Top Five Reasons Video Games are Good for Your Health" makes it clear that video games have several benefits, including making players more coordinated, better at reasoning and logic, and more social. Reggie realizes family is more important than video games and acts in a way that shows that he has heeded his father's words. Because of these conclusions, it is likely that the author of "The Top Five Reasons Video Games are Good for Your Health" would view games as a solution to a problem while Reggie would ask his family for solutions. Choice A is incorrect. Based on the passage, it is more likely that Reggie would find family time valuable. It is unlikely that Reggie would prioritize games over schoolwork, as he completed his homework before playing the game and realized that there is more to life than games. This means that choice B is incorrect. Because "The Top Five Reasons Video Games are Good for Your Health" is written to persuade people to play games, it is unlikely the author would simply want people to form their own opinions. It is also likely that Reggie would want people to understand the benefit of balance in life over gaming, so choice D is incorrect.

28. D: TEKS Standard (8.5)(E)

Both passages portray video games as being fun and exciting. "More Than Video Games" portrays this through Reggie's excitement, while "The Top Five Reasons Video Games are Good for Your Health" explains it more blatantly. Choice A is incorrect because only "The Top Five Reasons Video Games are Good for Your Health" explains the benefits of playing video games. Only "More Than Video Games" portrays video games as being a small part of life, so choice B is incorrect. Both Reggie and the author of "The Top Five Reasons Video Games are Good for Your Health" are excited about gaming, not indifferent, so choice C is incorrect.

Extended Response

29. TEKS Standard (8.11)(C)

Please use the rubric below to make sure your response meets these criteria. Try to have a friend or family member grade your response for you or take a break after writing your response and return to grade it yourself with fresh eyes.

Below is an excerpt of the STAAR Grades 6-EII Argumentative/Opinion Writing Rubric.

<table>
<tr><th>Score Point</th><th>Development and Organization of Ideas</th></tr>
<tr><td>3</td><td><ul><li>Argument/opinion is clear and fully developed
The argument/opinion is clearly identifiable. The focus is consistent throughout, creating a response that is unified and easy to follow. For grades 8 through EII, counterarguments are identified and refuted.</li><li>Organization is effective
A purposeful structure that includes an effective introduction and conclusion is evident. The organizational structure is appropriate and effectively supports the development of the argument/opinion. The sentences, paragraphs, or ideas are logically connected in purposeful and highly effective ways.</li><li>Evidence is specific, well chosen, and relevant
The response includes relevant text-based evidence that is clearly explained and consistently supports and develops the argument/opinion. For pairs in grades 6 through EII, evidence is drawn from both texts. The response reflects a thorough understanding of the writing purpose.</li><li>Expression of ideas is clear and effective
The writer's word choice is specific, purposeful, and enhances the response. Almost all sentences and phrases are effectively crafted to convey the writer's ideas and contribute to the overall quality of the response and the clarity of the message.</li></ul></td></tr>
<tr><th>Score Point</th><th>Conventions</th></tr>
<tr><td>2</td><td>Student writing demonstrates consistent command of grade-level-appropriate conventions, including correct:<ul><li>sentence construction</li><li>punctuation</li><li>capitalization</li><li>grammar</li><li>spelling</li></ul>The response has few errors, but those errors do not impact the clarity of the writing.</td></tr>
</table>

Revising

30. D: TEKS Standard (8.10)(Bii)

Choice D is a detail that makes sense between sentences 5 and 6. It gives the reader a clearer picture of what was happening before the family got in the car. It lets the reader know the attitude and behavior of each member of the family going on the trip. Choice A is incorrect because it is not a very relevant detail. It does not support the reader's understanding of any of the events in the passage. Choice B is incorrect because it contradicts the events in the second paragraph. The passage shows that all three siblings were happy and getting along well when the drive began. Choice C is incorrect because it does not support the reader's understanding of the story or give the reader helpful or relevant information.

31. A: TEKS Standard (8.10)(C)

Sentence 12 explains that the siblings are all looking for the next letter in the alphabet, and that they shout when they see it. In sentence 14, the author says that after long silences, they would see something and begin shouting. Based on the description of the game, the reader can conclude that *it* in sentence 14 is the next letter of the alphabet game. The alphabet game is not something that the siblings can look for or see, so choice b is incorrect. The family does not make it to the Grand Canyon until sentence 21, so the siblings would not be able to see it at this point in the story, and choice C is incorrect. Sentence 12 shows the reader that the siblings are looking for letters. Sentence 13 explains that they find the letters on license plates and road signs. They shout when they see the next letter on a sign, not when they see another sign, so choice D is incorrect.

32. TEKS Standard (8.10)(C)

Sentence 18 says that the author can look back at the challenges and be amused by them. Sentence 19 says that during the trip, the challenges seemed like tragedies. These ideas are contradictory, so the new sentence should show this relationship between the ideas. The following sentence correctly combines sentences 18 and 19: In retrospect, our challenges seem almost funny, but at the time, they seemed tragic. A sentence may be similar to this example and still be correct. The sentence should include all of the information in sentences 18 and 19 and show the relationship between the ideas in the sentences without repeating information. The new sentence should also be complete and free of errors in grammar and spelling.

33. C: TEKS Standard (8.10)(Bi)

Choice C is the best choice for a concluding sentence because it captures the author's feelings about the story overall. It also gives the reader a sense of closure by making it clear that the story is over. Choice A is incorrect because it focuses on one detail and does not refer to the whole story or theme within the paper. Choice B is incorrect because it contradicts the author's statement in sentence 18. The author is not regretful that these events happened. Choice D is incorrect because it does not capture the theme of the story or provide a sense of closure.

34. C: TEKS Standard (8.10)(Bii)

This paragraph is about the sources of the paint and binders that were used to create cave paintings. While every other sentence either explains where these materials came from or how they were used, sentence 8 describes how difficult it was for people at the time to get the materials. This information is not relevant to the paragraph, so choice C is correct. Choice A is incorrect because sentence 5 is the topic sentence of the paragraph. It lets readers know what the paragraph is about and helps them understand the information in the next two sentences. Choice B is incorrect because sentence 6 is a supporting detail that is relevant to the topic of the paragraph. It gives the reader more context and an example that supports the information in sentence 5. Choice D is incorrect because sentence 9 is necessary in order for the reader to understand the information in sentence 10.

35. C: TEKS Standard (8.10)(C)

Sentence 13 should clearly state that the Ancient Egyptians were the first people to apply dyes to a white powder base, which allowed them to create different shades of paint. Currently sentence 13 does not make it clear that applying the dyes to the white powder base created the new shades of paint. Choice C most clearly states this, so it is correct. Choice A is incorrect because it suggests that they also created new dyes to apply to the white base. This changes the meaning of the sentence and is not supported by the rest of the passage. Choice B is incorrect because its meaning is also not clear. Choice D is incorrect because it unnecessarily splits sentence 13 into three sentences.

36. B: TEKS Standard (8.10)(Bi)

Sentence 15 is currently vague and does not effectively prepare the reader for the rest of the paragraph. Choice B is correct because it adds details that let the reader know that the Ancient Romans made contributions that were unlike those made by other people and cultures. Choice A is incorrect because it includes the same information as sentence 16. This would not be an effective topic sentence because it would make the paragraph repetitive. Choice C is incorrect because it is not more effective than the current sentence. Choice D is incorrect because it gives the reader information that appears later in the paragraph. It would not be a proper topic sentence because it would make the paragraph repetitive.

37. D: TEKS Standard (8.10)(Bi)

Choice D is related to the passage overall, provides the reader with a sense of closure, and shows the reader why the overall point of the essay is important. Choice A is incorrect because it does not give the reader new information and does not conclude the whole paper effectively. Choice B is incorrect because it is unclear and because different cultures still produce paintings that use different styles and techniques. Choice C is incorrect because it adds new information without creating an effective conclusion for the paper.

Editing

38. D: TEKS Standard (8.10)(D)

Sentence 2 does not contain any misspelled words or grammatical errors, so choice D is correct. Choice A is correct because *military*, by itself, is a common noun and should not be capitalized. Choice C is incorrect because *is* is a singular verb that is used correctly to show the action of the singular noun *branch*. *Are* is a plural verb, so it cannot be used to show the action of *branch*. Choice C is incorrect because an apostrophe should only be placed after an *s* when the noun is plural.

39. B: TEKS Standard (8.10)(Dii)

Sentence 4 is in the present tense. *Seem* is a present-tense verb when used by itself. *Have seemed* is not a present-tense verb phrase, so it is used incorrectly in sentence 4, and choice B is correct. *This* is a singular pronoun, while *these* is a plural pronoun. In sentence 4, *this* is used to represent the purpose of the Coast Guard. Since the pronoun is used to represent one noun, a singular pronoun must be used, so choice A is incorrect. Semicolons are not used to separate clauses in a complex sentence. They must be used after independent clauses or in lists, so choice C is incorrect. Choice D is incorrect because changing *from* to *for* would change the meaning of the sentence and make it unclear.

40. D: TEKS Standard (8.10)(Dvii)

The word *too* has a similar meaning to *also*. The word *to* is a preposition. The word *to* is the correct word to use in sentence 5 since the sentence is discussing threats directed at the US, so choice D is correct. Choice A is incorrect because sentence 5 is talking about one, singular job, so the singular verb *is* is used correctly in this sentence. Choice B is incorrect because there is no need for a comma after *combat*. Though the next word is *and*, *and* is not used to begin a new independent clause or mark the end of a list with more than two items. Choice C is incorrect because *seas* is not referring to a specific sea, so it is a common noun that should not be capitalized.

41. B: TEKS Standard (8.10)(Dv)

Nationalities are adjectives that show which country a noun came from or belongs to. Nationalities must be capitalized. The word *American* is a nationality, so it must be capitalized. Choice A is incorrect because *mission* is spelled correctly in sentence 7. *Mishion* is an incorrect spelling. Choice C is incorrect because there is no need for a comma after *waters*. Choice D is incorrect because an apostrophe and *s* are not needed after *US*. In this sentence, *US* is used like an adjective to show which nation claims the coastlines.

42. C: TEKS Standard (8.10)(Dvi)

The word "Mary" and the phrase "Queen of Scots" are both appositives that give a different name for James's former rival. Since these are appositives that give new names for someone who has already been named, they should be set apart with commas, and choice C is correct. Choice A is incorrect because sentence 3 is in the past tense, but *is* is a present-tense verb. It should not be used to replace the past-tense verb *was*, which is used correctly in sentence 3. Choice B is incorrect because, in this sentence, Elizabeth has, or possesses, a cousin. A comma should be used to show possession, so *Elizabeth's* is correct. Choice D is incorrect because *Queen* is part of Mary's title, so it must be capitalized. Nouns that are usually common nouns are treated like proper nouns when they are part of someone's title.

43. created: TEKS Standard (8.10)(Dii)

Sentence 6 is in the past tense, so the verb that goes in the blank must be a past-tense verb or verb phrase. *Creates* and *create* are both present-tense verbs, and *will create* is a future-tense verb phrase. None of these can be used in the blank. The verb *created* is used to show that something was made in the past, so it is the correct answer.

44. D: TEKS Standard (8.10)(Div)

Sentence 7 is about a conflict that affects people in two different nations. In all parts of the sentence, two nations are being described, not one, so the singular pronoun *it* should be changed to *them*. Choice A is incorrect because punctuation should not be added after the word *developed* in sentence 7. Choice B is incorrect because changing *from* to *into* would mean that the conflict created the tensions, when the tensions actually led to the conflict. Choice C is incorrect because the words *with* and *in* can be put together to form the compound word *within*.

45. C: TEKS Standard (8.10)(Di)

Scholars is a plural noun, so it must be used with a plural verb. *Dismisses* is a singular verb, and *dismiss* is a plural verb, so *dismisses* should be changed to *dismiss* in sentence 8. Choice A is incorrect because *while* means that two events are happening at the same time, but *since* means that one event happens after or as a result of another event. In sentence 8, the author is saying that scholars are dismissing a theory at the same time that he or she is accepting it. *While* is the correct word to use. Choice B is incorrect because *scholars* is a common noun in this sentence, so it does not need to be capitalized. Choice D is incorrect because the word *cause* comes at the end of a dependent clause and before an independent clause, and the comma is needed to properly link the two clauses.

Practice Test #3

To take this additional STAAR practice test, visit our online resources page:
mometrix.com/resources719/staarg8rla

How to Overcome Test Anxiety

Just the thought of taking a test is enough to make most people a little nervous. A test is an important event that can have a long-term impact on your future, so it's important to take it seriously and it's natural to feel anxious about performing well. But just because anxiety is normal, that doesn't mean that it's helpful in test taking, or that you should simply accept it as part of your life. Anxiety can have a variety of effects. These effects can be mild, like making you feel slightly nervous, or severe, like blocking your ability to focus or remember even a simple detail.

If you experience test anxiety—whether severe or mild—it's important to know how to beat it. To discover this, first you need to understand what causes test anxiety.

Causes of Test Anxiety

While we often think of anxiety as an uncontrollable emotional state, it can actually be caused by simple, practical things. One of the most common causes of test anxiety is that a person does not feel adequately prepared for their test. This feeling can be the result of many different issues such as poor study habits or lack of organization, but the most common culprit is time management. Starting to study too late, failing to organize your study time to cover all of the material, or being distracted while you study will mean that you're not well prepared for the test. This may lead to cramming the night before, which will cause you to be physically and mentally exhausted for the test. Poor time management also contributes to feelings of stress, fear, and hopelessness as you realize you are not well prepared but don't know what to do about it.

Other times, test anxiety is not related to your preparation for the test but comes from unresolved fear. This may be a past failure on a test, or poor performance on tests in general. It may come from comparing yourself to others who seem to be performing better or from the stress of living up to expectations. Anxiety may be driven by fears of the future—how failure on this test would affect your educational and career goals. These fears are often completely irrational, but they can still negatively impact your test performance.

Elements of Test Anxiety

As mentioned earlier, test anxiety is considered to be an emotional state, but it has physical and mental components as well. Sometimes you may not even realize that you are suffering from test anxiety until you notice the physical symptoms. These can include trembling hands, rapid heartbeat, sweating, nausea, and tense muscles. Extreme anxiety may lead to fainting or vomiting. Obviously, any of these symptoms can have a negative impact on testing. It is important to recognize them as soon as they begin to occur so that you can address the problem before it damages your performance.

The mental components of test anxiety include trouble focusing and inability to remember learned information. During a test, your mind is on high alert, which can help you recall information and stay focused for an extended period of time. However, anxiety interferes with your mind's natural processes, causing you to blank out, even on the questions you know well. The strain of testing during anxiety makes it difficult to stay focused, especially on a test that may take several hours. Extreme anxiety can take a huge mental toll, making it difficult not only to recall test information but even to understand the test questions or pull your thoughts together.

Effects of Test Anxiety

Test anxiety is like a disease—if left untreated, it will get progressively worse. Anxiety leads to poor performance, and this reinforces the feelings of fear and failure, which in turn lead to poor performances on subsequent tests. It can grow from a mild nervousness to a crippling condition. If allowed to progress, test anxiety can have a big impact on your schooling, and consequently on your future.

Test anxiety can spread to other parts of your life. Anxiety on tests can become anxiety in any stressful situation, and blanking on a test can turn into panicking in a job situation. But fortunately, you don't have to let anxiety rule your testing and determine your grades. There are a number of relatively simple steps you can take to move past anxiety and function normally on a test and in the rest of life.

Physical Steps for Beating Test Anxiety

While test anxiety is a serious problem, the good news is that it can be overcome. It doesn't have to control your ability to think and remember information. While it may take time, you can begin taking steps today to beat anxiety.

Just as your first hint that you may be struggling with anxiety comes from the physical symptoms, the first step to treating it is also physical. Rest is crucial for having a clear, strong mind. If you are tired, it is much easier to give in to anxiety. But if you establish good sleep habits, your body and mind will be ready to perform optimally, without the strain of exhaustion. Additionally, sleeping well helps you to retain information better, so you're more likely to recall the answers when you see the test questions.

Getting good sleep means more than going to bed on time. It's important to allow your brain time to relax. Take study breaks from time to time so it doesn't get overworked, and don't study right before bed. Take time to rest your mind before trying to rest your body, or you may find it difficult to fall asleep.

Along with sleep, other aspects of physical health are important in preparing for a test. Good nutrition is vital for good brain function. Sugary foods and drinks may give a burst of energy but this burst is followed by a crash, both physically and emotionally. Instead, fuel your body with protein and vitamin-rich foods.

Also, drink plenty of water. Dehydration can lead to headaches and exhaustion, especially if your brain is already under stress from the rigors of the test. Particularly if your test is a long one, drink water during the breaks. And if possible, take an energy-boosting snack to eat between sections.

Along with sleep and diet, a third important part of physical health is exercise. Maintaining a steady workout schedule is helpful, but even taking 5-minute study breaks to walk can help get your blood pumping faster and clear your head. Exercise also releases endorphins, which contribute to a positive feeling and can help combat test anxiety.

When you nurture your physical health, you are also contributing to your mental health. If your body is healthy, your mind is much more likely to be healthy as well. So take time to rest, nourish your body with healthy food and water, and get moving as much as possible. Taking these physical steps will make you stronger and more able to take the mental steps necessary to overcome test anxiety.

Mental Steps for Beating Test Anxiety

Working on the mental side of test anxiety can be more challenging, but as with the physical side, there are clear steps you can take to overcome it. As mentioned earlier, test anxiety often stems from lack of preparation, so the obvious solution is to prepare for the test. Effective studying may be the most important weapon you have for beating test anxiety, but you can and should employ several other mental tools to combat fear.

First, boost your confidence by reminding yourself of past success—tests or projects that you aced. If you're putting as much effort into preparing for this test as you did for those, there's no reason you should expect to fail here. Work hard to prepare; then trust your preparation.

Second, surround yourself with encouraging people. It can be helpful to find a study group, but be sure that the people you're around will encourage a positive attitude. If you spend time with others who are anxious or cynical, this will only contribute to your own anxiety. Look for others who are motivated to study hard from a desire to succeed, not from a fear of failure.

Third, reward yourself. A test is physically and mentally tiring, even without anxiety, and it can be helpful to have something to look forward to. Plan an activity following the test, regardless of the outcome, such as going to a movie or getting ice cream.

When you are taking the test, if you find yourself beginning to feel anxious, remind yourself that you know the material. Visualize successfully completing the test. Then take a few deep, relaxing breaths and return to it. Work through the questions carefully but with confidence, knowing that you are capable of succeeding.

Developing a healthy mental approach to test taking will also aid in other areas of life. Test anxiety affects more than just the actual test—it can be damaging to your mental health and even contribute to depression. It's important to beat test anxiety before it becomes a problem for more than testing.

Study Strategy

Being prepared for the test is necessary to combat anxiety, but what does being prepared look like? You may study for hours on end and still not feel prepared. What you need is a strategy for test prep. The next few pages outline our recommended steps to help you plan out and conquer the challenge of preparation.

Step 1: Scope Out the Test

Learn everything you can about the format (multiple choice, essay, etc.) and what will be on the test. Gather any study materials, course outlines, or sample exams that may be available. Not only will this help you to prepare, but knowing what to expect can help to alleviate test anxiety.

Step 2: Map Out the Material

Look through the textbook or study guide and make note of how many chapters or sections it has. Then divide these over the time you have. For example, if a book has 15 chapters and you have five days to study, you need to cover three chapters each day. Even better, if you have the time, leave an extra day at the end for overall review after you have gone through the material in depth.

If time is limited, you may need to prioritize the material. Look through it and make note of which sections you think you already have a good grasp on, and which need review. While you are studying, skim quickly through the familiar sections and take more time on the challenging parts.

Write out your plan so you don't get lost as you go. Having a written plan also helps you feel more in control of the study, so anxiety is less likely to arise from feeling overwhelmed at the amount to cover.

Step 3: Gather Your Tools

Decide what study method works best for you. Do you prefer to highlight in the book as you study and then go back over the highlighted portions? Or do you type out notes of the important information? Or is it helpful to make flashcards that you can carry with you? Assemble the pens, index cards, highlighters, post-it notes, and any other materials you may need so you won't be distracted by getting up to find things while you study.

If you're having a hard time retaining the information or organizing your notes, experiment with different methods. For example, try color-coding by subject with colored pens, highlighters, or post-it notes. If you learn better by hearing, try recording yourself reading your notes so you can listen while in the car, working out, or simply sitting at your desk. Ask a friend to quiz you from your flashcards, or try teaching someone the material to solidify it in your mind.

Step 4: Create Your Environment

It's important to avoid distractions while you study. This includes both the obvious distractions like visitors and the subtle distractions like an uncomfortable chair (or a too-comfortable couch that makes you want to fall asleep). Set up the best study environment possible: good lighting and a comfortable work area. If background music helps you focus, you may want to turn it on, but otherwise keep the room quiet. If you are using a computer to take notes, be sure you don't have any other windows open, especially applications like social media, games, or anything else that could distract you. Silence your phone and turn off notifications. Be sure to keep water close by so you stay hydrated while you study (but avoid unhealthy drinks and snacks).

Also, take into account the best time of day to study. Are you freshest first thing in the morning? Try to set aside some time then to work through the material. Is your mind clearer in the afternoon or evening? Schedule your study session then. Another method is to study at the same time of day that you will take the test, so that your brain gets used to working on the material at that time and will be ready to focus at test time.

Step 5: Study!

Once you have done all the study preparation, it's time to settle into the actual studying. Sit down, take a few moments to settle your mind so you can focus, and begin to follow your study plan. Don't give in to distractions or let yourself procrastinate. This is your time to prepare so you'll be ready to fearlessly approach the test. Make the most of the time and stay focused.

Of course, you don't want to burn out. If you study too long you may find that you're not retaining the information very well. Take regular study breaks. For example, taking five minutes out of every hour to walk briskly, breathing deeply and swinging your arms, can help your mind stay fresh.

As you get to the end of each chapter or section, it's a good idea to do a quick review. Remind yourself of what you learned and work on any difficult parts. When you feel that you've mastered the material, move on to the next part. At the end of your study session, briefly skim through your notes again.

But while review is helpful, cramming last minute is NOT. If at all possible, work ahead so that you won't need to fit all your study into the last day. Cramming overloads your brain with more information than it can process and retain, and your tired mind may struggle to recall even previously learned information when it is overwhelmed with last-minute study. Also, the urgent nature of cramming and the stress placed on your brain contribute to anxiety. You'll be more likely to go to the test feeling unprepared and having trouble thinking clearly.

So don't cram, and don't stay up late before the test, even just to review your notes at a leisurely pace. Your brain needs rest more than it needs to go over the information again. In fact, plan to finish your studies by noon or early afternoon the day before the test. Give your brain the rest of the day to relax or focus on other things, and get a good night's sleep. Then you will be fresh for the test and better able to recall what you've studied.

Step 6: Take a Practice Test

Many courses offer sample tests, either online or in the study materials. This is an excellent resource to check whether you have mastered the material, as well as to prepare for the test format and environment.

Check the test format ahead of time: the number of questions, the type (multiple choice, free response, etc.), and the time limit. Then create a plan for working through them. For example, if you have 30 minutes to take a 60-question test, your limit is 30 seconds per question. Spend less time on the questions you know well so that you can take more time on the difficult ones.

If you have time to take several practice tests, take the first one open book, with no time limit. Work through the questions at your own pace and make sure you fully understand them. Gradually work up to taking a test under test conditions: sit at a desk with all study materials put away and set a timer. Pace yourself to make sure you finish the test with time to spare and go back to check your answers if you have time.

After each test, check your answers. On the questions you missed, be sure you understand why you missed them. Did you misread the question (tests can use tricky wording)? Did you forget the information? Or was it something you hadn't learned? Go back and study any shaky areas that the practice tests reveal.

Taking these tests not only helps with your grade, but also aids in combating test anxiety. If you're already used to the test conditions, you're less likely to worry about it, and working through tests until you're scoring well gives you a confidence boost. Go through the practice tests until you feel comfortable, and then you can go into the test knowing that you're ready for it.

Test Tips

On test day, you should be confident, knowing that you've prepared well and are ready to answer the questions. But aside from preparation, there are several test day strategies you can employ to maximize your performance.

First, as stated before, get a good night's sleep the night before the test (and for several nights before that, if possible). Go into the test with a fresh, alert mind rather than staying up late to study.

Try not to change too much about your normal routine on the day of the test. It's important to eat a nutritious breakfast, but if you normally don't eat breakfast at all, consider eating just a protein bar. If you're a coffee drinker, go ahead and have your normal coffee. Just make sure you time it so that the caffeine doesn't wear off right in the middle of your test. Avoid sugary beverages, and drink enough water to stay hydrated but not so much that you need a restroom break 10 minutes into the test. If your test isn't first thing in the morning, consider going for a walk or doing a light workout before the test to get your blood flowing.

Allow yourself enough time to get ready, and leave for the test with plenty of time to spare so you won't have the anxiety of scrambling to arrive in time. Another reason to be early is to select a good seat. It's helpful to sit away from doors and windows, which can be distracting. Find a good seat, get out your supplies, and settle your mind before the test begins.

When the test begins, start by going over the instructions carefully, even if you already know what to expect. Make sure you avoid any careless mistakes by following the directions.

Then begin working through the questions, pacing yourself as you've practiced. If you're not sure on an answer, don't spend too much time on it, and don't let it shake your confidence. Either skip it and come back later, or eliminate as many wrong answers as possible and guess among the remaining ones. Don't dwell on these questions as you continue—put them out of your mind and focus on what lies ahead.

Be sure to read all of the answer choices, even if you're sure the first one is the right answer. Sometimes you'll find a better one if you keep reading. But don't second-guess yourself if you do immediately know the answer. Your gut instinct is usually right. Don't let test anxiety rob you of the information you know.

If you have time at the end of the test (and if the test format allows), go back and review your answers. Be cautious about changing any, since your first instinct tends to be correct, but make sure you didn't misread any of the questions or accidentally mark the wrong answer choice. Look over any you skipped and make an educated guess.

At the end, leave the test feeling confident. You've done your best, so don't waste time worrying about your performance or wishing you could change anything. Instead, celebrate the successful completion of this test. And finally, use this test to learn how to deal with anxiety even better next time.

Review Video: Test Anxiety
Visit mometrix.com/academy and enter code: 100340

Important Qualification

Not all anxiety is created equal. If your test anxiety is causing major issues in your life beyond the classroom or testing center, or if you are experiencing troubling physical symptoms related to your anxiety, it may be a sign of a serious physiological or psychological condition. If this sounds like your situation, we strongly encourage you to seek professional help.

Online Resources

Due to our efforts to try to keep this book to a manageable length, we've created a link that will give you access to all of your online resources:

mometrix.com/resources719/staarg8rla

It's Your Moment, Let's Celebrate It!

Share your story @mometrixtestpreparation